Platonically Erotic

Embodied Tales of Asexual and Aromantic
Intimacy, Love, and Nonsexual Flourishing

Landa Love PhD

Published by Accessible Academics: Plymouth
First printed 22 September 2024

ISBN: 978-1-0687062-8-8

A copy of this book has been deposited with the British Library.

Library of Congress Control Number: 2024919598

For all of those who embrace the full spectrum
of human flourishing, who honor the unique and
varied ways we all experience and express love, and
who are open to the embodiment of nonsexual eros

They who dance are thought mad by those
who hear not the music.
Anon

And for M~D~C with love always
i will
touch you with my mind. Touch
you, that is all,

lightly and you utterly will become
with infinite care

the poem which i do not write.

E.E. Cummings

Contents

Preface

In embarking on this book, *Platonically Erotic: Embodied Tales of Asexual and Aromantic Intimacy, Love and Nonsexual Flourishing*, I find myself reflecting on the journey that led me to this point. This work is deeply rooted in my doctoral research, a period marked by intense exploration, both academically and personally. It is with immense gratitude and a sense of fulfilment that I offer this book to you, published through Accessible Academics, with a dedication to increasing the accessibility of impactful academic work.

Within this research I ventured into the multifaceted realm of asexuality and aromanticism. What began as an academic endeavor soon transformed into a passionate explorative journey to understand and articulate the lived, embodied experiences of individuals across the asexual and aromantic spectrum. This book weaves together narratives, theoretical insights, and creative expressions to offer a comprehensive exploration of nonsexual eros and the profound ways in which it enriches human relationships and personal flourishing. Although intended to be accessible to general readers, I have left in the references to journal articles and books to facilitate those who are conducting research into similar areas of interest or wish to utilize similar methodologies. I have also kept the same unusual structure as the thesis, in order that this book may act as a beacon for those scholars who wish to write in a way that differs from usual academic conventions.

My journey through this research was not merely an academic pursuit; it was a transformative experience that reshaped my understanding of intimacy, love, and the human condition. Through the narratives of co-creators, the analysis of personal and collective experiences, and the integration of creative methodologies, this book aims to challenge and expand traditional notions of the erotic and intimacy. It seeks to highlight the richness of nonsexual relationships and the diverse ways in which individuals can experience and express love.

The work is interdisciplinary in nature due to the complexity of asexuality and aromanticism. By combining autoethnography, sensory research, and poetic prose, I have endeavored to create a text that is both informative and engaging, encouraging readers to reflect deeply on their own understandings of desire and connection. This book is a call to acknowledge and celebrate the varied expressions of intimacy that exist beyond the confines of sexual and romantic norms.

In a world where sexual attraction and romantic relationships are often seen as the epitome of human connection, this book challenges the assumption that eros and intimacy must be contingent on sex. It argues for the recognition of asexuality as a legitimate and fulfilling orientation, not as a lack but as a rich and diverse way of being. By doing so, it hopes to contribute to a more inclusive understanding of human sexuality and desire.

I am profoundly grateful to those who mentored me during this project and to all the individuals who shared their stories and insights, your contributions have been invaluable. This book is as much yours as it is mine.

May this work inspire readers to embrace the full spectrum of human intimacy and to honor the unique and varied ways we all experience love and connection.

Landa Magdalene Love

Acknowledgements

I am profoundly grateful to Dr. Julie Parsons, Dr. Lyvinia Elleschild and Dr. Mike Sheaff for their unwavering support, guidance, and mentorship throughout this research endeavor. Their expertise, constructive feedback, and encouragement have been invaluable in shaping the trajectory of this project.

I would like to thank those who participated in this study for their willingness to share openly, for their dedication to co-creation and their time, experiences, and insights, without which this research would not have been possible. I also acknowledge all those who 'unofficially' participated through lively and enriching discussions in academic and creative contexts.

I am deeply grateful to my family for their unwavering love, encouragement, and understanding throughout the ups and downs of this research. Your belief in me has been a driving force behind my perseverance and success. This book also would not have been possible without feeling your unconditional love and your offering of quiet space and nurturance to enable me to focus on my writing. Our profound discussions of both my personal experiences and the literature shaped this book.

My heartfelt thanks go to Professor Gayle Letherby whose advice, writing workshops, auto/biographical writing, and sociological fiction have encouraged and inspired me greatly.

It is with great love and joy in my heart that I thank Professor Kitrina Douglas and Dr Tracey Collett for their celebration of my work, it has given me both the courage and motivation to seek to share it widely.

I would also like to acknowledge Debbie at *Retreats for You,* and all of the writing retreat participants who shared their comments and encouragement with me.

It would not have been possible for me to complete this work without the caring, therapeutic attention of Allison Trott at *Barbican Natural Therapies*. An hour with Alison always makes me feel like I have had a week's holiday.

And, most importantly, I wish to express my gratitude for the constant sense of Divine Love that holds and guides me.

Introduction

"I feel it in my fingers, I feel it in my toes, love is all around me, and so the feeling grows."[1]

These are the opening lyrics from perhaps the soppiest romantic love song of the 90s. It describes a state of joy that many long for and expect (or hope) to find through a connection with an idealized, romantic partner in an exclusive and sexual relationship.

However, this song could equally describe the experience of embodied ecstasy, an experience of the **nonsexual erotic** that sits outside of the social construct of the erotic being confined to, and erroneously conflated with, the sexual. One of the central arguments within this text is that the sexual is only one basic potential of erotic expression and that the libido is a lifeforce, not simply a sexual energy. I attempt to demonstrate that this libido, the energy of eros in the body, propels us towards creativity, love and connection, and can be directed to any activity. Within these pages you will find examples of lived experiences that describe how the pleasure of this energy is

---

[1] © 1994 Mercury Records Limited / currently distributed by Universal Music Publishing, Inc. These are the opening lyrics from *'Love is All Around'* a 1994 song by Wet, Wet, Wet, originally written by Reg Presley in 1967 and originally performed by The Troggs in 1968.

not only sexual in nature, but with somatic awareness[2], can be felt throughout the body during everyday activities. I explain how the lived experiences discovered during my research demonstrate that this state of energetic and somatic, mindful awareness can lead to states of erotic, ecstatic, spiritual ecstasy fueled by a sense of interconnectedness and 'being in love' without an object.

My journey from romantic addiction to a feeling of spiritual liberation, and then reintegration into a more embodied rational state is a complex one, which I have only begun to understand through the course of this research. This research was predicated on an 'academic epiphany'; an epiphany that asexuality exists as an identity, and that I fit the definition of asexuality given by AVEN (2022) which defines asexuality as a lack of sexual attraction and sexual desire. A definition I found limiting in its scope, but nevertheless it was a statement that could be applied to me.

I resonate with Gayle Letherby (2015), who, in her paper, *Bathwater, babies and other losses: a personal and academic story*, describes how her 'experience of reproductive loss led me to sociology and how, in turn, sociology has influenced my experience of loss' (p.128). My experience of psychological androgyny and celibacy once practiced, and now natural, led me to sociology and sociology has influenced how I now perceive this.

My asexual epiphany occurred during my PhD. It started with my supervisor Lyvinia Elleschild, introducing the term 'asexuality' during a supervisory meeting. It was our first meeting, and I was sharing some of my story. I explained that, wanting to delve more

---

[2] Somatic awareness is the ability to tune into and understand the sensations and movements within your own body. It involves being mindful of physical sensations, emotions, and your overall bodily state in the present moment. Cultivating somatic awareness through practices like mindfulness, body scan meditations and somatic movement practices such as tai chi and free form dance such as 'ecstatic' dance and contact improvisation, can enhance well-being, stress, and emotional management, and enhance the mind-body connection. It can also increase the awareness of the life energy in the body.

into the perceived gift of psychological androgyny, I had conducted a personal ritual, committing to myself and my 'inner marriage'. This included a vow of being celibate for one year. The year had become several years and, after about 18 months, was no longer a practice, but a way of being, however I only had the word 'celibate' to describe myself.[3]

Lyvinia responded, "That is very interesting. You will be able to write about asexuality then, there isn't much research about it, but I will send you some links."

I thought, "*Will I? What is an 'asexual'?!*"

I followed the links and found the papers interesting but, at the time, they did not grip me in the way that gender studies did. However, Lyvinia had sown a seed that would later grow into an asexual epiphany[4].

Following this epiphany and the refocusing of my research, I analyzed my journals written over the course of 22 years, which elucidated themes and questions that I investigated through the available literature and in collaboration with my co-creators[5]. Thus, applying my 'sociological imagination'[6] (Mills 1959) to the emerging asexual identity and the micro and macro societal factors that may

---

[3] When I say, 'describe myself', I was not looking for an identity label as such. It would be more accurate to say I was looking for a way to tell people in a concise way that I no longer wanted sexual or romantic relationships, but that it was not a practice of celibacy it was just a way of being. In doing that I wanted to also be able to encapsulate, neatly in a couple of words, that I was still open to nonsexual intimacy, and I felt erotically alive, just not sexually. The use of the world 'celibate' did not have the desired effect as a descriptor. I found it had the effect of the 'red rag to the bull'. When I told men who were interested in me that I was celibate, it seemed to make them more interested, like I was the ultimate challenge. They misunderstood, thinking that I wanted sex, but was trying not to have sex. The word 'celibate' infers a practice of not having sex, rather than a way of being.

[4] The event that led to my epiphany is narrated in Chapter 1, section 1.6.

[5] This is the term I use to describe those who participated in this research, due to the level of creative involvement and contribution made.

[6] See sections 1.2 and 1.3 for further discussion of this concept.

have influenced this emergence, and my desire to contribute to the knowledge of the lived experiences of being asexual.

As I analyzed these journals, I could see certain themes emerging. I noticed that my social conditioning had encouraged an obsession with romance and sexuality and that I had suffered a loss of meaning and ontological security at a young age due to the disintegration of my religious beliefs and a loss of connection to the transpersonal. I could articulate that the breakdown I experienced in my twenties was due to a disillusionment with the capitalist ideal that I had been striving for, and that a shift in my worldview became possible through exploring other cultures and more experiential forms of spirituality. It became apparent that the practices of mindfulness and emotional awareness had facilitated the realization of an addiction to romance and the beginnings of liberating myself from this. The links between the development of an experiential spirituality, the cultivation of a balanced psychological androgyny[7], and the redirection of my libido became clearer. I had discovered an embodied experiential spirituality based on movement, sensory awareness and nature connection, which led to a sense of joy and satisfaction that precluded my libido directing itself towards the sexual; a libido directed instead to full body ecstatic states, love (platonic and agape), creativity and community.

The search for an understanding of my experiences within the literature enabled me to gain understanding, not only regarding my own story but also about how this reflected some interesting developments in society[8].

---

[7] This is discussed in Chapter 4, section 4.8.1.

[8] See Chapter 3 for a full discussion of this in relation to the literature.

Inspired by Grounded Theory (Strauss and Corbin 1994)[9], I commenced the process of starting with my narrative and undertook an iterative process of analysis between this, the narratives of my co-creators and the literature. This analysis enabled me to begin to understand how asexuality is a product of this particular moment in time and how it could have the potential to disrupt capitalist power structures. I could also relate to the authors who posit that this can only occur if asexuality is examined and understood as a phenomenon and is used as a lens to deconstruct the discourse of compulsory sexuality and hypersexuality (Przyblo 2011, 2012, Vance 2018). Vance (2018) suggests that it would it be a wasted opportunity for such a deconstruction if asexuality is simply accepted as a fixed and accepted marginalized identity rather than as a lens to trouble our current notions regarding sexuality (Butler 1990, 1993, Przyblo 2011, 2012, Vance 2018).

The initial literature that I read regarding asexuality being an innate orientation did not fit with my experience of asexuality as a choice and a journey to becoming who I am today. It did not fit with my experience of asexuality as a flourishing rather than a lack (of sexuality) (Smith 2017). This research has been an exploration of shared narratives of asexual flourishing and existing theories that have not yet been applied to asexuality. These experiential narratives, alongside the theoretical investigation offer a rich opportunity to examine and understand an alternative narrative of asexuality that offers examples of how it is possible to flourish erotically without sex and romance, in order to deconstruct the current discourse of compulsory sexuality and hypersexuality and the primacy of 'romantic' relationships. This collaborative exploration has led to the

---

[9] Grounded theory is a qualitative research methodology utilizing an approach that is designed to systematically generate theory from empirical data allowing theories to emerge from the data rather than being imposed on it in advance. This offers a flexible and systematic approach for exploring and understanding social phenomena based on the perspectives and experiences of the participants.

creation of a definition that fits with my and the co-creators' experiences of asexuality, the definition of 'erotically embodied asexuality'.

The research has also led to the cultivation of a tentative new identity 'label' of 'platonically erotic' that the co-creators and I would be happy to apply to ourselves, should we wish to use an identity label. At the beginning of this research, I struggled with claiming a new 'identity label'. I reflected on this difficulty with accepting an identity category a few days prior to the writing retreat that was the final catalyst prior to my epiphany. The reflection was inspired by a gift my younger brother gave me with a gift tag that read 'Like you, some of the butterflies have broken free of the frame in which they were placed.' [10]

---

[10] The rationale for the layered format of this book is discussed later in this chapter.

Figure 1- Outside of the Box: A gift of recognition from my brother.

*   *   *

The following extract is a representation of the journal entry where I reflected on this personal struggle with identity, identity labels and social constructs:

(Journal entry, 7 September 2021)

Outside of the box

Each box I have broken out of has led to another for me to push against. On breaking out there is a sense of loss or perhaps lostness; wandering aimlessly, watching those still in the community of its confines and wondering 'what I am supposed to do now?'

Once the liminality becomes normal, it is replaced by a sense of freedom, which has to be maintained lest it dissolve into a state of emptiness.

Eventually, when I surrender to the emptiness, it is filled with a sense of joy and peace, and ease that fits better than the struggle to fit in the box. There is sometimes a back and forth between grieving for the life I was 'supposed' to live, the images and scenarios that play out in front of me, rubbing up against the cells of the body that were primed to play that part.

Life without a box is liberating, spacious and exciting. However, it can also feel like living out in the world without four walls to return to and be contained within; it can be over stimulating and tiring.

I observe now that I, like many people, seem to push out of one box only to put themselves into an alternative box.

Are the boxes, the social constructs, a means to create an illusion of order and safety that do not actually exist? Do they offer us a set of rules that absolve us of the effort of thinking and reflecting?

*   *   *

This book is a story of the quest to describe an experience that exists outside of current discourse. It is perhaps the journey of me trying to find a new home, a nice cozy box in which to sit with others whose worldview is similar to mine. However, I still struggle with 'labelling' myself. It is both an autoethnography of my journey to becoming asexual and an autoethnography of how my understanding of being asexual (and myself) has changed over the course of the research. It is a story woven with my endeavor to 'find a tribe', and the experience of collaboration with my co-creators. It does not make any claims to 'truth', it is a story. It aims to rhetorically challenge socially constructed commonly held views of both asexuality and sexuality in Western society. I hope that this story, belonging to me and my co-creators, if told repeatedly, will become a part of common discourse. It is the story of how the co-creators and I endeavored to create a definition of our experience of asexuality as a flourishing, not a simply as a lack of sexuality.

At first, I felt timid about sharing this story and this research. However, I now have the confidence given by finding that many people see themselves in this story. It surprised me at conferences and writing retreats that many people were interested in and engaged with discussing this research. How much they resonated with the stories I told them, whether they were sexual or asexual, although sometimes it seemed like quite an effort for them to come to an understanding of this alternative narrative. I assume this was because they were endeavoring to understand a foreign discourse that challenges many 'taken for granted' aspects of human experience, sexuality and the prevalent notions of identity and the importance of sexuality as an identity. I have found that those with experience of, or backgrounds in, cultures other than Western culture have less difficulty understanding the notion of an erotically embodied asexuality, perhaps because their cultures, or the cultures they have spent time in, have differing views regarding ecstatic body states and/or the nature of the erotic. There are many people that I have met during this research who are waiting to read this book and have expressed how important it is to them that I let them know when it is available.

One encounter stands out amongst the others and that was the interaction with Nadia[11] at a conference. She attended my presentation of poems that I shared to illustrate the experience of erotically embodied asexuality. At the end of the presentation, during the questions and comments, Nadia announced that she was asexual but that it was something she had never felt able to say before. She said, 'Landa I just loved it, because I would describe myself as asexual, but when you're black you can't be asexual. I *think* I'm asexual … I've just never had any interest in sex or having children'. At the end of the presentation, I met with her, and she explained further that, 'as a black woman it is more challenging to say you are asexual. Black women are seen as hypersexual and that being nonsexual is not an option'. She told me that if she tries to articulate that she is not sexual, she is met with ridicule and that people think 'she must be up to all sorts with everybody'.

Nadia is a strong vibrant presence full of 'bucket loads' of energy. What they are seeing is that she is full of what they *perceive* as sexual energy and yet, for Nadia, this energy it is not being directed sexually. When I described how the co-creators and I have strong libidos but that we do not experience this energy as sexual, but as a lifeforce energy that flows in all directions other than sexually, her eyes lit up with the joy of recognition. She said that she did not understand the obsession with sex and sexual orientations, that she was more interested in love rather than how people chose to express it. When I contacted Nadia to see if I could share this story, she replied with a message that I found encouraging, motivating and a little surprising.

---

[11] This is a pseudonym. This story is shared with permission.

She said how much it had meant to her meeting me, hearing my presentation, and talking afterwards, but that what had happened the next day was life-changing for her. I had to leave before the second day, but apparently quite a few other attendees at the conference, having heard her comments at the end of my presentation, approached her to say that they felt the same. She felt extremely grateful to have met people who felt the same as her and considered it a great gift. This struck me as an indicator of the importance of this research; it was a relatively small conference, so the fact that a reasonably high percentage of people there resonated with the narrative of erotically embodied asexuality seemed significant.

Once I had found this common theme of nonsexual erotic embodiment both in my narrative and the narratives of the co-creators, I found that the extant literature on asexuality did not reflect these experiences. I therefore scavenged for any academic literature I could find in order to expand my understanding of these experiences, and I connected some unconventional elements as a result of this search. This is a process that Jack Halberstam described as a 'queer methodology' that:

> [Is] a scavenger methodology that uses different methods to collect and produce information on subjects who have been deliberately or accidentally excluded from traditional studies of human behavior ... to combine methods that are often cast as being at odds with each other ... it refuses the academic compulsion toward disciplinary coherence (1998: 13)

This research does not therefore have a compulsion towards 'disciplinary coherence'. It is research into a specific unexplored alternative narrative of asexuality, within an unrepresented group of people, that necessitates 'a creative and idiosyncratic gathering of fragments of information on topics, groups, and individuals historically underrepresented or excluded from traditional knowledge production' (Smith 2017:16). To research an experience which has not yet been explored within academic research, I have undertaken a process of 'heterographic writing' (Scully 2010), a style of writing which can encompass multiple subjectivities and 'assumes difference, but also assumes the possibility of multiplicity of meaning' (2010: 32). Heterographic writing involves the integrating of multiple meanings and strands of information from various cultures, times and places and 'involves giving up a search for the 'whole subject'' (Scully 2010:32). Scully suggests that 'we might conceptualize such writing as a kind of cubist portrait in which planes of meaning intersect but do not, even when looked at in totality, render an illusion of having 'captured' the entire subject' (Scully 2010:33). She tells us that:

> ...one plane we might consider is the ways in which local cultural systems and meanings migrate through different spheres. These interactions occur not on the axes of peripheries/central, but rather through planes or angles. Meaning and its representations are always, in this vision, incomplete, challenging and suggestive of what we do not know as much as what we think we do (Scully 2010:33).

This project does not aim to capture the whole subject or make claims to empirical 'truth', it aims to offer new perspectives that can be viewed through different 'planes and angles', opening up possibilities, challenges and suggestions for alternative perceptions of asexuality. I have followed the guidance given by Åkerström (2013) to:

> Avoid societal or scholarly conventionality, even be disobedient to recommendations, if this blinds us to new meanings of our findings. The value of serendipitous findings lies in the fact that they diverge from conventionally held knowledge. Thus, we have to retain our curiosity, with the "strange intoxication" or passion that Max Weber wrote about in Science as Vocation. (Åkerström 2013:12)

This is a story. It starts with a story of how I created the methodology for this research, it moves on to my personal story and then to the story of me conducting the review of the literature that I undertook to understand my story. It shares the stories of my co-creators to add depth and similar, yet differing, angles to this developing narrative, the narrative of non-sexual erotic embodiment. It prioritizes embodied experience over rational knowledge in its aim to thickly describe an embodied experience. Smith (2017) describes how, in a similar way to a researcher of embodied experience investigating an unresearched experience, that the 'genealogist pieces together narratives out of fragments and does so not to capture a subject in its totality but rather to produce an alternative narrative to strategically undercut hegemonic discourses' (2017:16).

Within Smith's research, he utilized 'the history of Christianity' to 'challenge various taken for granted modern assumptions about sexuality, eroticism and asexuality' (2017:21). He does not go into explanations or justifications regarding Christian theology. He rather describes the practices, and the experiences of these practices, within Christian Mysticism, in order to challenge these 'taken for granted modern assumptions' that social theorists hold about eroticism and sexuality. I attempt to do the same, but by utilizing descriptions of practices within new religious movements and how these are experienced as 'mystical' erotic, nonsexual experiences by the co-creators within this research.

Weber famously said, in his 1905 book *The Protestant Ethic and the Spirit of Capitalism,* that you do not have to prove the existence of God in order to write about the sociology of religion. A view corroborated by Berger in his statement that 'the sociologist, qua sociologist, need not serve as arbiter among competing psychologies, just as … the sociologist of religion does not have to concern himself with the question of whether God exists' (1965:32). In a similar style to Weber's analysis (that is not concerned with theological or metaphysical questions about the existence of God) I will not be trying to validate the beliefs of the communities or new religious movements within which this research is located. I will be describing the embodied experiences of the asexual co-creators who articulate that some practices, located within 'new religions', were intrinsic to their flourishing as asexuals. In offering thickly described stories of these experiences of asexuals who are blooming with vitality and eros, I aim to offer an alternative discourse to the current concepts of what asexuality is and to challenge current discourse regarding sexuality and the erotic.

My research focuses on the experiential aspects of these practices and how they offer a window into how the co-creators discovered an erotic way of being nonsexual. It follows Weber's approach to the sociology of religion which is rooted in the idea that researchers can examine the social and cultural dimensions of religion without probing into questions of religious truth or seeking theological proofs. Taking this Weberian approach allows the researcher to explore how religion and religious practices influence human experiences and interactions, irrespective of religious beliefs or theological debates.

This research aims to add a further alternative narrative to Smith's alternative narrative of asexuality, the asexuality that is currently defined as a lack, a sexual orientation and an identity. I do not experience asexuality as a lack or an orientation. I do not have a sexual orientation, because I am not sexual. Smith (2017) described the practice of naming *not being sexual* as a *sexual* orientation as the 'asexual paradox'. There is literature that corroborates my experience and that of the co-creators' (as outlined in Chapter 3 and throughout the remaining chapters). However, trying to describe an experience of the erotic, the erotic that has been sexualized with language that has been purloined by sexuality, is challenging. Chapter 3 aims to offer enough background to asexuality and expanded views of asexuality and the erotic, in the hope that it can offer a framework for the reader to be open to a reading of the experience of embodied erotic asexuality within the following chapters. It tentatively holds open a doorway that could lead to new ways of becoming, living, expressing, and experiencing for those who do not resonate with sexuality as the full expression of their erotic selves.

This research prioritizes embodied experience as a form of knowledge formed from the experiential sensory interpretation of a somatically aware, integrated body and mind. The research aims to tell a story, the story of asexuality as a becoming[12] rather than as a fixed identity or orientation, the story of an erotically embodied asexuality and erotically infused platonic love. It does so to offer an alternative narrative to the commonly held definition of asexuality as a stable orientation and a lack of sexuality (rather than an experience in its own right).

It offers an autoethnography of my becoming asexual, my process and journey with the literature to understand an alternative narrative of asexuality, and creative representations of co-creators' stories to offer insight into the experience of the nonsexual erotic and nonsexual erotic love. It does not seek to make scientific claims about asexuality; it utilizes stories, the extant literature, materials gathered from my own journals and co-creators experiences to create a 'new story' of the erotic. It does so with the aim of dislocating sexuality from its sole, prime position within the erotic. Thus, opening up the possibility of full erotic expression and flourishing rather than the erotic being conflated with sexuality.

Although 'personal narratives can address several key theoretical debates in contemporary sociology: macro and micro linkages; structure, agency, and their intersection' and 'social reproduction and

---

12 Deleuze and Guattari (1980) use the concept of 'becoming' to refer to a philosophy of everything being in a constant state of change and evolution. The process of 'becoming' involves transcending stable identities or categories and emphasizes fluidity and diversity. Becoming involves a movement away from fixed structures and towards a more open, non-linear understanding of reality. Deleuze and Guattari use the concept to explore the ways in which individuals and entities can undergo continuous transformations, avoiding rigid categories and identities and embrace the complexity of the world.

social change' providing 'access to both the individual and the social and make it possible to see connections between them' (Laslett 1999: 392), this research only aims to offer insights into these macro and micro linkages and provide access to the individual and the social, it does not aim to find or tell the 'truth' of asexuality.

I have chosen to present the collected stories as creative outputs, which fits with the aim of offering an alternative narrative rather than a 'truth'. As Inckle (2010) explains, creative outputs offer an alternative to the conventional structure of quotes from the raw data followed by an analysis of the data, which offers a 'closed assertion or truth claim' (p.39). The strategy of presenting the research data as creative outputs, which are a combination of the 'data' and the analysis and interpretation, leaves the reader with 'thinking, feeling questions and open to a whole range of possible meanings and developments which much more closely reflected the dynamic experiences' of my research participants (Ibid.) This means that the creative outputs are not directly explained to the reader, leaving them with the space to make their own interpretations; the theoretical material preceding the creative outputs offers them a frame. They can therefore be read through the reader's own particular 'lens', allowing them to relate these to their individual life experiences and the temporal moment in which they are being read. This approach enhances the accessibility and engagement of the research for a broader audience.

In this way the creative outputs are both 'product and a process as/in critical research' Watson (2021: 4). I have utilized dramaturgical texts, sociological fiction, and poetry to share the experiences of the co-creators. Faulkner (2009) suggests that by composing poems, the researcher is compelled to engage in profound reflection on the data, its interpretation, and the associated meanings, resulting in a more nuanced comprehension and communication of the research. Faulkner also asserts that poetry has the power to captivate readers, prompting them to derive their own interpretations and conclusions. The poems are therefore left open to interpretation with no fixed analysis, in order to facilitate the open interpretation process outlined by Faulkner. This approach is similar to research where the data, analysis and interpretation are presented as a performance piece. The performer does not keep stopping and explaining what the last scene meant. The theoretical academic prose that precedes and follows the poem frames it, in a similar way to how a stage set frames and gives additional meaning to a performance.

In addition to utilizing creative methods to present my findings, I have also utilized an unconventional structure. Weatherall (2019) explains that rigid scientific structures for doctoral writing do not support studies which are experiential, reflexive, feminine and creative. I, like Weatherall, found it impossible to write up my academic research adhering to traditional structure. I felt blocked, unable to start until I started to write the whole thesis as an autoethnography. Then the process flowed. I therefore started the thesis by writing it as it had unfolded with the complexity and insight regarding existing theoretical material emerging on the page as it had through the research process (Weatherall 2019). Weatherall adopted a similar process within her doctoral thesis in an attempt to 'illustrate that the analysis didn't crystallize ideas in a single way, and that these are all different ways of seeing' (2019: 103).

Following the initial draft, I endeavored to restructure the write up as much as possible in the hope that it would be acceptable to meet academic examination requirements. It was challenging to present a more concise and regimented document from a protracted process of expansion, ideas and insight, which felt like the gentle unfurling of a flower's petals into a full and sensuous flourishing.

I could also not find a way to adhere to the traditional structure with the findings neatly confined to the 'findings' chapters. They have found their way into all the chapters, where they sit comfortably, for me, within the developing narrative. They are separated by three stars, in the hope that the stars enable a moment to pause, so that the process of moving from the theoretical to the experiential and creative is perhaps less jarring for the reader. This was a process utilized by Weatherall (2019) both within her doctoral thesis and subsequent writing about the process, where she oscillated 'between empirical and theoretical material throughout … drawing theory into immediate relief with lived experience'. She states that 'writing differently can open up the critical and creative potential of research to assist scholars in making a more interesting and creative contribution'. It is my hope that the unconventional style of 'academic writing' makes this book more interesting and pleasurable to read, it certainly made it more gratifying and motivating to write.

I endeavored to create a sense of narrative development with the structure I chose for my thesis; articulating and representing the research development and process rather than adhering to usual doctoral conventions. I included all the required elements, but not in the conventional order of 'introduction – literature review – methods – findings – discussion – conclusion' (Honan and Bright 2016, cited in Weatherall 2019). I have kept this structure within this book, so that it may be a resource for others who wish to write their doctoral thesis, or other academic writings differently.

I developed my methodology prior to writing my narrative. The first methodology chapter is therefore Chapter 1 and the presentation of my findings based on the analysis of my own narrative are presented in Chapter 2 before the literature review. This is because I undertook the review of the literature in response to the themes discovered in the writing of my narrative. The literature review is therefore presented in Chapter 3, at the end of this section I articulate the fully formed research question and the aims of the research[13]. The

---

[13] This is the traditional place for the formulated research question and aims, at the end of the literature review, in academic research. I also offer the initial questions and directions

next stage of the process was to start to communicate with the co-creators[14]. There is, therefore, a further methodology chapter, Chapter 4, which includes reflections on the research process, including ethical issues, sensitively presented descriptions of the co-creators, their selection, the influences perceived as contributing to their asexual 'becomings' and worldviews, and the experience of interacting and creating with them. The themes that arose within the co-creators' narratives of 'romance as eros' and 'becoming woman'[15] led to a further review of the literature in order to conceptualize these narratives and returning to my journals to extract my own reflections regarding these themes. This discussion of worldviews and influences means that this 'methodology' chapter also, unconventionally, includes theoretical and conceptual analysis and experiential creative outputs (or 'findings'). Chapters 5 – 6 are largely comprised of 'findings' although the 'findings' are also scattered throughout the document as explained previously and there is also some new theoretical discussion within these later chapters, that is necessary to understanding and the development of knowledge. The final Chapter, 7, is offered as an alternative to a conclusion and offers the reader an experiential reading of asexual erotic embodied experience, through a gallery of collaboratively produced poetry.

I have utilized the literary device of including pertinent quotes in shaded boxes at the beginning of chapters and sections. The use of shaded text boxes with relevant quotes at the beginning of chapters is a stylistic choice I have observed in much in literature and academic writing. I have employed this technique, within the gray shaded boxes at the beginning of chapters and some sections to introduce key

---

that I had after the review of my own narrative at the end of Chapter 2, these were modified following the literature review and my initial communications with the co-creators.

[14] Co-creators is the term I have given to the participants within this research as a mark of respect for their level of contribution and creative input.

[15] Discussed fully in Chapter 4.

concepts or themes, set the tone, provide context, or offer perspectives from notable figures in the field. I hope that this adds depth to the content and that it also engages the reader by providing a thought-provoking entry point to these sections.

The research is presented in a 'layered' (Ronai, 1995) format, which aims to facilitate more open analysis and knowledge. Rather than presenting the reader with a closed, fixed analysis, the layered account allows space for the reader to have a unique immersive, reflexive consideration of the intrinsic issues.

Each layer is separated with three centered stars to suggest a space to pause and grasp the meaning slowly. Journal entries have a light gray background and a 'handwritten' font. Section header quotes that are inserted for effect, but are not analyzed, are in light gray boxes. Poems that were produced from the analysis and interpretation of primary data, for the purpose of this research are presented centered on the page and with the usual header and white page background, whereas poems that were produced in previous journals or in my research journal, as a form of personal reflection, are presented as journal entries. Where the first person is utilized, the poem is based on my experience and when it is in the third person it is based on the co-creators' experience. Where a co-creator has largely produced the poem themselves with some collaboration, the poem will be in the first person but will have the marking 'CC' (to signify 'co-creator') at the bottom right of the poem.

The language that I utilize within many of the creative outputs may appear to carry sexual connotations. However, I have intentionally drawn on the language historically used by mystics to describe their ecstatic encounters—language that was later co-opted and confined within the realm of 'sexuality,' allowing it to dominate and overshadow the broader concept of the erotic. My aim in salvaging this language to express nonsexual erotic experiences is to help free the erotic and its associated language from the constraints imposed by sexual discourse.

I hope that through the utilization of an unconventional structure, presentation and the merging of disciplines, theoretical frameworks and the use of creative representations of findings, that I have met my aim of providing the reader with an engaging and experiential reading of erotically embodied asexuality, and that this book will be interesting and appealing to a wide audience of readers. My intention is to offer insight into the embodied nonsexual erotic experiences of the co-creators; how they interpret that experience and how it feels to them sensorially. I trust that I have met my aims of sensitively representing the voice of a marginalized group of people and offering more understanding and appreciation of an unrepresented way of being.

1. Though this be madness, yet there is method in't[16]

Within this chapter I aim to describe the process of selecting research methodologies that could meet the aims of the research and the epistemological ground for the research. Both aspects needed to fit with my worldview in order for me to be effective as the researcher. I decided to start with this chapter rather than following the standard structure within academic research because as an autoethnography, both of my life story and of this research, this foundational chapter is fundamental to the progression of the narrative. Within the flow of the sections that follow I aim to elucidate in a linear way, the somewhat chaotic, rhizomatic[17] process I embarked upon to piece together a theoretical framework, articulate my worldview and find methodologies and theories that could offer the possibility of gathering and articulating alternative narratives of asexuality. The process of finding the co-creators and communicating and creating with them is described in Chapter 4.

---

[16] Shakespeare's *Hamlet* Act 2, Scene 2.

[17] Within Deleuze and Guattari's (1980) work, the rhizome is utilized as a metaphor for complex and interconnected systems where ideas, knowledge, and connections can germinate and shoot out in multiple directions.

1.1 Maverick madness

> *But if the person's inner state cannot be emotionally shared by others,*
> *and a religious explanation cannot be constructed to fit his or her*
> *experiences, then we have the popular interpretation of the state as*
> *paglami, ordinary or secular madness*
> McDaniel 2018:16

The first time I handed in a draft of my autoethnographic writing my supervisor, Mike Sheaff, picked up on the fact that I commented within this piece of writing that I now saw 'this breakdown as a breakthrough'[18.] Mike commented that he had heard this somewhere before. He suggested that I might find Ken Gale's book *Madness as Methodology* (2018) of interest. On opening Ken Gale's book, I found the following quote on the first page:

> Madness need not be all breakdown. It may also be breakthrough.
> *Deleuze and Guattari, 2004: 143*

This was one of many synchronistic experiences that I had within the process of this research. I found it affirming and encouraging. I also found reading Gale's work and that of Deleuze and Guattari quite soothing to a rather beleaguered bodymind[19] which, having previously felt the rush of 'escape' from other uncomfortable boxes, was trying to squeeze itself back into another one.

Gale's book opens with the encouragement to the reader to 'engage with its content not in a linear, developmental manner, page by page, chapter by chapter, but rather in indeterminate and free-spirited ways' (2018:4). I felt instantly welcome, given permission to

---

[18] See Chapter 2, Act 4.

[19] The term 'bodymind is often used (in contexts such as somatic awareness and movement classes, Chinese medicine and body-centered therapy) to emphasize the interconnected unity of the body and mind, highlighting that they are not separate entities but rather two aspects of the same whole.

read how I wanted to read, and the reassurance that I was not being disrespectful to his work by doing so. He goes on to say, that in this erratic reading the reader may be 'driven by experimental inquiries and impulsive curiosities, moving from one plateau to another as an insect might move from plant to plant in search of food and sustenance.' (Ibid) It reminded me of something a teacher said to me many years ago, 'You remind me of a butterfly, flying from flower to flower, picking up many ideas and cross-pollinating.' I resonate with what that teacher said to me. Although perhaps now a little more grounded than a butterfly, I have always been a 'rhizomatic' thinker, a 'nomadic'[20] explorer who likes to be in the 'intermezzo' – the space between points, concepts, context and content, where there is a pause, a silence, a sense of possibility (Deleuze and Guattari 1980).

I have also physically travelled, picking up spiritual practices from many different cultures. These practices have opened more space for becoming[21] (Deleuze and Guattari 1980). They have opened new ways of sensing and being which are challenging to articulate and do not fit within our limited Western notion of 'five senses' (Barnes 2015: 18). I experience myself as being asexual. I have no desire for sex and, if I feel attracted to someone, it does not make me want to have sex with them. However, I also experience myself as highly erotic[22],

---

[20] Deleuze and Guattari use the term 'nomad' and 'nomadic thought' to describe a way of thinking which pushes against established hierarchies and structures and prefers a dynamic and fluid approach to knowledge and understanding. This metaphor is utilized because nomads are often associated with a state of continual becoming and transformation rather than settling into fixed identities or systems.

[21] Deleuze and Guattari (1980) use the concept of 'becoming' to refer to a philosophy of everything being in a constant state of change and evolution. The process of 'becoming' involves transcending stable identities or categories and emphasizes fluidity and diversity. Becoming involves a movement away from fixed structures and towards a more open, non-linear understanding of reality. Deleuze and Guattari use the concept to explore the ways in which individuals and entities can undergo continuous transformations, avoiding rigid categories and identities and embrace the complexity of the world.

[22] Within this book I am referring to the erotic as the fullness of the erotic, not eros confined to the sexual as is common in Western discourse. This definition articulates that sexuality is only one small part of or expression of the erotic, as defined by Marcuse (1974) Lorde (1978),

full of a non-sexual libido. I experience ecstatic states that do not fit neatly into any religion. I practice many things that individuals in the new age and neo-tantric[23] communities practice, but I do not resonate or feel comfortable within these communities. I sometimes feel like I am slightly mad. I have come to welcome the experience of breakdown as a herald for change, anticipating the feeling of breakthrough on the 'other side', and I do not seem to fit anywhere. I am the 'schizophrenic out for a walk'[24] (Deleuze and Guattari 1980: 2). I am grateful that this research has now led me to others who think in similar ways to me and whose 'becomings' have led them to a similar point.

McDaniel (2018) suggests that ecstasy is a topic avoided by both religion and theology, describing it as a 'hot potato' (p.2). She raises a

---

Griffin (1996), hooks (2010), Gafini and Kincaid (2017), Smith (2017) and Przybylo (2019). See Chapter 3 for a full discussion of this. The central premise within all of these texts, is that people can experience great satisfaction, personal effectiveness, and wellbeing 'when we embrace the full beauty of our embodied eros, not merely in the sexual but in every dimension of our lives.' (Gafini and Kincaid 2017: 8) This is introduced in depth in Chapter 3 sections 3.5 and 3.6, is discussed further in Chapter 4 and illustrated with findings from the research in Chapters 2, 5,6 and 7.

[23] Neo-tantra is a contemporary spiritual and sexual offering that is inspired by traditional Tantric practices originating in Eastern traditions. Unlike classical Tantra, which has deep roots in ancient Indian philosophy and spirituality, neo-tantra offers a modern reinterpretation of these traditions, adapted to Western contexts. There is an emphasis on the integration of spirituality and sexuality, aiming to promote personal and spiritual growth through various practices, including meditation, breathwork, and physical exercises. While classical Tantra has a rich philosophical foundation and is embedded in a broader spiritual context, neo-tantra receives critique for its selective and commercial approach, which focuses more on the enhancement of sexual experiences than spiritual growth. Some practitioners embrace neo-tantra as a path to explore consciousness and intimacy, while others view it with skepticism and consider it a simplified or diluted version of traditional Tantric teachings (Bishop 2019).

[24] Deleuze and Guattari are not referring to the mental illness termed 'schizophrenia', they are using it as another metaphor in a similar way as they use 'nomad'. I particularly relate to this metaphor and their description of it and would dearly love to be capitalism's 'extinguishing angel'. They describe it thus: 'As for the schizo, continually wandering about, migrating here, there, and everywhere as best he can, he plunges further and further into the realm of deterritorialization, reaching the furthest limits of the decomposition of the socius on the surface of his own body without organs. The schizophrenic deliberately seeks out the very limits of capitalism: he is its inherent tendency brought to fulfilment, its surplus product, its proletariat, its exterminating angel' (Deleuze and Guattari 1980: 35).

question about the perception of the study of ecstatic consciousness being non-scientific and asks whether this characterization is accurate. She also points to the dilemma of ecstatic states with religious content that are not accepted by current religious institutions and questions what should be done about them. McDaniel emphasizes that the challenge is that these experiences do not fit in with cultural and religious preconceptions. She suggests that while science serves as a learning method for many, for some 'it is an end in itself, and a justification for rejecting other forms of knowledge.' (p.11)

A physicist and Nobel laureate, Erwin Schrödinger shared this personal reflection in an interview:

> The scientific picture of the real world around me is very deficient. It gives a lot of factual information... [but] it cannot tell us a word about red and blue, bitter and sweet, physical pain and physical delight, it knows nothing of beautiful and ugly, good or bad, God and eternity. So, in brief, we do not belong to this material world that science constructs for us... the scientific world view contains of itself... not a word about our own ultimate scope or destination. (Cited in McDaniel 2018: 11)

This research prioritizes embodied experience as a form of knowledge formed from the experiential sensory interpretation of an integrated 'bodymind'. It does not aim to find the 'truth' of asexuality, it aims to tell the story of a unique perspective of asexuality and describe this experience in a sensory and multi-layered way. My passion is ignited by the goal of producing something that is located beyond scientific, rational knowledge, something written from embodied knowing, as Lorde (1979) explains:

> As we learn to bear the intimacy of scrutiny and to flourish within it, as we learn to use the products of that scrutiny for power within our living, those fears which rule our lives and form our silences begin to lose their control over us. (p.1)

My deepest desire is to share the erotic nature of nonsexual desire. Gale tells us that 'inherent in the objectification of desire is its very demise' (p.4). This writing aims to utilize my embodied, sensory 'sociological imagination' (Mills 1959) to create an alternative erotically embodied narrative of desire desiring itself.

1.2 Sociological Imagination

C Wright Mills (1999, originally published 1959) was the first sociologist to use the term 'sociological imagination' to describe the connection between internal (personal) troubles and external (public) issues. He saw this as being about understanding the relationship between biography and history (our own lives and our milieu). He said, 'it is by means of the sociological imagination that men and women now hope to grasp what is going on in the world, and to understand what is happening in themselves as minute points of the intersections of biography and history within society.' Mills (1999: 7).

Asexuality is a relatively new identity with limited representation. Research into asexuality is a relatively new and yet burgeoning field (see Chapter 3 for further discussion of this). This newness is reflected in my personal story, with my 'epiphany' (Denzin 2001) about being asexual occurring a year into my PhD studies, when I changed the focus of my study from gender queerness to asexuality. This fresh insider perspective allows a unique lens with which to view the phenomena, with direct experience, much 'primary data' in the form of journals kept over a period of 22 years, and yet few preconceived or formulated ideas regarding asexuality (see Chapter 2 for a presentation of this narrative).

However, when I first started to research the term 'asexuality' I was disappointed to find that the main definition provided by AVEN is that asexuality is a lack of something – a lack of desire for sex and sexual attraction, whereas I had experienced my asexuality as a flourishing, an embodied spiritual experience of erotic flourishing, an expression of my 'fullness' not as a lack of anything. Mark Smith (2017) noticed a similar problem during his ethnographic research into asexuality – that asexuals could not describe the *experience* of being asexual – they simply described the lack of experience, i.e. the experience of sexuality and their problems fitting in within 'sexusociety' and 'couples' culture' (Przybylo 2011). He looked to history to find and create a Foucauldian genealogy of asexuality, within which he linked asexuality with erotic and mystical experiences. During this process, he attempted what he termed a 'botched autoethnography'[25] into how spiritual practices affect the experience of asexuality, botched because he did not have the time to allow for these practices to have an effect. I aim to take up the parts of Smith's research which were unsuccessful. I do have over 20 years of undertaking such spiritual practices and I had access to a group of asexual individuals who also have a spiritual practice and who have been able to articulate their experience of being asexual rather than getting stuck on referring to a lack of sexuality or simply talking about their problems navigating relationships within sexualized society. In fact, their stories also contain a variety of experiences of erotically embodied asexuality. These stories have the potential to dislocate sexuality from its hegemony of eros. To borrow the words of Gale and Wyatt regarding the nature of this book:

---

[25] Smith (2017) describes his attempt at a mystical autoethnography thus, 'My readings on ascetic practices of sexual and self-renunciation as well as my readings on mysticism also prompted me to conduct a brief month-long experimental autoethnography in which I attempted to live an ascetic/monastic lifestyle and in which I attempted to more fully understand early Christian mysticism and the means by which to cultivate mystical experiences. During this month I read religious texts, conducted research on monastic and mystical practices, and engaged in customs such as meditation, chastity, and fasting for several days at a time. Ultimately, I call this experiment a "botched autoethnography," as I learned that it is far too tough to follow the mystical path to God in such a short amount of time—especially in the absence of a monastic infrastructure that ensures strict adherence to religious rules. Although this autoethnography is not discussed in the following chapters, it has deeply informed the writing of Chapters Two and Four on medieval mysticism and conceptions of eros, respectively.' (p. 19)

> This writing is experimental, it is transgressive; it expresses a desire to be curious, to destabilize and to trouble the givens of accepted discourses, knowledge constructions and ways of thinking and doing (Gale and Wyatt 2009: 8, cited in Carless and Douglas 2022: 155)

Transgressive writing has the potential to disrupt societal norms and explore the boundaries of human experience, including the erotic. This defiance against societal expectations can be inherently erotic, as it disrupts conventional boundaries and invites readers to engage with a narrative that may invite them to extend beyond perceived limitations or restrictions. Griffin (1996) also describes the writing of the 'history of the private life' as erotic, in her book *The Eros of Everyday Life* and says that it has 'an erotic edge, *not* because of the sexuality, which is part of private life, but because in doing so one penetrates a contained world' (p.184). This reflects Gafini and Kincaid's (2017) description of the erotic within all aspects of life (not merely limited to the sexual) as involving being on the 'inside' of the body, the experience or the shared field. The experience of expanding the limits of the personal to the transpersonal (for example with another individual, a group, art, nature, or more ethereal non-material dimensions).[26] This book is woven through with challenges to the sexualization of the erotic, erotic language and sexualized society, but the methodology, autoethnography, as a method that offers us a pathway to the inside of another's experience, is also inherently erotic. Through the application of my sociological imagination, I aim offer the reader an intimate reading of erotically embodied asexuality.

---

[26] Discussed in depth in Chapter 3.

1.3 Auto/biography and autoethnography

I am well aware that I have never written anything but fictions. I do not mean to say, however, that truth is therefore absent. It seems to me that the possibility exists for fiction to function in truth, for a fictional discourse to induce effects of truth, and for bringing it about that a true discourse engenders or 'manufactures' something that does not as yet exist, that is, 'fictions' it.
Foucault 1980:193

I utilize elements from both auto/biographical and autoethnographic methodologies. Sparkes states that autoethnographies are 'highly personalized accounts that draw upon the experience of the author/researcher for the purposes of extending sociological understanding' (2000:21). The auto/biographical approach emphasizes the interdependence of autobiography and biography (Parsons 2014). Parsons and Chappell (2020) discovered numerous advantages in embracing this approach, highlighting its ability to reveal the 'interconnectedness and interdependence of biography with autobiography, the self with the other' (p.8). Both address Plummer's concern that there is a need to counter the proliferation of scientific structural analysis which dominate the social sciences, and balance this with methodologies that privilege the human subject and the *Documents of Life* created by these human subjects, in order to create biographies and autoethnographies (2001).

Plummer states that 'social analysis and research is not something outside of social life and hence not something outside of stories' (2013: 216). This means that 'social science … needs to foster styles of thinking and writing that question and interrogate the documents of our lives, and which encourage the creative, interpretive story-tellings of lives' (Ibid.) Plummer values these *Documents of Life* as valuable and valid data sources for conducting research. Within these documents he includes:

> The autobiographies and life stories, the obituaries and the tombstones, the oral histories and the family histories, the desert island discs, the playlists, the diaries, the letters and the blogs. There are the bildungsroman, genealogies, therapeutic self-tales, memoirs and auto/ethnographies. There are narrative visuals: in art, sculpture, stained glass windows, architecture, photographs, film and video … the digital narratives of websites, e-mails, and YouTube videos, in Second Life realities and digital games fantasy, on social network sites and tweets. (Plummer 2013: 210)

Following my asexual epiphany, I was in the position of endeavoring to understand my identity whilst conducting my research. I had access to a wealth of *Documents of Life* spanning a period from 1996 to 2018. A period in which I explored sexuality, alternative sexualities, relationships, and celibacy within the context of alternative spiritual communities. This exploration took place alongside an adherence to various spiritual practices I learned whilst travelling extensively and undertaking facilitator and therapist trainings in the UK. My numerous ethnographical musings from within these contexts and my personal reflections in my journals offered me a messy text that formed a source of 'primary data' for the first stage of my research. This 'data' consists of 42 journals and some notes on scrap paper, written over the course of 22 years, which offered the opportunity for doing 'biographical work' (Scott and Dawson 2018) to extract the key biographical moments that led to me becoming asexual. This made it possible for me to offer an example of a non-essentialist asexual 'becoming' and present an alternative narrative of the experience of asexuality.

This wealth of personal 'data' offered a depth of material with a richness that would be challenging to amass from an interview with another. Therefore, my research starts with my own narrative; my analysis of this 'primary data' and the subsequent creative outputs provided me with the key themes for further exploration with co-creators.

These themes influenced my analysis of the literature and the focus of the explorations with my co-creators. I considered focusing solely on producing an autoethnography of asexuality, an approach utilized by Paula Stone[27] (2018) in her doctoral thesis based purely on an auto/biographical account of her personal narrative regarding class and education. However, alongside the depth of my own narrative inquiry, I wanted to increase the breadth of experiences by exploring the themes, emerging from the analysis of my experiences, in my dialogue with the co-creators.

In addition to including some raw quotations from my many journals, I will also be utilizing 'auto-netnography' (Villegas 2018) to look back over social media posts. By sharing this 'raw' personal data it enables a sharing of the view of the experience that I had at that point in my trajectory, without the filter of hindsight. This articulated reflexivity adds another dimension to the research by offering a window into aspects that have influenced my asexual becoming, from the perspective of me not realizing where my journey of becoming was headed.

There are risks associated with utilizing these methodologies within the context of academia. Many have warned about the personal exposure within the academic arena where the response to the content and the method can be oppositional (Inckle 2007; Parsons 2014; Letherby 2000; Sparkes 2002, Wall 2008). It is not a methodology to consider without acknowledging the potential of the impact on the researcher's emotional and social well-being and career trajectory (Inckle 2007; Parsons 2014, Letherby 2000; Ellis and Bochner 2000, Wall 2008). I have been gifted in this respect, with a 'tool kit' of well-being practices available to me for taking care of my own well-being, even in extreme and challenging situations (although I must say that this has been thoroughly utilized and at times almost exhausted). I

---

[27] I found Paula Stone's work inspiring, and it was also where I first discovered the technique of layering as advocated by Ronai (1995) and utilized in this book.

am also not seeking general acclaim; my hope is that this work will be useful to others who wish to gain an alternative understanding of (a)sexuality or who may feel reassured by my application of the methodologies I am utilizing, contributing in some way to the feeling that they have 'found their people' (Brown 2019). Throughout my research I have discovered, as Wall (2008), that I struggled with the acceptability of my autoethnography with both formal and informal reviewers.

Due to this struggle with 'acceptability', it was therefore important for me to have some benchmarks to aim for with my writing of an autoethnography. Sparkes provided some useful criterial for 'judging autoethnographies', which I am satisfied I have fulfilled within this project:

> First, any work labelled "autoethnography" should include personal experience and demonstrate, through thoughtful analysis, why this experience is meaningful and culturally significant ... Second, this personal experience must be reflexively considered through the use of extant theory, other scholarly writings about the topic, fieldwork, observations, analysis of artifacts (e.g. photographs), and/or involvement with others (e.g., interviews). (Manning and Adams 2015:205 cited in Sparkes 2022: 264)

Holman Jones, Adams and Ellis (2013) list the following characteristics:

> Purposefully commenting on/critiquing of culture and cultural practices; making contributions to existing research; embracing vulnerability with a purpose; and creating a reciprocal relationship with audiences in order to compel a response. (Sparkes 2022: 264)

In evaluating my research against this criteria, I find that this research makes an important contribution to challenging cultural assumptions regarding sexuality, relationships, the erotic and the libido, it utilizes vulnerability in order to destabilize compulsory sexuality and highlight the damaging effect of emotional and sexual commodification. It offers a highly personal engaging account that reaches out to those who have similar experiences. It enables them to feel validated and able to articulate their experience.

I also assessed my autoethnography utilizing the criteria for evaluating autoethnography offered by Chang (2022):

1. It draws primary data from a researcher's personal experience.

2. It engages a systematic and iterative process of qualitative research.

3. It seeks to understand the sociocultural meaning(s) of the personal experience within its context. (p.54)

Within my research I have covered all of these criteria; firstly, drawing my 'primary data' from my personal experience. Secondly, I have undertaken a systematic and iterative process of qualitative research (the iterative process involved collaborative work with the participants - or 'co-creators' - the term I use to describe those whom participated - to verify interpretation, meaning and the creative outputs). And I have met the final criteria as throughout this process I have been seeking to understand the sociocultural meanings of the personal experiences within their context through reading and interpreting multiple strands of literature with the lens of erotically embodied asexuality, the social context, and the current moment of history in which this experience is located.

Wall (2008) shares how she evaluated her research against some parameters offered by Caroline Ellis and that within her evaluation she looked at whether the research had enabled some change within her as the researcher saying, 'I not only challenged the received wisdom of the field but also learned to think about my experience as an adoptive parent in a way that challenged and changed me.' (p. 48). She then shares her concern that this challenge and change could be interpreted as being proof that 'the goal of a storyteller is therapy rather than analysis'(Ibid.) However, her conclusion is that she has made a contribution to the understanding of the process of international adoption and the 'fact that I learned something new in the doing of it was a wonderful bonus on the way to making a scholarly contribution'(Ibid.).

I too experienced this phenomenon of the research enabling some change within me as a researcher as described by Ellis and Wall. One of my research journal entries expresses this:

Journal entry, 18 October 2020

As I read and discuss, it changes my story – each puzzle piece changes my perception, and, as the perceiver of my past selves, their stories are therefore somehow changed by my new way of perceiving them.

* * *

I do not share a concern about this work being interpreted as navel-gazing or simply 'therapeutic writing'. Those who embark on the personal and academic challenge of writing auto/biographical or autoethnographic work will know that their motivations are far from doing this work to 'sort myself out' (Rothman 1986, cited in Letherby 2015). Everybody has personal 'issues' to deal with in their lives and 'for those of us whose work includes the responsibility of representing the lives of others, it is important that those issues do not cloud our presentation of the lives of others' (Letherby 2015: 137).

This often-challenging self-reflection and processing of challenging experiences is hard emotional work, it is understandable why many may avoid it. Gayle Letherby (2015) explains that 'critical scrutiny of the self is completely different than mere navel gazing and researchers and writers who do not engage in such self-reflection are not undertaking the reflexivity needed to properly represent the significance of the complex relationship between the self and other' (p.136). This 'critical scrutiny of the self' is necessary to avoid 'the narcissistic substitution of autoethnography for research' (Delamont, 2007: 3, cited in Letherby 2015). Chang (2022) tells us that:

> Although criticisms of this "unconventional" research method have persisted, advocates of autoethnography have directed social scientists' attention to the unique capacity of autoethnography that illuminates sociocultural phenomena through researchers ready and thorough access to their intimate and experiential data as native ethnographers (p.55).

Pelias (2022) affirms that:

> [T]his is not an act of self-indulgence, narcissism, or navel-gazing, as some would suggest. Instead, it is, as Goodall (2000) claims, "the process of personally and academically reflecting on lived experience in ways that reveal the deep connection between the writer and her or his subject" (p.137). Unlike personal absorption the reflexive gains its power by reaching for the cultural. Such introspection offers an intimate knowledge based on lived experience with others (2022:123).

Mills (1959) held this reflexive ability in high esteem: 'The most admirable thinkers within the scholarly community…do not split their work from their lives…. What this means is that you must learn to use your life experiences in your intellectual work' (p195-196). In order to utilize life experiences the researcher needs to take a position of 'theorized subjectivity' (Letherby 2013) which requires 'constant, critical interrogation of our personhood – both intellectual and personal – within the production of the knowledge' (Letherby 2015: 133). This is not work for the faint hearted. Wall (2008) tells us that 'the intimate and personal nature of autoethnography can, in fact, make it one of the most challenging qualitative approaches to attempt.' [2008: 39]

Denzin (2001) asserts that 'meaningful interpretations of human experience can come only from those persons who have thoroughly immersed themselves in the phenomena they wish to interpret and understand' (p.11). As I have had my own personal process and journey with asexuality, I considered it appropriate to utilize auto/biography as a research method as I could 'use my own social location as the starting point from which to engage research participants' (Inckle 2007:32). Auto/biography involves the researcher being explicit about their own position, which includes the researcher's reflections on their own subjectivity and emotions (Parsons and Chappell 2020).

This method enables the researcher to gain a deeper and richer understanding of the phenomenon they are researching (McIlveen 2008) by becoming a 'reflexive "key informer" attempting to bridge the gaps between lived experience and academic knowledge production' (Inckle 2007: 32). In addition to taking this 'reflexive key informer' position, interweaving my autobiographical reflexivity and insights into the academic text, I will also be utilizing my own embodied, sensory, 'thickly described' (Denzin 2001: 2) autoethnography, for interpretation and creative presentation (thus treating my own 'data' in the same way as the co-creators' stories). Inckle describes autoethnography as 'empirical sociology where the author's own experience forms the research material' (Inkle 2007: 29). Ellis and Bochner (2002) describe autoethnography as a form of autobiographical writing and research that intertwines personal and cultural perspectives which is often presented in the first person. They recommend that these narratives contain 'concrete action, dialogue, emotion, embodiment, spirituality, and self consciousness' (Ellis and Bochner 2002: 739), revealing relational and institutional stories influenced by historical, social, and cultural contexts.

Auto/biography and autoethnography are often utilized by authors who do not find any of the conventional practices of research adequate to convey the 'multifaceted, complex and emotive layers of embodied human experience' (Inckle 2007: 29). I find it helpful to use both terms to describe the two different roles I have undertaken in this research. There is the auto/biographical I who acts as 'key informer'; interweaving anecdotes and insights with the analytical, critical academic 'voice' and the autoethnographic I, whose voice introduces and elucidates the main themes of the research, and who weaves 'thickly described', multi-layered, creative, emotive expression into the poetical, fictional and dramaturgical texts.

Our efforts are undoubtedly
better spent in trying to speak of this experience and
in making it speak from the depths where its language fails,
from precisely the place where words escape it,
where the subject who speaks has just vanished,
where the spectacle topples over before
an upturned eye
Foucault 1963:40

My auto/biographical research interweaves a post-humanist perspective, as articulated by Deleuze and Guattari, particularly in *A Thousand Plateaus* (1980) and Gale (2018), with the framework of *Interpretive Interactionism* developed by Denzin (2001). Deleuze and Guattari's perspective accentuates rhizomatic structures and the idea that identities are not fixed but are constantly in flux, therefore rejecting traditional humanism and focusing instead on multiplicities, flows, and the interconnectedness of all entities. This perspective challenges the notion of a fixed self and explores the dynamic relationships between human and non-human entities. Interpretive interactionism, rooted in symbolic interactionism, focuses on the ways in which individuals create and interpret meaning through social interaction. It emphasizes shared symbols, language, and the negotiated nature of reality within social contexts, focusing on the micro-level of social interactions, and examining how individuals construct and communicate meaning in their everyday lives. It also acknowledges that the self is not a fixed entity and that it is continually shaped by social interactions.

Combining elements from interpretive interactionism with a post-humanist perspective, offered me a rich and nuanced approach for researching how individuals construct their identity through both human interaction and transpersonal interactions such as with nature or the divine. This combined framework allowed a broader, and more complete exploration of the complex dynamics shaping identity formation than interpretive interactionism could offer on its own.

Interpretive interactionism is a methodological framework that 'begins and ends with the biography and the self of the researcher. The events and troubles the researcher writes about are those that he or she has experienced or witnessed firsthand.' (Denzin 2001: 11) Interpretive interactionism shares roots with symbolic interactionism, which has key concepts 'such as negotiating meaning, career trajectories, social selfhood and pragmatic social action' (Scott and Dawson 2015: 4). Scott and Dawson tell us that in order to understand asexuality we need to recognize 'these relational aspects of becoming asexual, which emerge out of social interaction and are negotiated in relationships' and, that the concepts within symbolic interactionism can 'provide refreshing new insights into asexual identities and practices of intimacy' (p.4) This aspect of the research focuses on human interaction and the micro-level interactions that influenced individuals negotiating and constructing their identities within social contexts. Including individuals' perceptions of symbols, language, and shared meanings within interactions with others provides insights into how social constructs influence identity.

The addition of the post-humanist perspective allows for an examination of transpersonal interaction and an exploration of identity beyond the human-centric perspective. Including how individuals engage with nature or the divine in shaping their sense of self, opening up avenues towards understanding the interconnectedness of and interaction between human and non-human entities. Although the post-humanist approach often also includes the role of technology, this research does not focus on technology but examines other aspects of this perspective which look at the role of the environment, and spiritual or transcendent experiences in the formation of identity.

Drawing on Deleuze and Guattari's (1980) rhizomatic concept, allows this research to explore the non-linear and interconnected nature of identity. Rather than seeing identity as fixed and stable, this research looks at the multiplicity and fluidity of identity formation. It acknowledges the influences of various sources on identity, including human interactions and transpersonal engagements. Within this combined framework identity is a dynamic, relational process involving both human and non-human elements. Traditional dualisms between self and other, human and non-human are challenged and the intricate interplay between various factors in identity formation are acknowledged. Through utilizing post-humanist ideas it is possible to break down boundaries and recognize the entangled relationships that contribute to a developing sense of identity. This combination of interpretive interactionism with a post-humanist perspective offers an engaging mix of perspectives for researching asexual identity formation or 'becomings' and allowed for a subtle appreciation of an intricate web of influences, encompassing both human interactions and transpersonal encounters.

My choice of interpretive interactionism is due to its focus on the 'epiphany' and interpreting meaning (Denzin 2001:11-15). The (re)focus of this research followed my asexual epiphany, with my Director of Studies, Julie Parsons, recognizing this and directing me towards Denzin's work. Denzin describes the epiphany as:

> Those interactional moments that leave marks on people's lives [and] have the potential to create transformational experiences ... In these moments, personal character is manifested and made apparent ... Such moments are often interpreted, both by the persons who have them and by others, as turning-point experiences. Having had such a moment, a person is never quite the same again. (p.11)

I fully appreciate the strength of these moments. The impact of my epiphany was so great that it did not feel like a choice to change the focus of my research. The interpretation of certain moments in my trajectory and the meaning I attached to them altered my understanding and perception of my relationships, gender, and many other facets of my life.

The asexual identity is a relatively new identity in the sense that it only started to become an established identity around 20 years ago, largely due to the formation of the online community AVEN (Asexual Visibility and Education Network in 2001). This lack of recognition and representation means that most asexuals came to the realization that they identify as asexual after some confusion around why they could not fit into normative sexual and in some cases (if they are also aromantic) romantic couples' culture (Carrigan 2011). This means that asexual narratives are likely to stem from the perspective of the moment of 'epiphany' when, perhaps through a combination of self-reflection and moments of social interaction, the participant had the realization that they are asexual (Denzin 2001). I utilize creative methods of analysis and presentation to explore the 'biographical identity work' (Scott and Dawson 2015) that both I and the co-creators have done to make sense of our pasts from this new perspective.[28]

Utilizing creative methods enabled me to maintain a high level of ethics and safety for the co-creators in this project, offering a further level of anonymity through fictionalizing all the research findings

---

[28] This paragraph was utilized in a BSA conference abstract, published on their website (Love 2022).

within sociological fiction, poetry, and dramaturgical texts[29]. This use of fictionalized research outputs fits within the interpretive interactionist framework. Denzin (2001) explains that writers of interpretation must 'learn how to experiment with modes of writing that are not tied to mainstream and interpretive realist criteria of evaluation'. He advises that, 'they must experiment with alternative ways of presenting the interpretation' including presenting 'true fictions' through the mediums of 'films, novels, plays, songs, music, poems, dance, paintings, photography, sculptures, pottery, toolmaking, and architecture' (p.10). For this research I utilized fiction, poems, photos and dramaturgical texts.

1.5 Interdisciplinary Lens

In addition to the merging of frameworks, it was necessary to adopt an interdisciplinary lens in order to find literature that helped to make sense of the co-creators' stories. Many researchers have found that it can be beneficial to undertake interdisciplinary research to gain greater insight (Wardley and Belanger 2015; Balzer et al 2017; Fosl 2016; Scheff 2015; Shandas and Brown 2016). Wardley and Bélanger (2015) state that 'there needs to be a combination of integration of perspectives and methodologies, a complex issue that exceeds the borders of a single discipline, and cognitive advancement that would not be possible through the lens of single discipline' (p.47).

This research integrates insights from autoethnographic inquiry with literature largely from sociology, social psychology, religious studies, and theology. Although I attempted to focus on literature from these disciplines, I ended up taking a 'scavenger' approach[30], in order to gain a holistic understanding of asexuality, which led to

---

[29] See Chapter 4 for a discussion of ethics and the experience of the research process.

[30] See Introduction for a discussion of this 'scavenger' approach to the literature review.

following strands from psychology, anthropology, history, queer theory, feminist studies and sexology.

Working from an embodied perspective was also essential to this research for two reasons. Firstly, exploring asexual intimacy and experiences of attraction, the nonsexual erotic and desire would be impossible without direct reference to the experience of the body, and our understanding of these experiences is enriched by thick sensory description. Secondly, it is a match with my strengths, life experiences and philosophical perspective as a researcher. Like Jennifer Leigh, in addition to teaching marketing in academic settings, I trained and practiced as a mindfulness and mindful movement teacher, and somatic awareness and bodywork therapist. My somatic movement practice and training was key on my path to healing and self-development, and embodied experience is fundamental to the way I move through life and interpret my experiences.

1.6 Embodied Inquiry

Perception… is not the achievement of a mind in a body, but of the organism as whole in its environment, and is tantamount to the organism's own exploratory movement through the world.
Ingold 2000: 3

In their *book Embodied Inquiry* (2021), Jennifer Leigh and Nicole Brown describe an approach to research that 'privileges the lived, embodied experiences of the researcher and the researched' (p.101). The idea of immersion inherent in auto/biography and autoethnography resonates with embodied inquiry 'as it plays to the thought that we are interested in recording and capturing the sensations and substance of an experience.' (p.9) Pink (2015) advocates a similar, 'sensory ethnography', explaining that there is a need to understand the sorts of knowledge that ethnographies produce through methods that reference the sensory experiences inherent within them.

Williams and Bendelow (1998) propose that embodiment serves as the dynamic foundation of existence in the world, forming the basis for 'self, meaning, culture, and society' (p.1). They argue that the relationship between experience and representation is not a matter of choosing one over the other but rather of exploring their dialectical interconnection and the 'emergent properties' that arise from this relationship. The locus of embodiment establishes a holistic, non-dual position, transcending the limits of normative theoretical standpoints and methodologies, which are dualistic and disembodied, objectifying and distancing the very experiences they seek to explain' (Inckle 2007).

Embodied inquiry is particularly suited, although not limited to, research projects that have creative outputs (Leigh and Brown 2021). Working in a virtual way, as this research did, does not preclude this type of inquiry. Embodied inquiry does not require that the research is done in person it simply requires that the researcher and/or the participants are practicing embodied self-awareness (Leigh and Brown 2021).

Leigh and Brown describe the three principles of embodied inquiry as:

> The 'What?' of Embodied Inquiry - Embodied Inquiry is part of an ongoing process of self. It asks for reflexivity, an exploration, attention to and nonjudgemental awareness of self in addition to attention, exploration and nonjudgemental awareness of others' experiences. Awareness of every movement and moment is a skill that can be learned and practiced. It is likely to impact on life outside of the research study.
>
> Why? The starting point is that the body and mind are connected. By accessing the information, data and stories that bodies store, hold and tell, it is possible to reach deeper, emotional and authentic truths about lived experience than are accessed by more conventional research techniques.

> The 'How?' of an Embodied Inquiry is through conscious awareness, or the intention to incorporate this way of working into research. (2021: 2)

Leigh and Brown (Ibid.) explain that in order to embark on a project that includes sensory ethnography or embodied inquiry we need to be consciously self-aware by acknowledging and understanding information received from various sources such as senses, proprioception, thoughts, feelings, images, and emotions. They describe how this awareness is achieved through practices such as somatic movement therapy, bodywork, yoga, and mindfulness, which help individuals bring experiences from unconscious or unverbalized levels to conscious awareness and articulate them. This embodied awareness that they describe is part of the fabric of my being, and draws from strengths gained through my trainings, personal practice and over 15 years of working as a therapist and teacher in these fields.

The first step to realizing that I would be bringing this aspect of self to the research table was prior to my personal retreat to a log cabin in September 2021. The retreat was my 'turning point' the dawn of my epiphany that completely refocused my research. My supervisor, Lyvinia Elleschild, on hearing that I was retreating to a cabin in the woods to focus on my writing, guided me towards a book – *Sensory Ethnography* (Pink 2015). It felt like an invitation, an invitation to a part of myself that I did not feel would be welcome in academia.

My year of critical thinking and writing combined with the somatic practice and *Conscious Writing* (McCutchen 2015) practiced during my retreat allowed new insights and another voice to come through. This is my journal entry from the last day of the retreat:

(Journal entry, 18 September 2021)

Realizing that as I connected with an embodied sense of how I felt, who I was, what stage of the process I was at that there were three clear periods:

Confusion – teens and twenties
Liminality – 30s and early 40s
Integration – PhD, 2019 +

Although gender is intrinsic to my experience and the understanding of my experience – this is fundamentally about my relationship to relationships and asexuality.

*   *   *

When I am not giving conscious awareness to an aspect of self, I often find that I experience a 'nagging' internal voice that keeps suggesting something to remedy this self-neglect. If I listen and undertake the action it usually follows that greater levels of insight, integration, and (eventually) increased well-being arise. One of my favorite quotes regarding the importance of this balance is a proverb or axiom from India:

> Everyone is a house with four rooms, a physical, a mental, an emotional and a spiritual. Most of us tend to live in one room most of the time but, unless we go into every room every day, even if only to keep it aired, we are not a complete person (Godden 1989: 3).

In the first year of my PhD, I became focused on thinking, reading, totally immersed in the intellectual, mental realm. Consumed by my ideas and proving my standpoint, almost to the point of obsession. I felt, somehow, that I was looking for a missing piece of the puzzle that I could not find. I had neglected the somatic realm and the wisdom and insight that I find there. Even my daily movement practice had become focused on the western style (of simply stretching and keeping/building strength), rather than somatic awareness and the subtle aspects that were so dear to me. The difference is huge; when I focus simply on the movement as a form of exercise, I lay down to relax at the end of a session and feel like I am laying encased in a soft leather glove. When I also focus on the somatic, breath and energy awareness aspects of movement practice, when I lay down at the end, I feel like I have slipped into a soft leather glove lined with soft, silky cashmere.

In Wembury there is a place called Churchwood, with wooden cabins available to rent haphazardly placed within a lush woodland setting, nestled on the side of a valley overlooking a bubbling stream that winds down to the wild coastline. I drove past Churchwood regularly and my internal voice would say 'you should take time out to stay there and nourish yourself'. I ignored it with excuses about children, finances and time constraints and admonishments about the sheer frivolity of doing such a thing.

Just before I arranged my personal retreat the voice got louder and kept appearing in my journal, as I would sit to write some reflections on my research, it said:

(Four separate journal entries, August, and September 2021)

Do you have the courage to be yourself?

Making space for yourself in the world – broom – clean this up, clean this up.

Cleaning a fresh patch of space and feeling yourself grounded in it.

Where can I go that always feels supportive, strong and pure for my truest self – WEMBURY!!!

* * *

In retrospect I can see that this was an 'inner knowing' that being at Wembury would allow me to access something important, and indeed it did, as it was the location of my turning point, my accessing of key childhood memories and a reimagining of my life trajectory that would allow for my epiphany and refocusing of my research. Casey emphasizes a relationship between memory and place, making the point that 'moving in or through a given place, the body imports its own emplaced past into its present experience' (Casey 1987: 194, cited by Pink 2015: 44).

Pink explains the idea that the senses are connected and interwoven, saying that we cannot necessarily separate the senses in the way we experience them, but when we talk about our sensory experience, we divide them up into sensory categories. These categories (in Western culture) being; smell, sound, touch, hearing, vision. However, in other cultures, the same set of senses is not necessarily described in the same way.

Howes and Classen pursued this line of argument, claiming that:

The ways we use our senses, and the ways we create and understand the sensory world, are shaped by culture. Perception is informed not only by the personal meaning a particular sensation has for us, but also by the social values it carries (Howes and Classen 2014: 1, cited in Pink 2015: 32).

However, this does not preclude the understanding of sensory experience across cultures as these ideas about the interrelation of the senses also allow us to comprehend how, in various situations, similar meanings can be conveyed using 'different sensory modalities and media' (Pink 2015: 32).

As the co-creators and I undertake practices from varying cultures, the cross-cultural sensory pallet may differ from the standard western five-sense-system and categories and associated meanings will have to be elucidated. Pink noted that categories may have to be changed or adjusted to fit the sensory nature of the specific research, meaning that, for example, categories such as 'energy' or 'movement' are added as sense categories. Through this direct experiential description of embodied sensory awareness, the reader can gain a deeper understanding of and connection with the other's experience, perhaps dissolving social and cultural boundaries and the sense of self and other.

1.7 Embodied spirituality

Why, when God's world is so big, did you fall asleep
in a prison of all places?
Rumi

Embodied sensory awareness was one of the ways in which all of the co-creators in this research experienced 'everyday mysticism' or a sense of the sacred or a spiritual dimension to life (Soelle 2001). Canda and Furman (2009) define spirituality as a 'universal and fundamental human quality involving the search for a sense of meaning, purpose, morality, well-being, and profundity in relationships with ourselves, others, and ultimate reality, however understood' and religion as 'an institutionalized (i.e., systematic) pattern of values, beliefs, symbols, behaviors, and experiences that are oriented toward spiritual concerns, shared by a community, and transmitted over time in traditions' (p. 59). I will be utilizing these definitions within this research.

Pargament (1997) suggested that religion is the vehicle through which spirituality is commonly expressed. It seems from an examination of the cross-disciplinary literature that this is not the case in the modern era, with religion being only one way in which spirituality is expressed (Griffin 1996, Soelle 2001, McDaniel 2018). New terminology is needed to articulate a shared spiritual experience whilst still honoring the traditions, rituals, and practices of each religion. I find that the terms spiritual and religious are useful categories and they do not need to be mutually exclusive. Some of the co-creators considered themselves broadly spiritual, although they chose to participate in one structured religious institution.

The important point here is that whether one connects to something either deeply within themselves or outside of themselves, this process gives life meaning and can lead to erotically ecstatic states. It is this process of merging with the 'Other' that brings pleasurable sensations and a feeling of liberation. This can be through sexual merging and pleasure, but this is only one expression of something that can be much more expansive. This idea will be explored throughout this book, both through theoretical analysis and the experiences of those who identify as erotically embodied asexuals.

All of those who participated in this research have varying spiritual, psychospiritual[31] or religious beliefs. Some relate to God,

---

[31] The term 'psychospiritual' has become part of discussions in psychology and religion, loosely representing the merging of psychological and spiritual aspects. This broad term

although all have different definitions of what this means (personal, love, energy, cosmos etc.) Some have spiritual experiences based on an atheistic psychospiritual connection, applying Jung's ideas within their personal process, and merging within, with the unconscious aspects of their soul. For some, they find their release within meditation and an associated conscious deconstruction of all social programming and identity labels. For some the erotic is found within an animistic perspective of Spirit within nature. For some, like me, they experience a combination of all of these, with Spirit being present within all realms, the essence of their human flourishing and a sustained feeling of being held by love.

The foundation of my becoming an erotically embodied asexual was my journey to re-enchantment and rediscovering a spiritual connection. First through the 'neo-mysticism' (Berger 1965) of Jungian psychology, working with Jungian psychological models and utilizing meditative techniques to gain peace of mind, and liberate myself from social conditioning, which could be classed as a form of 'spiritual atheism'. In line with my meditation practice, I became interested in Buddhism, joining a Buddhist community, undertaking a training in 'counselling with a focus on mindfulness' and, in particular, adopting the regular practice of 'metta meditation'[32] also

---

encompasses various relationships between psychology and spirituality, including the integration or conflation of the two domains. Typically, it is employed to characterize therapeutic systems that view the spiritual dimension as integral to mental well-being and complete human development. These systems employ a holistic, integrated approach to healing and inner growth, utilizing both psychological and spiritual methods such as meditation, mindful movement dream-work, and breathwork.

[32] Metta meditation, also known as loving-kindness meditation, is a mindfulness practice originating from the Buddhist tradition. It involves cultivating feelings of love, compassion, and goodwill towards oneself and others. Practitioners typically focus on the area of the heart and repeat phrases or intentions wishing happiness, health, and peace for themselves, loved ones, acquaintances, unknown neighbors and those they have difficult or challenging relationships with. The practice aims to cultivate a mindset of kindness, empathy, and connection towards all beings.

known as 'loving kindness meditation', which is a meditation designed to develop benevolence, universal love or love of mankind.

This expansive and non-particular feeling of love altered my practice into a more outward focused spirituality and a desire to serve and create for the benefit of all. As my practices broadened into somatic awareness practices, ecstatic dance and nature connection, my spiritual feelings developed further with an 'animistic' sense of Sprit in nature which I felt as an effervescent, joyful, tingling both in my body and in the space around me. The feeling of 'love of mankind' or loving compassion, (referred to as Agape in Greek) and Spirit within nature gave an erotic feel to everyday interactions, tasks and activities. Griffin describes how 'the alienation of human society from nature has led to many different kinds of destruction, not the least of which has been the fragmentation of consciousness' (1996:14). She goes on to describe the erotic connection to love, the body and earth that I was experiencing:

> If human consciousness can be rejoined not only with the human body but with the body of earth, what seems incipient in the reunion is the recovery of meaning within existence that will infuse every kind of meeting between self and the universe, even in the most daily acts, with an eros, a palpable love, that is also sacred (1996:15).

The 'spiritual atheism' that I explored at the beginning of my journey does not fit neatly into a religious or spiritual category. Mc Daniel explains that the modern trend is to pigeonhole any ecstatic experience into 'existing institutional or religious categories' 2018:18). A central premise of many books on non-religious mysticism is that if you change the state of the unconscious mind, you can change your experience of the world and how you interact with others and the world around you. Berger (1965) would locate this type of psychospiritual experience within the prevalent 'psychologism'[33] as a type of 'neo-mysticism' with a focus on individualistic transformation through the use of psychological models, which 'brings about a strange reversal of the disenchantment and demythologization of modern consciousness' (1965:40-41).

The psychospiritual offers a consumable spiritual experience, filling a gap created by the secularization of Western society, the 'loss of the sacred canopy'[34] Berger (1967) and 'the death of God' (Foucault 1963). Eva Illouz (2008) explores this 'psychologism' in her book *Saving the Modern Soul*, delving into the commodification of the psychospiritual realm and discussing how emotional experiences, therapeutic practices, and spiritual quests have become marketable commodities within consumerist, contemporary society. She raises concerns about the potential loss of authenticity, the distortion of spiritual practices for commercial purposes, and the creation of unrealistic expectations for individuals seeking emotional or spiritual fulfilment within a consumer-driven culture. Berger states that 'Sociology, like psychoanalysis occupies a fairly unique position in the American cultural situation. There is probably a common reason behind the cultural prominence of these two disciplines of *collective introspection*' (1965:28 – emphasis in original).

Despite the rampant commodification of the psychospiritual, both psychology and sociology offer an opportunity in secularized society to become free of the social constructs and programming that keep us imprisoned as consuming and producing subjects. I have found that the two disciplines are both necessary in order to change the consumerist and hypersexual programming that individuals may be subject to within Western culture; that it is not enough to simply work

---

[33] Berger used the term 'psychologism' to describe 'a psychological model operative in the taken-for-granted-world of everyday life in our society' (1965:34).

[34] Berger (1967) introduced the concept of the 'sacred canopy', which is the religion which every human society builds over its world to give it meaning.

on a psychological level in order to unravel conditioning, that there is a need to take a sociological perspective and examine the institutions and interactions within which this programming has been developed.

Soelle (2001) describes capitalist society as a kind of prison with the constraints of our prison as heedless consumerism which has even led to identity becoming commodified. Soelle reminds us that we are 'we are all mystics' (2001:9), offering many examples from the wonder of childhood to ecstatic connection within nature. She argues that experiences of mysticism are available to all of us, and are not limited to monastics, sadhus and saints. She defines a spirituality that is 'within the tangible world of experience' (2001:9). An exploration of the psychospiritual and the sociological can offer a glimpse of an 'atheistic spirituality', a mystical and possibly ecstatic liberation from the 'capitalist prison'.

Just as a sociological lens can lead to a deconstruction of social constructs within the individual's psyche, many Eastern spiritual traditions, such as Buddhism can lead to this sense of liberation from a 'Western' mindset. Both lead to a point where we find our commonality. This feeling of commonality and not being 'special' leads to greater compassion and morality, and also points to that which was there before social construction, such as the natural material world from which we are all made and to which we will return when we die. Griffin (1996) points towards a 'shift in the deepest levels of meaning we share. An early, still fragile meeting in consciousness between care for nature and a care for human society' (p.14-15).

The Self that is discovered through the meditation practices shared within the Eastern spiritual traditions, such as Buddhism, does not have a fixed identity although it does have a sense of continuity as the observer of all the content and concepts that present themselves. It might be conceived of as the strand forming a cord that weaves through our lives, a strand that is not static. The constituent threads of this cord can undergo changes—becoming frayed or strengthened, 'continuously spliced', or interwoven with other threads—resulting in its ongoing transformation over time (Jackson 2007:7); this cord may be complex and have many threads.

This view of the Self acknowledges the Self as an 'experiencing subject' with some agency and that although constantly changing in response to content, concept and context, including social interaction, it has a continual sense of both the disruptions and unity within the psyche (Stanley, 1993). It also acknowledges the actuality of experience and events in the past (Jackson 2007) and points towards the fact that change can be painful, with the image of 'fraying'. Identity could be seen as the various unchangeable physical qualities of the cord and, in the case of chosen identity labels, as a strand in the cord that an individual has a perception of being constant or integral to the stability of the cord over time and wishes to name as a continuous thread (and be seen by others as having this thread). The metaphor could also be expanded to include that the cord is made of the same substance within everyone, although it may have different qualities and subjective evaluations of, or ways of naming those qualities.

Tentatively touching that commonality, the fundamental context from which variable contexts, content and concepts arise is thrilling to me. It is thrilling within academic studies intellectually probing to the ideas behind the ideas. It is thrilling to contact the body fully from the inside, it is exhilarating whilst meditating to feel the expansive liberating clear horizon of 'no mind'. It is electrifying in moments of activism within a group of disparate people united in the passion of a shared cause expressed in action. I have found it overjoying to feel the opening of the heart in moments when I have served this common humanity in acts of care and support. I feel the thrill in somatically sensing the reciprocal movement of particles and waves within nature; a bodymind understanding itself as an integral part of a rhizomatic ecosystem. Griffin explains this sense of underlying connection; 'by the science of ecology it has been established that all phenomena in nature, including human beings, are interconnected' (1996:15).

This sense of the interconnectedness of all things within nature can be simply an animistic and grounded sense of the sacred. However, Christian Theologians, such as St Athanasius (c. 338 [2017]) explain that God can be seen and experienced through the created world, often referred to as the 'general revelation'. This is the belief that God's attributes, power, and existence are evident in the natural world, and because of this, people can discover some aspects of God's nature through observing and connecting with nature and studying the order of the universe. This idea can be seen in biblical passages such as Psalm 19:1-4, which speaks of how 'the heavens declare the glory of God.' In conjunction with this 'general revelation', Christianity also teaches the concept of 'special revelation', which is the unique and definitive revelation of God through Jesus Christ (St Athanasius c. 338). In Christian theology, Jesus is considered the perfect revelation of God in human form.

An everyday revelation or mystic experience (Soelle 2001) can be found within the embodied embrace of mindful somatic awareness. By delving into intimate dialogue with our own bodyminds, our own bodily temples, the co-creators and I unearthed a profound understanding that we are not separate from nature but integral to its majestic tapestry and that the sacred is not only beyond but within, manifested in the beauty of the human form. This realization, which echoes the wisdom of Griffin (1996) and Soelle (2001), resonates with the ancient notion that the divine is not confined to heavenly realms but is palpable in the very fabric of creation. Although the co-creators have varying spiritual views and practices, one commonality was that we all include various forms of somatic awareness and mindful movement as a disciplined practice in which we find the sacred not only in cosmic realms but in the subtle movements of our own breath and the beat of our own hearts; a heightened awareness that allows us to attune to the vibrant pulse of existence.

1.8 The Embodied Embrace

A worldview is a commitment, a fundamental orientation of the heart, that can be expressed as a story or in a set of propositions (assumptions which may be true, partially true or entirely false) which we hold (consciously or subconsciously, consistently or inconsistently) about the basic constitution of reality, and that provides the foundation on which we live and move and have our being (Sire 2004:122).

This embodied embrace of mindful somatic awareness has been fundamental to my emotional wellbeing and a sense of safety within spiritual development. My personal narrative is woven through with 'a wish for a meaning that might weave oneself and the world together. Not dictated from above the earth but palpable, embedded and experienced in daily life' (Griffin 1996:34) a search that stemmed from my experience of 'disenchantment'[37] in early childhood. Within my personal experience of becoming asexual, there is an intrinsic story; one of losing a worldview, investing in 'unhealthy gods' and then searching for, and discovering alternative worldviews, and finally integrating the learnings that resonated with me in a personal way; a reformulation of a worldview, or in the words of Sire (2004) discovering my 'elephant all the way down'[35].

---

[35] Sire's (2004) book title derives from a metaphor that runs throughout the book. The metaphor begins with an introductory anecdote in which a father, in response to his son's inquiry about what holds up the world, playfully asserts, "A camel." Although this answer satisfies the child temporarily, he later questions, "Dad, what holds up the camel?" The father's response is "A kangaroo," and this pattern continues with the father attributing the support of each creature to another, concluding with an exasperated declaration that the elephant (which is supporting the entire chain) is an "elephant all the way down." (p.6-17).

I will articulate this intrinsic wish and my worldview more explicitly here – how embodied experience has become *the* ground on which I locate all of what I may *think* I know. Knowledge which, although may be based on my beliefs, rational interpretation of experience, and on other's theories and experiences, is always subjective and constantly evolving. I will articulate how my experience has been one of exploring social constructs through a 'social constructionist' rational mind, or from the Eastern spiritual context, the witness or 'observer consciousness', and how these practices of rational observation and mediative contemplation merge seamlessly together for me and lead me to a common 'root' or context. However, it is essential for me that my acceptance and integration of rational theories or spiritual beliefs and practices, lead me to an embodied experience.

This is due to my history – my journey to healing from my 'disenchantment'[36] to an embodied 're-enchantment'. It is important to my ontological security[37] that my re-enchantment is based on embodied experience, because being 're-enchanted' was a painful process for me. I did not simply want to 'believe' something on a rational level or 'feel' it on a heart level. That could be taken away from me again.

---

[36] Weber (1905) introduced the idea of the 'disenchantment of the world' to describe the rationalization and secularization of Western society. This occurred when traditional religious and magical beliefs were replaced by rational, fixed, and systemized ideals. I experienced a 'disenchantment' of my personal world early in my childhood, which is related in Chapter 2.

[37] Ontological security was a term originally introduced by R D Laing in *The Divided Self* (1990), in reference to a 'continuous person' that benefits from stability in an unbroken sense of reality. Ontological security is a sense of mental stability that an individual feels when there is a sense of order and coherence in their life events and individual experiences (Giddens 1991). Giddens argues that a sense of ontological security is fundamental to the ability to give meaning to one's life. It affects the individual's perspective on their self-image, the society they live in and the nature of their future. This sense of meaning derives from the experience of favorable and consistent emotions and an absence of turmoil and angst. When something is experienced that is not compatible with the meaning of the individual's life it can disrupt the sense of ontological security.

Once I have experienced something fully and somatically, that cannot be taken away, it is not just a 'belief', I have experienced it in a grounded way that is not based on ideas or feelings, it has substance. The spiritual meaning I give to this experience is subjective and of course there can be acceptance of others' subjective understanding of my experiences and the meanings that I give to them. But it is *my* experience, it is firmly rooted, my 'elephant that goes all the way down'. It is this feeling of it going 'all the way down' that offers security - no one can 'pull the rug out' from under this elephant.

The metaphor of 'naming the elephant'[38] was fundamental in the process of this research. Whilst I was desperately trying to fit my work into a social constructionist worldview, it did not work, because I was not naming my 'elephant that goes all the way down'. The social construction viewpoint is only a part of my worldview. I experienced trying to fit writing and research into a framework which did not fully express my worldview as a sense of reimprisoning myself. Susan Griffin articulates her experience of this misfit saying that she 'can remember a feeling of inward panic, as if my mind were being enticed into a small windowless place, while the larger world I was so excited to enter slowly disappeared from sight' (1996:33).

I found the inspiration to move out of this 'small windowless place' and to 'name the elephant', following my reading of Mark Smith's (2017) thesis (which was unembargoed until 17 June 2023)

---

[38] The expression 'naming the elephant in the room' is a commonly utilized metaphor describing a situation where there is an obvious, significant issue or problem that everyone is aware of but that is deliberately being ignored or avoided in conversation. The 'elephant in the room' represents the problem or issue (and that it is a substantial issue), and 'naming' it means openly acknowledging and discussing it. When someone takes the step of 'naming the elephant in the room', they are addressing the unspoken issue, making it explicit and bringing it into the forefront of the discussion. It may be experienced as difficult or uncomfortable to do this, as people can avoid discussing such issues due to their sensitive, controversial, or awkward nature. However, it is essential to address the unspoken issues in order to resolve conflicts, find solutions, and promote open and honest communication.

and shortly after, meeting Jamie Barnes at the International Conference of Autoethnography (July 2023). Jamie directed me towards Dorothee Soelle's book *The Silent Cry: Mysticism and Resistance* (2001). Both of these 'meetings' gave me the permission and courage, not only to name my 'elephant' but to allow it to be fully present in my work. These readings enabled me to see deeper layers within the theory, the themes and the experiences; both my own and those that had been shared with me. The shared narrative demonstrated that adopting the constructionist viewpoint had allowed for the dissolving of constructed viewpoints and identities, which led to the possibility of embodied spiritual experiences. Allowing the embodied spiritual in allowed my writing to flourish in the same way that it allowed my bodymind to flourish erotically. Audrey Lorde (1978) speaks of how the dichotomy between the spiritual and the political is false and that it results from:

> [A]n incomplete attention to our erotic knowledge. For the bridge which connects them is formed by the erotic – the sensual – those physical, emotional and psychic expressions of what is deepest and strongest and richest within each of us, being shared: the passions of love, in its deepest meanings. (p.11)

My journey first started with the practice of silencing the mind and becoming the quiet witness, this witness consciousness[39] led to the examination of the social constructs and programming that had shaped me, which facilitated the endeavor to consciously reprogram my mind and my way of thinking (and *not* thinking – meditation gives a welcome break from the constant chattering of the mind). This meditative process also led to a Butlerian disintegration of a sense of

---

[39] This 'witness consciousness' is the mind watching all of the thoughts, emotions and events and knowing that 'I am not that'. It is practiced in meditation and then flows out into the rest of life. It leads to a liberation from attachment to anything that does not serve you and to not grasping objects, other people or yourself as a fixed entity. It is very like the 'unself' described by Quinn (2011).

any attachment to identity labels or a fixed identity. I cannot say it was a wholly pleasant experience.

Although liberating, it was painful. Like a 'death of the self'. I went through a grieving process; I grieved for that 'me' I had thought was substantial and real. A sense of safety started to evolve again with somatic awareness and movement practices, which led to a sense of embodiment and a trust of body. I stopped feeling like a disembodied 'mind' floating above a mechanistic body and had a sense of being an integrated 'bodymind'[40]. Again, this was a painful process. Although now feeling fully embodied is a resource and I experience ecstatic embodied states, the process to getting there was excruciating at times; meeting the trauma and memories that had been 'pushed down' into my body.

However, once I felt grounded and able to trust my sense of 'full body knowing' I then opened again into more 'spiritual' realms of experience through an animistic connection with nature. I needed this gentle progression back into the spiritual, to be grounded, to have a sense of the body for me to know it was an authentic experience rather than 'spiritual bypassing'[41]. This point in my life, where I

---

[40] The term 'bodymind is often used (in contexts such as yoga, Chinese medicine and body-centered therapy) to emphasize the interconnected unity of the body and mind, highlighting that they are not separate entities but rather two aspects of the same whole.

[41] Spiritual bypassing is a term first introduced by Robert Masters (2010) to describe unresolved or ignored psychological issues which can be masked as spirituality, including self-judgment, excessive niceness, and emotional dissociation. It refers to a defense mechanism in which individuals use spiritual beliefs and practices to avoid or bypass dealing with emotional and psychological issues, unresolved trauma, and personal growth challenges. In essence, it involves using spirituality as a way to escape from confronting and addressing real-life issues and emotional pain. It is important to note that spiritual practices and beliefs can be powerful tools for personal growth, healing, and that they can complement psychological therapy. However, when they are used to avoid facing real life challenges and emotions, it can hinder authentic, grounded personal growth and emotional wellbeing. This is discussed in more detail in Chapter 4.

experienced this new combination of embodied and spiritual experience is when I started to have the experience of nonsexual erotic embodiment. The point I am trying to make in articulating this process is that I cannot simply rely on the rational, the philosophical, spiritual belief or transcendental intuition. For me to have a sense of ontological security and epistemological grounding, the ground for what I think I 'know' must be in embodied experience. Firstly, I grasp an idea on a superficial level, I then experience something for myself. If the experience feels worthwhile, I delve into it deeply, embody it and then I am ready to read or hear more about the theory behind that which I have experienced.

1.9 Embodied knowing

Imprisonment which was at one and the same time understood as the imprisonment of the female mind has a larger boundary, and that is the shape of thought itself, within Western civilization.
Susan Griffin 1996:185

This balanced way of knowing and coming to knowledge is something I aim to reflect within this book, although due to my worldview the research privileges the knowledge gained from embodied experience over that of rational theories or scientific knowledge. Whilst remaining conscious of the extensive contributions of theoretical frameworks and scientific methodologies to our understanding of phenomena, my epistemological stance privileges the nuanced, experiential wisdom found within embodied knowledge. This emphasis on lived experience, tacit understanding, and embodied awareness honors the inherent complexity of human experience that eludes rational approaches. I aim to contribute to a more inclusive and holistic epistemological stance, one that recognizes the multifaceted dimensions of human understanding beyond the confines of theorization and scientific inquiry. Jamie Wallis Barnes begins his PhD thesis with a story to illustrate the 'dynamics of authoritative knowledge' (2015:8). It is a birth story and rather than share the same story, I will share my own to illustrate a similar point.

For the birth of my first child, I had decided to have a water birth, at home with my mother and my partner present to support me. As soon as I read about water birth I knew it was the right thing for me on a heart-felt, body-sensing level and subsequently researched the benefits and potential risks, so that I would be equipped to justify my decision to those who may question it. I hired a birth pool and wrote a birth plan. I went to some birth training organized by the National Childbirth Trust, which appeared to promote more 'natural' methods than traditional birth preparation classes. Determined to have a 'natural' birth, I had somehow conflated the term 'natural' with easy. Although I had much information and advice regarding birthing, birthing techniques and what creates a good birth experience for the baby, once I was feeling vulnerable and exhausted, I started to go against my birth plan and to allow the midwives to guide me. I allowed internal examinations, which were excruciatingly painful and during the second stage, when I was feeling my body wanting to take a natural pause, I pushed when I was told to push, causing much pain, exertion and tearing.

Although the birth was natural, calm, candlelit and bonding for us all, I was left feeling that if I had trusted my body, it could have been less painful and demanding. I embarked on further research. I read about the birthing practices of women in other cultures. I watched a video on 'orgasmic birth', with films of others' births (one was even in the sea with dolphins). I signed up for 'hypnobirthing' birth coaching in order to try to undo my social conditioning regarding what birth is like. I learned that my body's knowing in the second stage of the last birth was correct. That as the baby's head is making its way through the vagina, it is supposed to come down a little to gently stretch the passage and then it goes back up again. It is a slower but less painful process if you do not push and allow this to happen naturally. I found out the correct way to breathe, move and position myself based on practices from other cultures. Watching the ecstatic births of others reframed my perception of the possibilities of the birthing process.

The second birth was a family occasion. We had a birth pool again. Both of my parents came, and my younger son came downstairs for the moment of birth. The midwife who attended would not believe that I was in labor and said she would have to do an internal exam. My partner informed her that would not be happening as it caused me pain during my last birth. When I said I felt it was time to get in the pool she said that she did not think I had progressed far enough (that I may not even be in labor at all) and that it could stop the labor, with a strong warning that if my labor did not 'start soon' I would have to go into hospital because my waters had broken some hours ago.

I got into the pool, I squatted down, and five minutes later calmly informed the midwife that my baby's head had just moved through my cervix. She looked quite shocked. My partner delivered our son in the pool around 20 minutes later and cut the cord once it had stopped pulsating. There was no forced pushing. I trusted the process of my baby making his way out into the world and that his head would retract each time he made a little progress. I trusted the natural waves of my internal muscles to move him along, I knew how to breathe to harness the power of those waves. Luckily for me, I trusted both the embodied knowing from my previous birth and the sensitivity of my body in that moment to know exactly what stage I was at, and I did not succumb to the pressure of the medical professional's authority and rational knowledge.

The birth story in Jamie's thesis is similar to my first birth story, where the woman submits to the authority of the medical professionals, being directed to pause the birthing process to wait for an examination by a delayed medic and causing herself unnecessary pain, just to have her feeling of what she should be doing verified by the medical professional on his arrival. Both stories illustrate 'the dynamics of authoritative knowledge present within this social context' (Barnes 2015: 8). This dynamic is one where 'certain knowledge "counts" (i.e., biomedical knowledge, the physician's knowledge etc.) and certain knowledge doesn't "count" (i.e., the woman's knowledge of her own body)' (Ibid: 9) and the woman's embodied wisdom is therefore dismissed. Jordan (1997) explains that:

> Frequently, one kind of knowledge gains ascendancy and legitimacy. A consequence of the legitimization of one kind of knowing as authoritative is the devaluation, often the dismissal, of all other kinds of knowing. Those who espouse alternative knowledge systems then tend to be seen as backward, ignorant, and naïve, or worse, simply as troublemakers.' (Jordan 1997:56, cited in Barnes 2015:8-9).

Griffin (1996) affirms 'alternative knowledge systems' positing that 'those tears and laughter with which we meet this moment are as much a part of intelligence as any reason and can move us deeper to the core of things' (p.172). But she is careful not to dismiss the mind in the equation saying that 'Nor is the life of the mind irrelevant in this critical, tragedy-bearing time. By what and how we think, we coerce, confine, distort and damage or sustain, encourage, create, coax ourselves and otherness into a fuller realization of being' (Ibid.) Lorde (1978) prioritizes erotic knowing saying that 'Beyond the superficial, the considered phrase 'it feels right to me' acknowledges the strength of the erotic into a true knowledge' (p.10) and that 'The erotic is the nurturer or nursemaid of all our deepest knowledge.' (Ibid.)

My birthing stories have given me courage to trust the teamwork of my heart, mind, and body, including the erotic flow of intuition, to value perspectives from other cultures. When I combine many kinds of knowing, I find there is usually a more balanced, harmonious, and beneficial outcome than when I prioritize one type of knowing. In this scenario I had a heartfelt intuition and a somatic sense that a water birth at home was the right thing for me and my baby. This was verified and backed up by research, which enabled a more rational appreciation. I learned that I could and should trust the wisdom of my body from my first birth experience, a knowing verified by cross-cultural research and somatic awareness during my second birth. This merging of knowledge streams, including my somatic sense led to the second birth being both natural and easeful; more fully infused with the erotic.

This cross-cultural search for something that 'fits me better' is a theme of my asexual narrative, not just my birth story, and will be explored throughout the book. I found like Griffin, that 'the awareness grows that something is terribly wrong with practices of European culture that have led to both human suffering and environmental disaster' (1996: 36). Lorde (1979) describes how discovering a consciousness outside of Western constructs is essential to forming a more balanced view:

> [As] we become more in touch with our own ancient non-European consciousness of living as a situation to be experienced and interacted with, we learn more and more to cherish our feelings, and to respect those hidden sources of our power from where true knowledge, and therefore, lasting action comes. (p.2)

I found the PhD process painful at times. For much of my young adult life, I felt like a disembodied or floating head, utilizing my rational mental capacities for financial reward, doing cerebral tasks in boxes (both conceptual boxes and physical offices that resembled 'boxes'). I undertook the endeavor to still my mind and free myself from boxes. I then went through a protracted and challenging process of becoming embodied, which slowly transformed into the bliss of being embodied. I found the pleasure of peace, switching the flow of thoughts off, sitting in silence, moving with freedom, appreciating the flows within and feeling grounded.

In order to undertake this academic project, I had to engage my mind in a concentrated and conceptual way that I had not visited for many years. Once it was reignited, it would not shut up! I was back in the mental realm, having to fit my cross-cultural, embodied, spiritual experiences into 'Western thought' (Griffin 1996). At times it felt as if my brain was swelling and pushing up against my skull. The constant stream of thought was not welcome, even if it was substantive thought. At times, as my head pounded, I would cry, longing to be doing a mind-less physical or creative task where I could feel present with my heart and the fullness of my being and becoming.

David Carless (2022) shares how, during his PhD, he would start each day playing his guitar. He describes this as 'A needed time to deal with some of the tensions, contradiction and doubts that my scientific research training is already raising.' He shares some lyrics from one of the songs that arose on one of those mornings:

> At this time in the morning
> when breathing is too loud
> Your heart is a fire
> your brain is water that puts it out (Carless and Douglas 2022: 158)

I resonate with this struggle between heart and mind, with the potential for academic rigor and empiricism to extinguish the passion of my heart. Griffin explains that 'without the body, it is impossible to conceive of thought existing. Yet the central trope of our intellectual heritage is of a transcendent, disembodied mind' (1996: 185). She goes on to say that as her essay 'moved further away from meditation and reflection, further from what we call "confessions" and closer to science, with its claim of objectivity, it began more and more to resemble this celestially detached brain.' (Ibid.)

When I changed my process from one of trying to start with a 'literature review' and started my autoethnography, even writing about the literature in an autoethnographically reflective way, I found much more joy and flow in the process. Once I had written my narrative piece (see Chapter 2) and identified the themes that I intended to explore with my co-creators the mental tasks became enthused with a different timbre. Inspired by Wall (2008) who approached her 'autoethnography with a desire to "converse" with the literature rather than just to interject my perspectives into identified gaps in the literature' (p.40), I adopted Deleuze's suggested method for reading, as shared by Gale (2018: 8):

> There's nothing to explain, nothing to understand, nothing to interpret. It's like plugging in to an electric circuit. I know people who've read nothing who immediately saw what bodies without organs were, given their own 'habits,' their own way of being one. This second way of reading's quite different from the first, because it relates a book directly to what's Outside. A book is a little cog in much more complicated external machinery . . . This intensive way of reading, in contact with what's outside the book, as a flow meeting other flows, one machine among others, as a series of experiments for each reader in the midst of events that have nothing to do with books, as tearing the book into pieces, getting it to interact with other things, absolutely anything . . . is reading with love. That's exactly how you read the book. (Deleuze, 1995: 7–9)

I understood exactly what Deleuze was referring to. When I read the term 'body without organs' (Deleuze and Guattari 1972), I had an embodied feeling of what this meant, I had an erotic feeling of merging with the text as a unified bodymind, a body without organs with flows of desire rippling over it with no hinderance, goal or final resting place; the simple pleasure of feeling desire with no need to offer it an object, no striations within which it can be hindered and uncomfortably concentrated. This 'reading with love' fit with other strands from Deleuze and Guattari's work which had both validated and inspired me. I stopped trying to fit my autoethnography into a disciplinary 'gap' and instead traversed a treasure map, in a seemingly synchronous finding of theoretical jewels, reading and 'plugging in' to the 'electric circuit' of the ideas found. Then, I found that my academic work, rather than limiting my 'lines of flight', upheld me with an updraft of support with theories and concepts that matched my flight pattern.

Once I started to communicate with the co-creators and write fiction and poetry in collaboration with them, I found ecstatic moments in the creative process. Within the fiction, the sense of 'becoming' in the character development and the trajectory of the writing, with me immersing myself in the co-creators' stories so thoroughly that the writing took on a life of its own, was an intense feeling of being 'on the inside' (Gafini and Kincaid 2017). Whilst writing the poetry, I felt a sense of spirit, of the nonsexual erotic in my own body as I wrote the bodies and energy bodies of others, allowing them to flow over my 'body without organs'. I experienced a sense of urgency in desiring to articulate a desire for desire itself. I wanted to 'converse with the literature' to give 'updraft' to co-creators' stories. I felt the erotic 'ménage à trois' of mind, heart and body.[42]

Griffin (1996) speaks of her frustration at the 'domination of Western thought' which 'expands even now throughout the world' and articulates her hope for 'an experience of knowledge as *intimacy* rather than power' (p.11, my emphasis). Once I felt this permission to allow my reading to be rhizomatic and match my cross-cultural rhizomatic way of thinking, there was no resistance, and I felt able to

---

[42] A French term to describe romantic relationship with three partners (in contemporary language this is known as a 'throuple'). I deliberately use this term in conjunction with the non-sexual erotic, to challenge the assumption that feelings we associate with romance are associated with sexual desire or that they only arise towards a human 'other'.

engage with and feel gratitude for my 'good mind'[43]. The 'good mind' was a shorthand utilized by one of my Buddhist teachers to suggest that the goal of mindfulness and meditation practice is not to dismiss the mind entirely, that it is a valuable tool for thinking, but it should be used thoughtfully and mindfully to cultivate meaningful and profound insights rather than being dominated by unproductive or frivolous thoughts. I did not fully understand the concept of 'good mind' and its value until undertaking this academic endeavor.

During a break from a Thesis Writing Retreat held by the Doctoral College, another postgraduate student and I were standing on the sixth-floor balcony at the top of Rolle building. We were looking out across a miniaturized Plymouth towards the sparkling sea and an uninterrupted, blue-skied horizon. We were silent for some time and then I gave voice to my imagination, "As researchers, we need a balcony in our mind, a place we can climb up to gain a spacious perspective. From that place we can see it 'all at once' in its condensed form, organized into distinct areas with all the roads and pathways that link the various suburbs, edifices, and monuments, with the delicious addition and inspiration of a clear and uninhibited horizon."

It is impossible to attain a single 'truth', there is no route to attain a worldview or understanding of the real or natural world that is 'correct'. There is no point that we can reach a 'God's eye view' (Putnam 1999) that is free from conditioning, context, concepts and content. However, it is possible to 'think outside of the box' in order

---

[43] 'Good mind' is a term utilized by my Buddhist teacher on the 'Counselling with mindfulness' training that I did in 2006. She used it to point towards the notion that the goal of mindfulness and meditation is not necessarily to entirely shut down or eliminate the mind but to achieve a more focused, clear, and insightful state of mind. Meditation can help individuals reduce mental clutter, distractions, and frivolous thinking, which allows for deeper and more profound understanding of thoughts and experiences. What my teacher meant with this shorthand, was that by quietening the mind and reducing the constant stream of distracting thoughts, the thoughts that do arise during meditation or in daily life can be more intentional, meaningful, and profound.

to achieve a more nuanced understanding. We first need to be aware that we are in the box and be fully aware of the contents of the box. Through meditation we can start to become witness to the constantly arising and dissolving thoughts, which starts to put us on the outside of the box. This watching of the thoughts and emotions and realizing that they do not constitute 'who we are' can lead to a dissolving sense of a fixed identity or a continuous need to 'hold it all together' and make it 'make sense' as a solid identity within a world and self that is constantly dissolving. The world is constantly 'becoming', as are we.

This releasing from the confines of the conditioned mind can lead one into the body and utilizing the body to 'make sense' in the ever-changing moment. To literally sense with the whole bodymind and be present, engaging with whatever is being done, with a sense of the energetic flows and intelligence of the body and that which is 'touching' the body.

This union of body and mind can then follow through into the writing process. Pelias tells of how his 'body and mind work in concert, sensing the wisdom of Gingrich-Philbrook's poetic insight: "My body makes language. It makes language like hair" (2001: 3). I am my body speaking, I am a mind/body fully engaged. I am a thinking and feeling agent trying to assemble some sense of experience, trying to let the cognitive and affective guide my way' (2022: 124). I resonate with the quote he shares from Spry (2011) articulating that the body can function 'as a site from which the story is generated by turning the internally *somatic* into the externally *semantic*" (p.63, italics in the original, cited in Pelias 2022: 124).

1.10 Creative sociology

Stories animate human life: that is their work …
Narrative makes the earth habitable for human beings.
Frank 2010: 46

Representation through stories, poems or dramaturgical texts is often utilized within research into issues that are 'sensitive' in nature (Renzetti and Lee 1993), as these creative methods are suited to conveying the complexity of 'embodied, emotional, manifold and ambiguous' human experiences (Inckle 2007: 29). Watson tells us that 'fiction and other arts practices can generate multiple meanings, and often intentionally do so' (2021: 4). These creative methodologies open 'multiplicities in meaning-making instead of pushing authoritative claims' (Leavy 2020: 27). Sociological meaning may be evoked 'through the cumulation of … poetic and aesthetic details across a story' (Watson 2021: 4). The layers of complex meaning and embodied sensory impressions that can be conveyed within creative outputs allow an attempt to offer a subtle, almost ungraspable understanding of experiences that are challenging to narrate.

Richardson (1994) understood writing as part of the process and not just the output of the research, stating that 'writing is also a way of 'knowing' – a method of discovery and analysis. By writing in different ways, we discover new aspects of our topic and our relationship to it. (p. 515, cited in Letherby 2015: 138) Through utilizing creative methods and collaboration with co-creators in this process, these layers of knowing and discovery were opened up to all those participating, not just the researcher. Through my dialogue with the literature and the co-creators and writing in response to both, I came to know and understand my becoming and the apparently disparate aspects of my journey. By writing creative outputs in response to the co-creators' experiences they gained greater access to the meanings within them. I found that much of the writing did not make it into this book, but that it was instrumental to the insights and outputs that are shared here.

My use of these creative methods, although encouraged by Denzin (2001) within the articulation of the interpretive interactionist approach, is largely inspired by Kay Inckle's (2007) work *Writing on the Body: Thinking Through Gendered Embodiment and Marked Flesh*, particularly the final chapter, which is written as a series of fictional stories linked together by a common setting, 'not simply as a convenient means of creating a shared environment in which to connect the women but, rather, to highlight the diversity of lives and experiences that converge in such a place' (p.204). This way of concluding the book is utilized to replace the 'conventional conclusion' and is 'intended to counter the style, content and purpose of such normative constructs' (p.203). Inckle describes how by utilizing this approach 'the imperatives to analytic tidiness, dualistic categorization, and the reformulating and fixing of experience, are replaced with an open, fictional and messy text' (p.203). I have utilized this approach in this book, and Chapter 5 shares this sociological fiction. I have also utilized Inckle's approach to an unconventional 'open' conclusion, with a gallery of erotically embodied poetry.

The utilization of creative representation also holds within it a greater level of anonymity for my 'participants' and for myself as a participant in the research. I find that when I am reading research that offers 'anonymity' through a pseudonym, whilst still using the participant's exact phrasing, it builds such a strong picture or sense of the person that I would likely recognize them if I knew them within my social or professional sphere. This is of particular concern for this research due to the asexual population being relatively small (Bogaert 2004), making participants even more likely to be recognized. By utilizing stories, poems and a dramaturgical text I could reassure my co-creators that they should not be 'easily recognizable'. This proved to be an important factor in the co-creators agreeing to engage with this research project.

Inckle, reflects on the use of creative outputs instead of the traditional presentation of chunks of data followed by analysis saying that rather than offering a 'closed assertion or truth claim, I wanted to leave people with thinking, feeling questions and open to a whole range of possible meanings and developments which much more closely reflected the dynamic experiences of my research participants' (2010: 39). Inckle's work challenges 'how we come to make and privilege certain kinds of knowledge' (2010: 39). Watson (2021: 4) speaks to the value of fiction as a *product* and a *process* in/as critical social research (a value also epitomized by Satchwell *et al.* 2020).

Satchwell *et al* utilized stories as findings in their collaborative research as a core method of 'hearing and amplifying' the voices of the participants. They share that 'meanings were made' in an 'iterative process of capturing resonances in the different stages of the research, resulting in the creation of stories filtered through many different participants' (2020: 874). The iterative process of interpreting meanings, checking meanings, the making of creative outputs and then sending the outputs back for comments was a long and challenging process, especially as many outputs were based on the stories of multiple co-creators. It was, however, a rewarding endeavor and due to the rigorous process involved I am satisfied that these creative outputs are valid research findings and that they will offer voice for life stories that would otherwise not be heard. Plummer (2013) verifies that stories enable us to listen to 'significant others' and their 'different voices' offering a broadening of 'our circles of empathy' and the 'moral universes' in which we can exist (p.217).

Gayle Letherby (2015) suggests that 'some, taking a traditional view of the relationship between fact and fiction, might suggest that fiction is the opposite of explicit auto/biographical writing' and that this is not her view. Letherby's view is that it is 'another way to tell our auto/biographical stories – either drawing specifically on respondents' narratives or more generally on our research and our own experiences.' (p.138). Plummer (2013) describes stories as 'representations of reality' that increase understanding, saying that 'stories must always pose questions about their relationship to truth, fiction, reality, copying. Where might reality start and story end; or story start and reality end?'. He goes on to present the question 'although stories provide their own narrative reality, there is surely a reality beyond the text?' and to state that stories 'must take us to this further land' and help us 'see bridges to wider understandings' (p.212).

This form of creative sociology has been referred to as 'the new writing' (Denzin 2003: 118) which 'privileges evocation over cognitive contemplation' (Denzin 2003: 119). Denzin describes this as a 'writing form that moves from interpretation and evaluation to praxis, empowerment and social change' (Denzin 2003: 133). Griffin (1996) explains how story 'and even more the poem' fits with an embodied approach to research because 'in fiction the whole life of the body, of sensuality, is opened to view' (p,185). She explains that these creative representations allow 'the reader to enter imagined experience as if within a body' as 'pain, pleasure, color, taste, sound, smells are evoked.' (Ibid.) Thus the literary devices of these fictionalized outputs can elucidate embodied experience and even offer an embodied experience for the reader.

Pelias speaks about how 'autoethnography benefits from its acquaintance with the personal, poetic, and performative as it goes about the business of creating its accounts' (2022:129). He tells us that:

> [T]he poetic and the autoethnographic can come together to speak from the heart, from the body's joys and sorrows, from the most exalted to the most tragic. They can join together to name, to write into the commonality of the human condition, to note the differences that matter. (2022: 124)

I found poetry a useful way of telling of multiple stories with disparate meanings that appeared within one narrative. Carless and Douglas (2022) speak of this in relation to songs, which, to me, seem to have a similar nature to poems:

> My body is more than one story, and others too have multiple stories written on, in and through their bodies. Songs, it seems, can hold story fragments that escape a unified temporal plot, allowing differences and diversity to coexist in harmony (p.157).

The benefit of the 'poetic form' is that it 'recognizes and incorporates the emotional and embodied … lost within a transcribed text (however coded)' (Inckle 2007:34). Poetry 'relies on interpretation, feeling and metaphor to convey "truth" and meaning' and it 'enables us to engage on an experiential level: emotional, intellectual, visceral and corporeal with a range of human experiences' (Ibid.), allowing the reader to explore and connect with these experiences. Within the outputs, particularly the poetry, I have utilized the third person, to ensure that I am not appropriating the co-creators' experiences. In the poems where the first person is utilized, it is because the co-creator had a larger part in producing the poem than me, and I have indicated this by putting a 'CC' in the bottom right of the poem.

In her book regarding utilizing poetry to present research findings, Faulkner (2009) argues that poetry allows researchers to convey complex emotions, experiences, and insights that might be difficult to capture and express using traditional academic prose. This was particularly important within this research as I needed to write about experiences of erotic embodiment and spiritual ecstasy which are not easily communicated through words. She also suggests that the use of metaphor, imagery, rhythm, and language in poetry can provide a more nuanced and visceral understanding of lived experiences, again an important factor for conveying the sense of somatic experiences within this research. She explains that poetry has the added benefit of offering an efficient presentation of findings as much information can be transmitted through very few words.

Faulkner also states that poetry can entice readers in and encourage them to draw their own meanings and conclusions, making the research more engaging and accessible to a wider audience. She suggests that through crafting poems the researcher must reflect deeply on the data, the interpreting of the data and the meanings which leads to a more nuanced understanding of the research.

I am not a trained poet. I know nothing about the structure of a poem or how to analyze poetry. I do love poetry though. I have written poetry without particular form or with reference to convention from a young age. I enjoy it. I have utilized poetry to try to articulate my own and co-creators' experiences within this research. I also included poems from prominent, erudite, and published poets within my research, where the reading of these poems helped me to grasp a theory or understand my own and others' experiences with more ease. The knowledge of a philosopher is based on study of texts and their writings are musings and application of these rational findings. The knowledge of the poet is based on the study of experience and their writings are musings and application of these experiential, and somatic or intuitive findings.

Like Inckle, I find that these creative methods address 'ethical concerns around representation and knowledge and sit comfortably within an embodied position' and that they 'not only represent an ethics of transformation but are also precisely a part of that process' (2007: 29). Asexuality is a 'fundamentally embodied' experience and as such is suited to methodologies, which are 'equally embodied and able to contain and represent the complex, emotive, fluid and dynamic nature of these experiences' (Inckle 2010: 27).

1.11 The performance of a lifetime

The book you hold in your hands is not, therefore, a respectable work of scholarship. It has not benefited from editorial oversight and contains little verifiable fact. It is just a story.
I have written it anyway, for two reasons:
First, because what is written is true. Words and their meanings have weight in the world of matter, shaping and reshaping realities through a most ancient alchemy. Even my own writings — so damnably powerless - may have just enough power to reach the right person and to tell the right truth, and change the nature of things.
Second, my long years of research have taught me that all stories, even the meanest folktales, matter. They are artifacts and palimpsests, riddles and histories. They are the red threads that we may follow out of the labyrinth.
Alix E. Harrow *The Ten Thousand Doors of January*: 53 – 54

The chapter that follows, Chapter 2, *Becoming - An Alternative Narrative of Asexuality*, offers a view into an alternative narrative of an asexual becoming that challenges an essentialist view of asexuality as a stable identity and orientation and describes an erotically embodied asexuality. It also offers an insight into my worldview, how it has changed over the course of my life and how it has shaped me. It aims to offer transparency into the ground of this research. It offers descriptions of the alternate worldviews that have shaped me. It gives the reader a small window into my heart and mind.

Plummer's work *Documents of Life* (2001, originally published in 1983) has become a classic text within social research. Within this book Plummer critiqued social science's anti-humanist methodology. In contrast, he advocated the use of life stories and encouraged the use of personal documents, such as journals and diaries, in producing these life stories. Plummer verified these 'life documents' as a valid form of data, equal to the validity of data or life stories captured within qualitative interviews. Although Wall (2008) does acknowledge the possible stress for the researcher in taking such an approach to using these 'documents of life' saying that 'the intimate and personal nature of autoethnography can, in fact, make it one of the most challenging qualitative approaches to attempt (p.39)

The pieces (or 'acts' from my life) that I share in the next chapter stood out as the most significant from the many I have found in my journals, and some that I have recalled. I endeavor to keep the original essence of these past interactions, whilst acknowledging that I am viewing these through my present lens of asexuality and my wish to create a desired future self.

My personal account of my asexual becoming is presented in 11 'Acts', utilizing creatively represented extracts from the 'biographical identity work' that I undertook, utilizing my extensive journals, in response to my asexual epiphany. An epiphany radically transforms a person's life and means that they may have the need to re-evaluate the past and seek new meanings in order to make sense of the trajectory of experiences that led to where they are now and leave them free to move on into the future with a cohesive sense of self. Scott and Dawson named this process as biographical identity work (2015).

* * *

All the world's a stage,

And all the men and women merely players;

They have their exits and their entrances;

And one man in his time plays many parts,

His acts being seven ages.

William Shakespeare, *As You Like It*, spoken by Jaques.

* * *

The writing of this piece as 'Acts' is inspired by the work of Erving Goffman (1959), who first brought the term dramaturgy into the sociological realm. Goffman utilized theatre as a metaphor to look at social interaction as a theatrical performance. The performance, or presentation of self, is executed to gain acceptance from the audience (the other participants or observers in the social setting). When the performance is successful, the actor is viewed as they wish to be viewed by the audience (Goffman, 1959).

Whether this leads to a true sense of acceptance is debatable; by playing a part or multiple parts it means that no one knows the true person one feels themselves to be or understands the multifaceted nature of their personality. Goffman tells us that often those observing the performance, the audience 'assume that the character projected before them is all there is to the individual who acts out the projection for them.' (1959: 48) By presenting my story as 'acts' I am acknowledging this constantly changing 'self', that has been influenced and changed by social interaction, often wearing a mask in order to be accepted and validated. It is also inspired by Pelias (2022), who advocates the approach of delivering a 'performance on the page', saying that 'I am most satisfied when my autoethnographic accounts are performative, a performance on the page that plots the drama of living' (p.130).

I am inviting the reader to be the audience, to participate in the theatre of my life, a stage where I performed many roles in order to receive social acceptance. I am lifting the mask and allowing myself to be seen. In the words of Pelias (2022) 'I stand as a member of a community of autoethnographic scholars, to offer an autoperformance, a "mystory" (Ulmer, 1989, 1994), a testimony on behalf of the personal, on behalf of what marks our humanity' (p.124).

The next chapter, in the same way as the other chapters, is presented in a 'layered' (Ronai, 1995) format, which aims to facilitate more open analysis and knowledge. Rather than presenting the reader with a closed, fixed analysis, the layered account allows space for the reader to have a unique immersive, reflexive consideration of the intrinsic issues. This is important, allowing the time for the meaning to reveal itself, allowing a pause for interpretation. Plummer describes how time is necessary to appreciate stories because 'stories are never transparent all at once: they are rarely immediately clear. Narrative understanding requires the space to sit and stare, ponder and puzzle' and that 'like a slow-moving veil or curtain, the wisdoms of our stories' can only 'be revealed gradually' (2013: 212).

Each layer is separated with three centered stars to suggest a space to pause and grasp the meaning slowly. Journal entries have a light gray background with a shadow, quotes that are inserted for effect, but are not analyzed are in light gray boxes. Poems that were produced from the analysis of primary data, for the purpose of this research are presented centered on the page and in an italicized font, whereas poems that were produced in previous journals or in my research journal as a form of personal reflection are presented as journal entries.

Within the following chapter all of the poems are representations of my own data or are presented as they were originally written in my journals. In subsequent chapters, where the first person is utilized, the poem is based on my experience and when it is in the third person it is based on the co-creators' experiences. Where a co-creator has largely produced the poem themselves with some collaboration, the poem will be in the first person but will have the marking 'CC' (to signify 'co-creator') at the bottom right of the poem.

*　*　*

> Listening to the stories of *the lives of others whose world may be different from yours* is a prerequisite for democratic functioning, for the working of societies seeking a *respect and recognition for human differences*.
> Plummer 2013: 217

2. Becoming

An Alternative Narrative of Asexuality

There was no part of me that I could withhold from the dispositif de sexualité…There was no outside to the sexual identification system, no place for me to be a human being without any sexual identity at all…'from within' was the only possible location for resistance.
Ladelle McWhorter 1999: 100

Although my understanding of my experiences has developed throughout the course of this research, I present here my narrative as presented in 2022. This trajectory was created in May 2022 and presented at the British Sociological Association Auto/Biography Summer Conference 2022, on 14 July 2022. It offers my view at that point. My understanding of my experiences from the analysis of my journals, my *Documents of Life* (Plummer 2001). It also articulates the themes I identified, which then informed my dialogues with the co-creators.

I have kept this piece largely as it was when I created it, to offer a sense of narrative development within this work. My aim is for this book to not only be my story and the story of the co-creators, but for it also to be a story of the research process and how our understanding of asexual erotic embodiment developed over the course of our collaboration, and the reading of the literature. In keeping my presentation as it was, I aim to take you on the journey undertaken within this research as it unfolded. I hope that, in the previous chapter, you walked with me as I wrestled with articulating my worldview and gained the courage to let this guide the research. I aimed to articulate how this worldview shaped the methodology and structure of the research and its presentation. In the chapter that follows this one, I will articulate the linear progression or story of my reading of the literature, which by necessity had to widen outside of the asexuality literature in order to encompass my experiences and those of the co-creators.

This piece was written following the examination of my *Documents of Life* (Plummer 2001[44]) from the perspective of the realization that I am asexual. This followed the epiphany I had one year into my PhD[45] and the 'biographical identity work' (Scott and Dawson 2015) that I undertook in light of this epiphany. I read the journals I had kept for a period of 22 years from 1996 – 2018 in which I reflected on an intense period of self-development, therapist and mindful movement teacher trainings, and my time within the new age and neo-tantra communities. I added post-it notes to the entries that stood out to me as 'breadcrumbs on the path' that may have acted as food to grow an identity outside of sexuality, if the crows of my social conditioning had not swept down to feed on them, stopping me from noticing and following them.

Following this initial analysis of my journals, I constructed a rough narrative timeline with the key events, in order to try to fit the selected entries into a linear 'story'. I reflected on each of these points

---

[44] See Chapter 1 section 1.3 and 1.10 for further discussion of this method.
[45] See introduction.

regarding their significance and the feelings I had about them now. I drew together the entries that stood out as significant. Some of these were not descriptions and reflections of events that were taking place as I wrote them, they were reflections on past events that had 'come up' during therapy or therapeutic trainings for processing. Once I had extracted these key entries, I created poems, reflections and dramaturgical texts from them, in a similar way to the way in which I analyzed, processed, and then made creative pieces with the co-creators' scripts.

This narrative reflection, therefore, not only guided the research and the themes to be explored, but also served as a practice run for the more complicated process of analysis and creative work that would be done after collecting the co-creators' stories. The use of creative mediums such as poetry enable a greater span of experiences and meanings to be presented with greater impact and utilizing less descriptive text. These creative methods provide an engaging and open way of concurrently presenting the data, interpretation and analysis with room for the reader's own experience and interpretation (Faulkner 2009). It is presented, in the same way as the other chapters, in a 'layered' (Ronai, 1995) format, which aims to facilitate open interpretation. Rather than presenting the reader with a closed, fixed analysis, the layered account allows space for the reader to have a unique immersive, reflexive consideration of the intrinsic issues. Each layer is separated with three centered stars.

With these selected 'Acts', I aim to challenge essentialist views of asexuality by illustrating an asexual narrative which troubles AVEN's definition of asexuality as a lack and as a stable orientation. This trajectory is counter to the essentialist 'prevalent trajectory' found by Carrigan (2011: 476) and assumed by many researchers since (Bogaert 2012, Brotto and Yule 2017, Mitchell and Hunnicutt 2018, Chasin 2019, Kurowicka 2021). I aim to illustrate how my identity was formed through social interaction and constructs; firstly by generally accepted social constructs and the social conditioning within my family of origin, and secondly, by two significant 'biographical disruptions'.[46] The first occurring within childhood, where I experienced the trauma of 'disenchantment'[47] and the second in my twenties, when I realized that the 'capitalist carrot' and ideal romance I had been chasing were in fact plastic dummies with no sustenance; that what I had been desiring and chasing was empty and worth nothing to me—a disruption soothed by a period of travelling and discovering beneficial cross-cultural influences and spiritual practices. In short, my journey is one of *becoming* (Deleuze and Guattari 1980), not being, it is a journey of searching for an identity outside of the confining 'box' of sexualized culture and finding a 're-enchantment' with roots (see Chapter 1 section 1.7 and Chapter 4 for further discussion of this worlding).

At the end of the Chapter, I include the key themes that I formulated in response to creating my narrative piece at that stage in my research. These are themes that influenced both my reading of the literature (detailed in Chapter 3) and the dialogues with co-creators (described theoretically in Chapter 4 and within creative outputs in Chapters 5, 6 and 7).

It is apparent that a new identity needs clear definitions, a removal from any association with pathology and boundaries, so that it can be politically effective and defend against obscurity (Gressgard 2013).

---

[46] Bury (1982) utilized the term 'biographical disruption' in his work on serious illness. He defines biographical disruption as "the kind of experience where the structures of everyday life and the forms of knowledge which underpin them are disrupted" (p. 169). There are three stages in biographical disruption: the disruption of taken-for-granted assumptions and behaviors, a fundamental rethinking of the individual's biography and their self-concepts, and the mobilization of resources in facing an altered situation (Bury, 1982: 169). The individual attempts to repair the damage to their self-identity utilizing cognitive capacities such as toleration and normalizing in order to preserve meaning in life (Bury, 1991).

[47] Weber (1905) introduced the idea of the 'disenchantment of the world' to describe the rationalization and secularization of Western society. This occurred when traditional religious and magical beliefs were replaced by rational, fixed, and systemized ideals. I experienced this on a micro level within my childhood.

However, I find the parameters offered by AVEN (2022) limiting and excluding for many stories of asexuality, including my own, and those of the co-creators.

In Mark Carrigan's research (2011) he found a 'prevalent trajectory' of asexual stories: 'individual difference, self-questioning, assumed pathology, self-clarification and communal identity' (p.476)'. He found that for most participants the identity process started early, around adolescence. However, there were those who deviated from this due to 'temporal displacement', caused by those around them questioning their apparent difference as 'a phase'. Asexuality is often denied due to social expectations and sexualized couple's culture with phrases such as 'late bloomer' and 'finding the right one'. The assumption in Carrigan's trajectory (and his reasoning as to why certain asexuals do not follow it) is one of an innate sexual orientation that is to be discovered, rather than one that is shaped by the social setting and social conditioning experienced throughout a lifetime.

My trajectory does not follow the pattern outlined by Carrigan. Perhaps due to the state of my mental health, I did not have enough sense of self until later in life to realize that I was different and to seek an alternative to the master narrative presented to me, or perhaps my asexuality is a result of my social conditioning and social interactions.

My trajectory is more like this:

> Confusion and addiction – teens and twenties
> Breakdown, breaking away – late twenties
> Liminality – thirties
> Integration – forties

My story also does not conform to AVEN's ideal of an asexuality that is intrinsic and not associated with celibacy or trauma. AVEN's definition of asexuality is 'An asexual person is a person who does not experience sexual attraction' (AVEN 2022). They go on to say:

> Unlike celibacy, which is a choice to abstain from sexual activity, asexuality is an *intrinsic part of who we are* just like other sexual orientations ... Most asexual people have been asexual for their entire lives, although not all of us have been aware of the term or the community for as long as we've recognized this. (AVEN Overview 2022, my emphasis)

The 'biographical identity work' (Scott and Dawson, 2015) I share within this chapter attempts to illustrate how I reconstructed my narrative from the point of realization. I aim to illustrate an example of how 'Asexuality is not just a state of being, achieved through individual reflexivity, but also a life-long process of becoming, developed via meanings that are negotiated through interaction.' (Scott and Dawson, 2015:15). I aim to show that asexuality can be linked to the practice of celibacy (indicating a level of choice and how a thing once practiced can become a way of being) and trauma (indicating that asexuality is a valid choice for those who have experienced trauma, rather than trying to 'fix themselves' in order to fit into sexualized culture). I also aim to tell a narrative of asexuality that is not based on a lack but that is a story of flourishing and fullness. A story that I told with some trepidation at the conference, as it was not a narrative, at that point, that I felt was 'substantiated'. I had not yet had the validating experience of seeing my story reflected in others' stories, and of finding myself within the reading of literature regarding *ars erotica* and the expanded erotic.

*   *   *

Act 1 - Special cuddles

I asked mummy why I couldn't stay up after daddy got home. She said it was because daddy has to come first. She said that one day we will all leave her and daddy will be all she has. That sounds scary. Mummy and Daddy are each other's special person. I think daddy is most special because they share the special cuddles that men and ladies share only with one person. Mummy told me about those. Maybe that's why they laugh when I try to get inside when they are dancing cos they think it's silly ... my cuddles will never be as special as theirs.

I want to have a special person that loves me better than anyone else. I will give them lots of special cuddles to make sure they are always my special person and I won't be left alone.

Being up here makes me feel sad. I feel like I have a hole in my tummy, but I had my dinner with my brother before bedtime. I wonder if they are having the same food or if they have special food too.

* * *

This is presented as a creative piece from the child's perspective[48]. The content came from several journal entries I made during therapy and therapy trainings. They did not 'shout out' to be understood until I had the perspective of my asexual 'epiphany', it seems that my perceptions from childhood had been influencing me in the shadows and waiting for a context to illuminate them.

---

[48] This approach was inspired by a piece called *Poppy* written by Gayle Letherby (2017), published on ABC tales online, which is written from the child's perspective and her perceptions of events and interactions.

From my current position I view these perceptions from my childhood as the starting point of my multiple relationships in which I invariably had sex far too soon, as a strategy to make someone 'my person' rather than from a place of sexual desire.

My family context inflated my view of the importance of romantic relationships. Last year, I was watching the Disney film, *Raya and the Last Dragon* (2021) with my children; a film where a young female warrior goes on a quest to save the world. As I watched the film, I was suddenly struck by the memory, from early adulthood, of watching films with the hero's quest theme. I would have thoughts such as, "They're out on their own in the middle of nowhere, what's the point of their life, they can't have a relationship!"

When I reflect on this, I remember how my mother hindered any natural inclination to admire independent, single women. I had two great aunts, one each on the maternal and paternal side of the family, who were single and had never been married. They had certain similarities. They went travelling to exotic places, were property owners, were interesting to talk to and seemed to have a younger more playful demeanor than other women of their age. Whenever my mother would refer to them, however, it would be with a comment such as, "They never had someone, it is so sad really, such a waste."

Although their lives seemed exciting to me and I did not observe them being sad, my mother's evaluation was the one that stuck with me.

The most challenging aspect of my asexual epiphany was the anger I felt towards my parents. I felt disillusioned by how much time and energy I had wasted on relationships and saddened by the prevalence of consensual, unwanted sex within my relationship history. It was not all negative with regards to sex. I had one relationship where I thoroughly enjoyed love making and it felt healthy, pleasurable and natural, and I also had one relationship in which we shared ecstatic states, both through mindful sexuality and the non-sexual erotic. However, in other relationships the sex was performed to maintain the relationship, to receive attention and validation, or even just to get some peace from constant advances. Although I know there are many societal influences that shaped me, the feelings of resentment were directed towards my parents, particularly my mother.

I took a break from my PhD studies and returned to see a psychotherapist I had worked with in the past to process my feelings. I wanted to be able to discuss asexuality in an objective and critical way, without raw emotion clouding my work or my work becoming therapy.

Following this, I was staying with my parents and talking with my dad, about how my research was going. I read him a poem I had written and unexpectedly broke down crying. My mum came into the kitchen to join us at that point, and I explained about how my epiphany had led to me feeling so angry with them. I went on to say that following my talking therapy I no longer felt anger, but now felt ashamed for feeling angry with them, and that I could not connect fully with them as this was causing a barrier.

This led to an open, refreshingly honest, and tear-soaked conversation about relationships and sexuality. It struck me after our conversation that the path I have walked almost seems as if I am trying to resolve and integrate my parent's (previously unexpressed) issues. By daring to open this 'Pandora's box', rather than the troubles within silently consuming us, we were liberated by them. The interaction was a cathartic and connecting experience. Since this, I have felt more loving towards my parents, genuinely enjoying, and seeking their company.

My interactions with my mother continued to be somewhat challenging going forward, however. For instance, sitting on the beach about a year ago, my mother said, "It makes me feel sad when I see women of my age on their own."

Once I had taken a couple of fortifying breaths, I dared to ask, "Why?"

The unsurprising reply, "Because it means they are lonely, they must have lost their partner."

I gently pointed out that they might be perfectly happy and choosing to be alone. Although I understood that her comment came from her fear of losing my dad, it was still quite grating to me.

Another conversation, regarding my future, later that week, saw my mother stating, "You never know, you might meet someone!"

On this occasion, I managed to remind her that I do not want a relationship, to which she emphatically replied, "NEVER?!"

I explained that I know that I do not want a relationship to the same degree that most people seem to know that they desperately want one; that it has become a fundamental part of who I now am, not just an idea or a phase I am going through. This explanation seemed to be absorbed, and I have not received any further comments like this. My youngest brother refers to my relationship status as a single person as 'a lifestyle choice' whenever it comes up in conversation with friends. I feel both acknowledged and supported when he does this.

*　　*　　*

Act 2 – Disenchantment

As a child and a young teenager, I had a passion for Jesus. I always found the monotony of the church service difficult to tolerate, but I adored singing devotional hymns both in and out of church. It felt like my whole being lit up.

I felt like I wanted to marry Jesus, to become a nun. When I shared this with my brother he laughed and said, "there is no way you're going to be a nun." Perhaps he was right. I thought that the joyously unrestrained, erotic way I express my spiritual fervor would be unlikely to be welcome in a nunnery [this was a preconception at the time but following reading Mark Smith's (2017) research in 2023, I realized that this is not necessarily the case]. I also recently came across the following letter from a nun which seems to express this spiritual fervor:

Figure 2: First Holy Communion 1980

When you have loved [him] you shall be chaste;
when you have touched [him] you shall become purer;
when you have accepted [him] you shall be a virgin.
Whose power is stronger, whose generosity is more elevated,
whose appearance more beautiful, whose love more tender,
whose courtesy more gracious.

In whose embrace you are already caught up;
who has adorned your breast with precious stones...
and placed on your head a golden crown as a sign [to all] of
your holiness.

Clare of Assisi: First Letter to Blessed Agnes of Prague: FF, 2862

*   *   *

I felt my faith dwindling around the age of 10. I had just found out that Father Christmas was not real. I asked my mother, and she responded by asking me if I really wanted to know. I was devastated, not just about losing the sense of magic, unconditional love, and giving I had connected to this mythical figure, but that my parents had lied to me about something special in the transpersonal realm. What else had they been lying about? Was there anything beyond physical reality that was real? My next question was, 'So does that mean fairies aren't real too?'

My mother's answer, confirming my fears, destroyed my sense of wonder and my trust in my parents for many years. I remember crying myself to sleep.[49]

The seed of doubt had been sown. Later in my teenage years, finally losing my connection to religion was devastating. It felt like a severing of a connection to a vital essence that gave meaning to my life. My spiritual connection was bound up with an institution with which I no longer wished to associate. An institution where I was starting to observe warped power structures, abuse, and dogmatic views—faith had already been diminished by my childhood loss of other mythical and magical things that were dear to me.

*   *   *

---

[49] With my children, I did not lie about Father Christmas. I told them the story of St Nicholas, we celebrated St Nicholas day on 6 December, by placing nuts, fruit and some chocolate in each other's slippers (they filled mine before I got up, thus participating in the ritual). At Christmas, we all participated in the story of Father Christmas as equals. They understood that their stocking was filled by me, but that the original purpose behind honoring the St Nicholas story is that it is a celebration of the joy of giving without receiving anything in return (i.e. the gift given in secret is not reciprocated in kind by the thanks of the receiver). We were able to play act the rest (mince pies and wine left out for 'Santa', carrots for the reindeer and muddy reindeer hoof prints and chewed up carrot all over the place in the morning) as equals. It was like a piece of participatory theatre. It did not feel any less magical because of the co-creation and aware participation of my children.

Act 3 - Spear

He was twenty-five, I sixteen

He resembled a Romcom actor

I thought I loved him

His name was Lance

Appropriate really

His sharpness nearly killed me

I saw the light of love in his eyes

Actually, the glint of power

The hunter's joy, eying its prey

I wanted to give myself to him

Join as one

Make him my special person

He was aggressive

Not tender or loving

I still thought 'perhaps he loves me'

He told me it was deliberate

"To kill the confidence"

Perceived in conversational challenges

He told me to get a knife

Waiting, back turned, for me to stab him

I said, "That would make me worse than you"

I bought some pills

Downed with vodka

Retched up

Something had died

Something inside

Yet my body stayed alive

*   *   *

I flailed my way through life like a zombie from this point, trying to establish a carbon copy of a life that was supposed to heal my pain. Numb and still clinging to the ideal of romantic love as a savior, I got married at nineteen, a disastrous relationship that lasted a couple of years, followed by a continuing plethora of unhealthy relationships.

*   *   *

As I reflect on this, I find it challenging to unpick the different layers. The interaction between us was highly charged, but perhaps more around the ego than the sexual. I was playing power games with a man over ten years my senior. At sixteen, I felt like a woman, but now as a woman, I can see that I was still a child, barely at the age of consent.

Looking back, I can see we were engaged in a mental game of chess, always trying to outwit each other with a clever remark. It seems that the sexual to him was the final move in his arsenal, 'check mate'. He had found my 'Achilles' heel'[50], my vulnerability. In the sexual and romantic he was the experienced, dominant party and my conditioning regarding romantic and sexual relationships left me vulnerable and eager to please in order to secure my romantic ideal.

His pursuit of me sexually was about a bid for power, and not about fulfilling a sexual desire per se. Browning et al (1999) found that it is common that sexual behavior is tied up with a desire to experience power. However, the pursuit of power is not the only factor—there is another dimension to this episode. After arriving at his house, his actions were not loving, they were dismissive and bordering on violent. At this point I was not enjoying the situation, and did not wish to continue being intimate with him. I did not articulate this though and continued. Although, following the incident I felt like I had been raped, not just physically, but mentally by his articulation of his intention to hurt me, it is clear that I was not raped. I have found that this would be classed as 'consensual unwanted sex'.

Consensual unwanted sex, which sits within the spectrum of sexual violence and coercion (Dempster et al. 2015, Foster 2011, Walker 1997) is not defined as rape because the non-desiring partner consents to sexual activity either explicitly or by not saying 'no' (Walker, 1997).

Froemming (2020) found that individuals who participated in a higher frequency of unwanted consensual sex, had an increased risk of adverse mental health, including somatic symptoms, depression, and anxiety. This is similar to the negative mental health outcomes

---

[50] A critical weakness, which leads to downfall despite overall strength. In mythology, this was originally a physical vulnerability. However, it has become common to use this metaphor to describe other attributes that can lead to downfall.

associated with other forms of sexual coercion and violence (Acierno et al. 2002, Burnam et al. 1988, Winfield et al. 1990). Heldman and Wade (2010) reported that many people have consensual unwanted sex in the hope that it will lead to a committed relationship. This is of concern within the context of asexuality, when viewed alongside the finding that many asexuals view sex as the 'admission price' of a relationship (Brotto et al 2010: 607).[51]

*   *   *

Act 4 - Breaking down

I had a breakdown

On the M40

Not one fixable by the AA[52]

(Well not the AA that comes in a van)

I had been climbing

The social ladder

Career, fitness, relationship, popularity, education

Yet the view (from the top)

Vast, excruciating emptiness

I simply stopped

In the fast lane

(An irony not lost on me)

Screaming until the breath ran out

Windows steamed to capacity

---

[51] This is explored further in Chapter 3 and 4.

[52] The AA is an abbreviation for The Automobile Association – a car breakdown service in the UK. It is also an abbreviation for Alcoholics Anonymous – a service that offers recovery programs to addicts.

I felt numb

All emotion frenziedly outpoured

My only reference

The mirror of shock

On my boyfriend's face

I was herded

Like a sheep

To the doctor

Given pills to keep me numb

Functioning, coping, existing

*　　*　　*

In retrospect, I now see this breakdown as a breakthrough[53]. I interpret this as the point where the oppressing force of my social conditioning coming from the outside collided with the expanding sense of internal emptiness coming from the inside, creating an explosion of some magnitude. The anti-depressants I was prescribed enabled me to cope and function in my everyday life and to continue working, until I had saved enough to go travelling—a physical journey to discover other cultures and their philosophies, and to learn spiritual practices that enabled an inner journey of self-discovery.

*　　*　　*

---

[53] See the story at the beginning of Chapter 1 regarding how my supervisor, Mike Sheaff, enabled me to find the work of Ken Gale and Deleuze and Guattari after reading this reflection.

Act 5 - Breaking away

The Road Less Travelled[54]

A book given

By an exasperated boss

Sick of romantic rollercoasters

Unhealthy attachment theories

A revelation

For a co-dependent woman

Tired of feeling trapped by need

"Dependency may appear to be love"

("the myth of romantic love is a dreadful lie")

Signpost quotes

For a shattered heart

Looking for another direction

*   *   *

My identity started to shift following the breakdown in my mid-twenties, an event caused by two complimentary strands of dis-ease. Firstly, the realization that the capitalist dream was in fact, shallow and devoid of meaning. Having reached 'the top' of the ladder I had been diligently climbing, in the position of a Chartered Marketer with

---

[54] Peck (1978). These theories, and my and co-creators' experiences in relations to them, are discussed further within Chapter 4 and 5.

an international management position and an MSc, completing the London Marathon, and socially successful, the view from the top was sadly disappointing. Lured by the capitalist 'carrot on a stick' of success and status, enabled by my privileged position, I had reached the point of truly being able to take a bite of that carrot.

I realized that this carrot that had been dangled before me was not the juicy nourishing morsel I had anticipated but was in fact a plastic dummy devoid of any nourishment or meaning. Secondly, the realization that the myth of the idealized romantic relationship was little more than a fairytale, a shiny veneer to a harsh reality; like many of the other fairytales and myths I had been sold as a child, such as Father Christmas, fairies and happily ever after. The romantic ideal, an ideal that I had latched onto and formed an acceptable addiction to (an obsession encouraged by my social conditioning), had also become devoid of meaning to me. This critical and shocking lens on my habitus[55] led to a habitus clivé[56] and a cross-cultural search to find meaning of an experiential nature, rather than a meaning based on ideas, belief, and ideals.

I was born into a lower middle class, white, catholic family, which had the underpinning principals that the primary romantic relationship took precedence over everything else, and that the maintenance and success of this relationship was of the upmost importance. The status quo was that this relationship should constantly keep its romantic 'spark'. It was also guided by aspiring capitalist ideals of success, acquisition of assets, and that all endeavors, such as education and work, were to be focused on the

---

[55] A term utilized by Pierre Bourdieu, which refers to the ingrained dispositions, attitudes, and behaviors that individuals acquire through their socialization and experiences, shaping their perceptions and actions (Stone 2018).

[56] The term 'habitus clivé' refers to a concept used by Pierre Bourdieu to describe a situation in which an individual undergoes significant and transformative changes in their life, leading to a sense of dislocation and internal division. This occurs when the conditions of existence change dramatically, causing a person's ingrained dispositions and habits to lose coherency, resulting in a fragmented or divided sense of self (Stone 2018).

attainment of qualifications and career pathways that would lead to greater financial gain and status.

From my privileged position of a 'white, middle-class woman', I had the advantage of reaching the 'top of the ladder' academically, professionally, and socially, enabling me to realize that it was not somewhere I wanted to be. I am aware that without reaching 'the top', I could have wasted a lifetime striving to get 'there'. My privileged position and economic capital also allowed me time to 'take time out' to explore and discover who I did, and did not, want to be.

*   *   *

Act 6 – Liber-Eat Pray Love[57]

In this poem, I attempt to describe the impact that my outward journey to the countries I travelled to had on me and the effect that the practices I learned there had on my inner journey. It comprises words that attempt to illustrate the sensory impressions and qualities that imbued me during my journey. It is not an attempt to describe or define the country and culture or the practices in their fullness.

---

[57] This is a play on the words used in the title of Elizabeth Gilbert's memoir *Eat Pray Love* (2007). This book and the subsequent film created from her memoir (2010) were intrinsic to my understanding of my relationship addiction. I use Liber-eat instead of 'eat' as my journey was also one to overcoming an addiction to food and it is a play on the word 'liberate'. My journey also mirrors that of Elizabeth Gilbert, in that she went on a journey through cultures and practices outside of her habitus in order to liberate herself from unhealthy patterns.

The outward journey ...

Tender-hearted Thailand

(Chilled-out, radiant kindness)

Thai Wai[58], gentle joy from simplicity

Incredible India

(Surreal, sensually vibrant, Spiritual)

Unity in Diversity, Jugaad स्वडेशी, Swadeshi स्वडेशी[59]

Grounded Guatemala

(Wise elders and sacred sites)

Rainbow weave huipils[60] of reverence and beauty

The inner journey ...

Meditative expansion

(Nature of mind, no fixed identity)

Present moment awareness

---

[58] The Thai Wai is a traditional Thai greeting and gesture of respect. It involves placing the palms together in a prayer-like gesture with fingers pointing upwards, accompanied by a slight bow of the head. The wai is commonly used as a greeting, farewell, or to show respect.

[59] Swadeshi स्वडेशी - self-sufficiency, sovereignty. Jugaad जुगाड़ - making things work out with all you have.

[60] A huipil is a traditional garment worn by indigenous women in parts of Mexico and Central America, particularly in Guatemala, Mexico, and parts of Honduras. Huipils are known for their intricate designs and vibrant colors, often featuring elaborate embroidery, patterns, and symbols that reflect the wearer's cultural heritage and community identity.

Mindful movement

(Nature of lifeforce, bodymind integration)

(W)holistic vital liberation

Ancient Animism

(Nurture of Earth, Divine Spirit within Nature)

Heart guided ceremonial ritual

*   *   *

This image was taken at the time when I started to feel the 'breakthrough' that occurred following my breakdown. It was taken at a festival I attended following my travels. It was the first festival that I had attended within the 'new age' community. I found there some western interpretations of practices I had discovered on my travels and people who seemed to 'speak the same language' as me.

Prior to that point I had been met by glazed expressions

Figure 3 An image that encapsulates how I felt at this point in my life: 21 June 2000

when I spoke to people within my family and work environment, who had no resonance with the experiences, practices, or ideas I had picked up on my travels. Although the 'new age' community was not the 'perfect fit' for me it allowed me to integrate back into Western society and gave me an environment where I could express myself more fully.

Act 7 – Healthy Substitutes

When I returned from my travels, I had started to eat healthily; inspired by the food I had tried whilst travelling, and in an attempt to follow a vegan diet, as advised by my yoga teacher. I found myself in the kitchen one night at 10pm frantically stuffing avocados and dates. An inner voice warned, "This is the same problem, in a healthy disguise." I was still trying to fill the hole inside and suppress my emotions with food. I was fooling myself that it was ok because the food was healthy. Once I withdrew completely from using food as a prop, it was excruciating. I found a poem in my journal from that time entitled *'hunger at the heart of me'*.

It is interesting to note the similarities. With my food addiction I replaced binging on junk food with avocados and dates, realized what I was doing and went 'cold turkey' to break my habits. This process was comparable with the process I underwent regarding relationships. Having pulled away from dependent relationships and romantic obsession, and inspired by what I had started to learn from different cultures, I started to break the pattern further by exploring alternative relating and intimacy practices. I had replaced an unhealthy, yet acceptable addiction, with a healthier alternative.

In my exploration of alternative relationships, there was a period where I explored polyamory[61]. My experience of this is a huge 'breadcrumb' on my path that I cannot believe I did not pick up at the time. Once the door was flung open and I was no longer restricted by my current primary relationship, I had absolutely no inclination to have a sexual or a romantic relationship with anyone else. I felt free in the fact that I could connect in the realm of innocent intimacy (such as cuddles, rituals, dancing, touch and massage) with whomever I

---

[61] Polyamory is a distinct type of consensually non-monogamous relationship where people typically engage in romantic love and sexual intimacy with multiple partners (Moors, Gesselman and Garcia 2021).

chose. I had the safety of a primary partner in the background, which I used as a way to say, "I want to connect with you, and my partner is cool with that, but sex is off the table". This can now be replaced with the statement "I am asexual and aromantic."

I see now that the exploration of alternative relationships and intimacy was still an obsession, moving from one relationship and straight on to another. I had swapped something less healthy for something more nourishing, but I was still trying to soothe my emptiness with a compulsive behavior.

Elizabeth Gilbert describes relationship addiction eloquently in her memoir *Eat, Pray, Love* (2007):

> Addiction is the hallmark of every infatuation-based love story. It all begins when the object of your adoration bestows upon you a heady, hallucinogenic, emotional speedball. Soon you start craving that intense attention, with the hungry obsession of any junkie.

* * *

Act 8 – Acceptable Addictions

The struggle with the addictions I have battled with is that they are both accepted and encouraged within Western society. The poem below attempts to illustrate this by incorporating statements and encouragement that were often voiced to me about food and relationships. These statements have a translation, in brackets underneath, as to what an equivalent phrase might be if someone were giving similar advice to someone with an unacceptable addiction, such as drugs.

Acceptable Addictions

You'll find the right one for you
She says
You have to kiss some frogs to find a prince
(You've only tried marijuana and ecstasy
You need to experiment to find your perfect high)

Have some banoffee pie
She says
I know you've given up sugar, but it won't hurt
(There's a needle in the bathroom
Why don't you go and jack up?)

There's plenty more fish in the sea
She says
Just get out there and make an effort
(There's plenty more hits on the streets
Stop moping around, go out and find a fix)

Relationships are about compromise
She says
You have to keep your man happy
(Go and sell your body my dear
You need a way to fund your score)

*   *   *

Act 9 - InTEAmacy

During my period of celibacy, I met and had a potent platonic relationship with an androgynous man. We seemed to be mirrors for each other. We shared an erotic intimacy that was not sexual in nature. I include a poem illustrating an example of this nonsexual erotic intimacy; a ritual which I named the *'Tantric Tea Ceremony'*.

She warms the pot
Delicately adding the leaves
Slowly pouring water
Gushing, rippling

She cups the bowl
Tenderly turning in her hand
Gently placing down
Faintly, clinking

She lifts the pot
Carefully serving tea
Precisely spiraling
Liquid love

They hold the bowls
Infusing tea with their energy
Sending from heart to hands
Silently, intently

They gaze deeply eye to eye
Looking into the depths
Swapping bowls
Soft touch

They drink the tea
Absorbing the essence within
Infused by the other
Reverently digesting

He leans towards her
Whispering in her ear
Telling her fluid quintessence
Quietly, sincere

She shudders with delight
Absorbing his recognition
Returning her appreciation
Lyrically passionate

*   *   *

There was electric energy between us. I experienced this as exuberant vitality, not as sexual energy. I had no desire to have sex with him.

*   *   *

Act 10 Waiting

My commitment to celibacy opened the space for me to appreciate what was genuinely occurring for me, rather than viewing my experience through the lens of sexualized couple's culture.

The androgynous man I was having a queer platonic relationship with was unusually attractive and I enjoyed his beauty; comparative to how I appreciate the splendor of an exquisite landscape, yet more fascinating and charming. I now understand this as 'aesthetic attraction'[62], a term utilized by the asexual community to describe an attraction towards the way somebody looks or presents themselves.

---

[62] Aesthetic attraction is often equated with sexual or romantic attraction, a lens through which we have been conditioned to view people. Assuming that aesthetic attraction leads to sexual attraction can be problematic and has been for me.

He was also aesthetically attracted to me. He used to deliver long and lyrical soliloquies about how beautiful he found me. What I did not realize at the time was, that to him, this aesthetic attraction was linked to sexual attraction and that he was (and thought that 'we' were) 'waiting' for my year of celibacy to be over.

*   *   *

An interaction with a female friend regarding a troubling incident, led to insight regarding the nature of the relationship and my patterns. With hindsight, the conversation was a spark that ignited self-awareness and the beginning of my practice of celibacy transforming into becoming asexual[63]:

Me: We were at the party, and I was cuddling a man that he is attracted to, I turned around and he was leaning up against the wall, looking at us with a look I can't describe.

Friend: Desire?

Me: No don't be silly, he's gay.

Friend: Or perhaps bi?

Me: He told me he is gay.

Friend: Uh huh?

Me: Well, he did say he had related with women in the past the other day …

Friend: Okaaaaay. So, what happened then?

Me: He said, "Look at you cuddle bunnies", and walked over and sidled between us.

Friend: How did that feel?

---

[63] i.e. something that was practiced – celibacy - abstinence from sex - became a way of being. I simply *was* 'asexual', rather than practicing celibacy by deliberately rechanneling my libido to fuel other pursuits and activities, my libido was naturally sublimated into an expanded nonsexual erotic way of being (see Marcuse 1955). I no longer experienced sexual attraction or desire and therefore fit the definition of asexuality, something I did not realize until Lyvinia Elleschild (my supervisor) pointed this out to me.

Me: Ok, I guess, maybe slightly uncomfortable ... controlling or something.

Friend: So, you all just cuddled?

Me: No, he leaned in towards me.

Friend: And you *kissed him*?

Me: No, I just bent my forehead towards his so our foreheads were gently touching in a forehead kiss, but he couldn't kiss my mouth.

Friend: Did you not want to kiss him?

Me: I don't know, it just felt, because of our friendship, that it would have meant too much.

Friend: Ah, it would have *meant too much.*

Me: Hmmmm.

Friend: So, just supposing he does want to have a sexual relationship with you, would you?

Me: I don't know, I don't really want to, but I guess I would if not doing it meant the end of our relationship.

Friend: Right, so you *would* even though it's not what you *want.*

*   *   *

Act 11 – The Blessing of Solitude

The 'platonic' relationship ended soon after this, my friend's voice saying, "So you *would* even though it's not what you *want*" became a haunting mantra that stayed with me on repeat. I realized that I could not betray myself, as I had in the past, by offering more than I wanted to for the sake of a relationship.

At the time of taking my vow of celibacy[64], I had only intended for it to last for a year. However, on the other side of the emptiness and

---

[64] I made vows I made to myself in a private fire ritual I held for myself at the beginning of my intended period of celibacy. My practice of celibacy continued after the prescribed

struggle that I felt during the months after this queer-platonic relationship ended, was a wholeness I had not experienced before.

I genuinely had no desire for a coupled relationship, I sought solitude as a blessing and my libido or lifeforce, no longer directed towards sexual relationships, became a source of vitality, an electrical power that could fuel my creative pursuits, parenting and community giving. The addictive feeling of being in love that I had desperately sought with another person had become something that I accessed naturally in the everyday.

I found it in the sweet nectar of a flower's scent, in the bittersweet tang of a berry, in the whoosh of a bird's wings, in my body free flowing through rippling water, in glistening beams of light tantalizing my eyes. The feeling of 'being in love' had become an internally accessed sensation not particular about its object.

*   *   *

Curtain call

Whether asexuals want a relationship or not they have to create a viable life and relate in the context of sexualized couple's culture (Przybylo 2011, Budgeon 2008). Many asexuals compromise as they think that sex is the entry fee in order to have a relationship (Brotto et al 2010). Even David Jay, the founder of AVEN – described as the 'poster boy' of asexuality in an Observer newspaper article (Swash 2012)—says that he would consider having sex if it allowed him to have a life-partnership with someone (Chevigny and Davenport 2012).

---

period and became a way of being rather than a practice and led to the discovery of asexuality.

My initial discovery of the limited definition of asexuality provided by AVEN, combined with the analysis of my own narrative illuminated themes that I wished to explore further through reviewing the literature, exploring with co-creators and the subsequent creative representation of my own and others' experiences. These themes were:

- Motivations for asexuals participating in sex and the consequences of consensual unwanted sex

- Acknowledgement of the potential link between sexual trauma and asexuality

- The distinction between asexual intimacy and the sex act

- Asexual romance and aromance

- Asexuality, celibacy and spiritual practice

- The nature of asexual desire and the asexual libido/lifeforce

- The fluidity of sexuality and the asexual spectrum

I am certainly not the poster girl asexual. I have a history of trauma and mental health struggles. I have practiced celibacy and I have had a sex life and children. I cannot say "I have always been this way". However, I hope that by that by listening to and telling more asexual stories of 'life experiments' and experiences of flourishing in non-sexual ways, I can offer further understanding and representation of alternative ways of blooming and thriving as a non-sexual person.

I hope that the emotionally demanding work of self-reflection and analysis that I have been able to undertake will help others to navigate this terrain and offer some encouragement, the language and confidence to seek and negotiate for levels of intimacy that are truly nourishing for all those involved.

*   *   *

After the creation of this narrative, the themes that I went on to explore and the focus of the research were refined, due to further reflections on my experiences during exploring co-creators' narratives, and the reading of the literature (these aims, and focus are articulated in the conclusion of Chapter 3). The aspects of my narrative, that only appeared important following this expanded understanding, gained from the co-creators' stories and my reading, will be shared in Chapter 4. Chapter 4 examines our process of finding a way of being that felt right to us from within a hypersexualized culture, in relation to concepts and theories found within the literature.

3. Investigating a Mystory[65]

Following the analysis of my journals, the writing of my personal asexual becoming (shared in the previous chapter) and locating the themes to be explored within this research, I undertook a review of the literature, endeavoring to unravel the mystery of my-story and in response to the themes emerging within the beginnings of my communications with co-creators. I wanted to understand and locate my experience and those of co-creators within the theoretical material, not only for the purpose of the research, but because it felt urgent and was personal. I therefore scavenged for any sources I could find in order to expand understanding of these experiences and I have pieced together some unusual puzzle pieces in the process.

---

[65] A term utilized by Ulmer (1989, 1994), cited in Pelias (2022:124).

I start with sections on 'foundations' and 'identity, community and relationship choices' which review the literature on asexuality. Within these initial sections, I include some poetry based on co-creators' narratives of deterritorialization (Deleuze and Guattari 1980) and asexual identity formation[66], in the layered format (Ronai 1995) that has been utilized in previous chapters and continues to be followed throughout this book. These are separated from the theoretical analysis with three stars. I also include some journal entries within this layered format. This differs from the usual academic practice of quoting raw data and then interpreting the data. The poems are a representation of the interpretation of the raw data and will not be analyzed in the way that raw data would be in conventional academic research (Faulkner 2019). The theoretical text around the poems will frame the poems and give them context.

I then move into a broader review of the literature that is relevant to my story and the life stories that I had started to gather from co-creators. These sections include the themes of asexual (mis)representation, the nonsexual erotic, the nonsexual libido as the erotic life energy (or lifeforce), nonsexual erotic pleasure (or jouissance) – with a focus on the nonsexual erotic pleasure of desubjectification, which is often related to the spiritual practices that are practiced by me and the co-creators, and which we all feel contributed to us becoming erotically embodied asexuals. I finish the chapter with the revised aims and objectives that arose from the literature review.

3.1 Foundations

The asexual identity started to become an established identity around 20 years ago, with the formation of the online community AVEN

---

[66] The process of creating these poems in collaboration with the co-creators is described in Chapter 4.

(Asexual Visibility and Education Network) in 2001. The ability to connect, discuss and form this new identity has grown due to social media, with many asexual groups forming on Facebook, Reddit and Tumblr, and channels with an asexual focus appearing on YouTube. Brown (2016) tells us that 'social and digital technologies are changing conceptualizations of self and identity' and that selfhood and identity are 'far more complex than when they existed only in the physical world' (p.194).

AVEN's definition of asexuality is 'An asexual person is a person who does not experience sexual attraction' (AVEN 2022). This definition has been expanded over the past twenty years, with a complex variety of identities emerging under the umbrella of asexuality. These identities, that create a spectrum of asexualities, accommodate the varying types and intensity of attraction experienced with asexuality acting 'as a common point of identification rather than constituting a shared identity per se' (Carrigan 2011: 467). Chasin (2013: 405), offers a variant on the AVEN definition of asexuality as 'a lack of sexual attraction combined with one's identification as asexual' this definition emphasizes the importance of self-identification, helping to deter anyone who would place the label of 'asexual' on another person without consent. Online forums, linked to AVEN and some independent of AVEN with similar goals, are active in other countries, for example Baidu Post Bar of Asexuality in China (Wong and Guo, 2020: 79).

Bogaert (2004) produced formative academic research into asexuality. His study endeavored to both estimate the prevalence of asexuality and the causes of asexuality. This study showed 1.05% of participants identified with the statement: "I have never felt sexually attracted to anyone at all" (Bogaert 2004: 281). The notion of human asexuality did appear in some previous studies, such as the "group X" in Kinsey's 1948 report, although the focus of his report was male sexuality not asexuality. Roughly 1.5% of respondents placed themselves in the "X" category, which indicated 'no socio-sexual contacts or reactions.' Within Kinsey's 1953 follow on research, it was estimated that 1 to 4% of male interviewees, and 1 to 19% of female participants were asexual. Bogaert continued researching asexuality proposing that it should be treated as an orientation not a pathology (2012, 2015).

This dislocation from the realm of pathology is reflected within the 2013 edition of the *Diagnostic and Statistical Manual, DSM 5*, asexuality is listed as an occurrence separate from FSIAD/HSDD (female sexual interest/arousal disorder / hypoactive sexual desire disorder). The text regarding this topic reads: "If a lifelong lack of sexual desire is better explained by one's self-identification as 'asexual', then a diagnosis of female sexual interest/arousal disorder [or male hypoactive sexual desire disorder] would not be made" (APA, 2013: 434 and 443, cited in Kurowicka 2021: 41).

Among the many terms and definitions associated with the asexual spectrum are 'demisexual' (a person who only feels sexual attraction once a relationship with an emotional bond has been formed) and 'graysexual' (a person who only experiences sexual attraction on rare occasions or at a low level of intensity). There are also definitions for different types of attraction, including romantic attraction, which helps distinguish between homo-, bi-, hetero-, pan- and aromantic asexuals (Decker 2014). The identity definitions given here are only the most commonly used and popular definitions among the multitude of subtypes within asexuality, they do however demonstrate the complicated nature of the asexual identity.

The aromantic identity, which is when an individual has no interest in or desire for romantic relationships, is distinct from but sometimes correlates with asexuality. However, many asexuals seek traditional romantic relationships and marriage and these relationships may be with either asexual or sexual partners (Scott and Dawson 2015, 2018). There has been little research published on the aromantic identity, with searches only revealing three studies (Lang 2018, Antonsen *et al* 2020, Elgie 2020).

Those asexuals who are also aromantic can face the concurrent challenges of navigating both sexualized society and couples' culture. One co-creator found herself in a community, which although understood and embraced asexuality, was biased towards her lack of interest in romantic relationships. The following poem articulates this experience:

*   *   *

Spock

Sex wasn't a problem

Who would?

Want that

Sweaty

Messy

Entangled

Romance was different

Who wouldn't?

Want that

Swoony

Magical

Exciting

The shock

Called 'Spock'[67]

For showing

Love differently

Yet

Fully

Committedly

Not fitting in

It's a sin

To not want

The white dress

A ring

Coercivity

Exclusivity

*   *   *

Asexual research is in its infancy, although literature can be found across a variety of disciplines. The psychological literature studies asexuality as a sexual orientation, exploring the frequency of asexuality and its conjunction with other personal variables (Bogaert 2012, Brotto and Yule 2017 and Chasin 2019). Sociological research has looked at the impact of the emergence of asexual communities

---

[67] Spock is a character in the long running TV series and multiple motion picture series *Star Trek*, produced by CBS. Spock is a Vulcan, which is an imaginary alien race who do not experience emotions.

online and how asexuals form their identities (Carrigan 2011, Scherrer 2008, Scott and Dawson 2018, Mitchell and Hunnicutt 2018).

Research by queer and feminist academics views asexuality through a more political lens. Scholars in these fields have utilized asexuality to examine social theories and constructs, challenge assumptions about compulsory sexuality and to imagine alternative ways to relate and form community (Barounis 2014, Renninger 2015, Przybylo 2019).

The body of cross-disciplinary asexuality research is affirming and offers validation that asexuality is a legitimate identity. It has facilitated increased asexual representation, awareness, and visibility. Asexuality has also been utilized as a lens through which to question the dominant discourse regarding the essential role sex plays in human life and society (Przybylo 2011, 2019).

However, although asexual research and representation has increased, asexuality is still often seen as an individual being repressed, is defined by being a *lack* of something (sexuality) rather than being a distinct experience set apart from sexuality, and is still frequently viewed as a pathology which needs fixing (Smith 2017, Chasin 2015, MacInnis and Hodson 2012). There is also the problem of the 'asexual paradox' (Smith 2017) of non-sexuality being defined as a sexual orientation, which reflects the hypersexualization[68] of society (Smith 2017, Gupta 2013, 2025, Przybylo 2013, 2019, Carrigan 2012).

This type of 'asexphobia' (Kim 2014) highlights how asexuality is denounced and how in 'couple culture' (Budgeon 2008) sexual relationships and being in a couple are privileged above being single or other forms of relationships. Many scholars espouse that romantic love, sexuality, and secular marriage (the societally normative and highly commercialized manifestation of a romantic and sexual

---

[68] Discussed further in Chapter 4.

coupling), are historical and cultural constructs, constructs shaped and maintained by social, economic and political conditions (Steven Seidman 2014, Illouz 1997, 2007, 2017, 2021). 'Couple culture' establishes societal norms, for example the presumption that everyone desires a sexual relationship or that this coupled, sexual relationship should be the primary or most important form of relating to the individual, and, furthermore, that this is necessary for health and contentment (Budgeon 2008, hooks 2001). This has also been labelled as 'sexusociety' (Przybylo 2011), 'compulsory sexuality' (Rich 1980, Chasin 2011, Emens 2013, Gupta 2015) and 'sex normativity' (Gupta 2013). Carrigan (2012) argues that asexual practices may negate the culturally wide belief that all adults' life energy is sexual in nature and that healthy individuals desire sex within romantic relationships. He called this the 'sexual assumption'.

Eva Illouz's large body of work focuses primarily on the relationship between capitalism and love, and the ways in which love, romance and sexuality are shaped by larger social and cultural forces such as capitalism and psychologism[69] (Illouz 1997, 2007, 2008, 2017, 2021, 2022). However, Illouz's broader critique of the commodification of love and sexuality can also be applied to the experiences of aromantics and asexuals, who face unique challenges in a culture that values romantic love and sexual desire as the norm. Erich Fromm dismisses the western notion of 'romantic love' describing this as a form of 'immature love' (Fromm 1957), a view shared and developed by Scott Peck (1978). Both Illouz (1997, 2007, 2017, 2021) and hooks (2001) critique the romanticization of love and the sexualization of intimacy. They discuss the problems inherent in romanticizing and individualizing a primary force that is essential to

---

[69] Berger used the term 'psychologism' to describe 'a psychological model operative in the taken-for-granted-world of everyday life in our society' (1965:34).

the cohesion of a society, and inspiring and enabling group or community action for societal change.[70]

It is important to note that, although asexuality challenges the supposition that a relationship including sexuality is the norm, it is not intrinsic to the asexual identity to be averse to forming a couple as a form of relating. Some asexual narratives are likely to verify and some to rebel against this ideology. Scott and Dawson's and (2015) symbolic interactionist paper tells us that:

> ... contrary to the idealism of poststructuralist anarchism, dominant discourses may not simply be rejected, but rather retained as meaningful by those in the relationship. For example, an asexual–non-asexual relationship may still involve sex (albeit perhaps motivated by altruistic love rather than physical lust), children, and other components of heteronormative expectations, indicating that a desire for, and choice of, 'tradition' and/or 'convention' can still play a central part in asexually intimate lives. (p. 14)

They continued their exploration of asexuality (Dawson *et al* 2018) prioritizing lived experience over conceptualization. This research explores how asexuals form and navigate intimate relationships. They argue that asexuality is not as radical/queer as many other researchers have suggested. Their research shows that, rather than challenging existing structures of relationship, asexual people negotiate intimacy within these structures. The problem with this is that it does not recognize the power of structure in qualifying some lifestyles whilst curbing others or that knowledge and discourse can negate possibilities by rendering them incomprehensible. Many co-creators articulated a problem with navigating the issue of intimate erotic encounters being conflated with an ultimate progression into the sexual. These experiences are represented by the following poem:

---

[70] This is discussed in greater depth in Chapter 4, 5 and 6.

*　　*　　*

Just Jouissance

"You're a prick tease"

"You should do something about it now I'm aroused"

"You shouldn't date sexual people"

"What I am supposed to do with this now?"

Not allowed

To kiss

Snuggle

Sensually touch

Enjoy the energy

The warmth

The rush

It must have an ending

One that is 'happy' for some

It's not really pleasure

Until he's able to cum

*　　*　　*

According to Brotto *et al*'s (2010) study, roughly 25% of asexuals state that they have sex with their partners, despite the fact that they feel no sexual attraction. Some asexuals perceive sexual contact as a 'price of admission' for being in a relationship (Brotto *et al* : 607) and for some the opportunity for intimacy is more valuable than avoiding sex (Carrigan 2012).

Despite the varying points of view regarding what asexuality is and how it is navigated, one of the contributions that asexuality studies make to society in general is to facilitate a questioning of how we view fundamental concepts such as sexual attraction, sex, desire, intimacy and romance, and the compulsory nature of these (Wilkinson 2012). The spectrum from asexuality to allosexuality[71] and from aromantic[72] to amatonormativity[73] allow a greater level of self-understanding, choice and self-expression for any person wanting to understand and fully articulate their orientation and preferred mode of relating.

3.2 Identity, community, and relationship choices

Asexual individuals find themselves outside of normative sexual identity and often seek alternative communities in which they can explore alternative identities that fit them better, and where it is easier for them to articulate their preferred way of relating. Carrigan (2011) found that although the details of his participants' stories were 'biographically specific' there was a 'prevalent trajectory' among participants: 'individual difference, self-questioning, assumed pathology, self-clarification and communal identity' (p.476).

For most participants in Carrigan's study the identity process started early, around adolescence. However, there were those who

---

[71] Allosexual pertains to individuals who do not identify as asexual, indicating those who consistently feel sexual attraction, irrespective of their sexual orientation.

[72] An individual who feels minimal or no romantic attraction to others.

[73] Amatonormativity is a term coined by Elizabeth Brake (2012) to describe the belief that 'everyone is better off in an exclusive, romantic, long-term coupled relationship.'

deviated from this due to 'temporal displacement', caused by those around them questioning their apparent difference as 'a phase'. For others this was caused through their own reflections, in which they understood their difference in terms of the circumstances they were experiencing (such as postgraduate studies or travelling around the world, where they explained their difference being due to it being easier not to have a partner). Participants shared some of the advice they received if they tried to express their difference to others with many hearing that their asexuality was 'just a phase', that 'some day they would find 'the right person'' or that they are simply a 'late bloomer'. Carrigan explains how damaging this dominant discourse about sexuality and coupledom is to someone who is 'trying to come to a sustainable understanding of their apparent difference' (2011: 473).

Scott and Dawson critique Carrigan's emphasis on individual choices or thought processes to reach a fixed and final identity. They contrast this with the Symbolic Interactionist model of 'processual becoming'. They point out that this and other literature has depicted the asexual as an 'essential' type of person, saying that:

> This is problematic because it keeps the analysis at the level of individual thoughts, decisions and behaviours, while neglecting to consider the social context in which these are negotiated and the cultural discourses through which they are given meaning. [Research would be] more usefully grounded in Symbolic Interactionist concepts, such as social selfhood and negotiated transformations of social identity. (2015: 4)

With regards to sexuality, essentialism holds the notion that sexuality is a natural force and that sexual orientations exist before discourse, social life, interactions and contact with institutions (Rubin, 1984, cited in Kurowicka 2021). Essentialist ideas regarding sexuality have generally searched for the 'truths' of sex to explain the essential nature of the person (Foucault, 1978:56). These views are found in medical, psychiatric, psychological, and academic studies of sex and sexuality (Foucault 1978, Rubin 1984 - cited in Kurowicka 2021). An example of the essentialist model in asexuality research is Scherrer's (2008) study of the process of coming to an asexual identity. The essentialist view of asexuality is prevalent, with many participants expressing how they had 'always been this way' or concluding that they had 'always been asexual, even if I didn't have a handy label to stick on' (p.630). The AVEN website supports this viewpoint by claiming that:

> Unlike celibacy, which is a choice to abstain from sexual activity, asexuality is an *intrinsic part of who we are* [my emphasis] just like other sexual orientations ... Most asexual people have been asexual for our entire lives, although not all of us have been aware of the term or the community for as long as we've recognized this. (AVEN Overview, 2022)

This is quite a strong generalization, with some hedging in the use of the word 'most'. The vision held by AVEN/the AVEN community is that of a stable asexual orientation and identity. Despite this being a fixed and perhaps limited definition of asexual identity and how it is formed, the development of a communal identity defends against pathology and obscurity, with individual differences acquiescing to a sense of a communally shared trait. This facilitates both clarification and self-acceptance, which may have been absent before (Gressgard 2013).

Scott and Dawson (2015) tell us that, 'social identities are viewed as meaningful phenomena, and these meanings are not just privately held by individuals but rather shared, defined and negotiated through interaction' (p.8). The asexual online spaces and community are crucial to asexuals as a source of information, support, and a space where they feel safe and accepted, that they are 'normal' (Robbins *et al* 2016). One qualitative study of asexual narratives found that online communities are regarded as fundamental for the discussion of the complexities of asexual identities (Mitchell and Hunnicutt 2018). Co-creators who felt they had always been asexual articulated the 'crushing' experience of realizing that their life trajectory may not follow that which had been expected. The following poem aims to capture the essence of these experiences.

*　　*　　*

Weight of her difference

The weight of her difference

Is crushing

The realization breaking

Apart

Everything expected

She will never

Love quixotically

Passionately

Marry

Create family

She will not be

The person

Assumed

Acknowledged

Accepted by kin

*　　*　　*

Due to a lack of asexual representation until recent times, finding the asexual community online is often an essential step in the creation of an asexual identity. Much of the research discussed here indicates that an asexual identity usually only becomes established once an individual has discovered, and perhaps made contact with, the asexual community. Before this discovery, it is not probable that an asexual person would have the necessary representation or language necessary to articulate their experience (Chasin 2011).

It has been documented that researchers' attempts to understand asexual experience have been limited by the definitions and discourse of the AVEN community (and other similar communities) due to the constant referral to sexuality and societal norms rather than an exploration of the lived, embodied experience, of asexuality (Smith 2017, Gupta 2015, Przybylo 2019, Scott and Dawson 2015, 2018). The observation by these scholars that asexual discourse was being limited by the scope of AVEN's definition and rhetoric inspired me to locate my research participants within an online group[74] where there are participants who previously had extensive experience within the new age/neo tantric community and still incorporate conscious movement (such as somatic awareness, dance or mindful movement) and spiritual and/or religious practices (such as meditation, prayer, chanting or mindfulness) within their daily lives.[75]

---

[74] This is a private group where members with therapeutic skills offer free support and signposting to those who may have been traumatized by their experiences within the new age or neo tantra communities. Members also share positive experiences that have emerged from their participation and recommend legitimate, reliable, and regulated classes, groups and teachers to each other.

[75] It should be noted that the researcher and the co-creators within this research project no longer participate in these communities (also see the note in Chapter 4 regarding the sample). Although many of the associated practices have been an essential catalyst within their life journeys and narratives and they still have some elements of 'spiritual or religious' practice (see Chapter 1 for a definition of these terms) as an essential part of their lifestyle, this is not to be taken as a recommendation for these practices or the communities. The information given about these communities (and details of some of the practices in Chapter 4) is included to frame and offer background to the experience of erotically embodied

These asexual individuals tend to have heightened embodied awareness and a discourse about sexuality and non-sexuality that differs from that of mainstream Western society or the AVEN community. Along with my own narrative these co-creators offered the chance to develop and write an alternative narrative of asexuality.

The difficulty with locating an alternative narrative of asexuality is expressed by Mark Smith (2017), who became disillusioned and frustrated within his autoethnographic research into the experience of asexuality. He found that all of the discussions he had with asexual individuals defined asexuality in terms of sexuality, i.e. as a *lack*; a lack of a drive or experience that is considered normative rather than an experience within its own right. He therefore decided to redirect his research towards a historical understanding of the asexual erotic, based within ancient Christianity. He found there the articulation of religious ecstasy, experienced by Christian mystics whose practice was sexual renunciation.

The way that they articulated their experience sounds 'sexual' by modern western standards[76]. However, Smith suggests that this language was in fact appropriated by western *scientia sexualis* (Foucault 1978) at the moment of the 'death of God' (Foucault 1963) when human experience came to be defined in psychological terms and became individualized (contained within the limits of the individual) rather than religious/spiritual (contained within limitlessness or a connection to the divine). This implies that the loss of divine connection limited the experience of eros to the sexual and

---

asexuality that this research aims to articulate (details of the literature critiquing these communities is offered in Chapter 4). In the words of Peter Berger (1965:31): 'The sociologist, qua sociologist, can be of no assistance to distressed individuals hesitating before the multiplicity of healing cults available on the market today, just as he can be of no assistance in the choice of the many religious or quasi-religious *Weltanschauungen* which are engaged in pluralistic competition in our society'.

[76] See section 3.5 for examples of this and further discussion in Chapter 4, 5, 6 and 7.

thus limited our articulation and recognition of eros to that of the sexually erotic.

3.3 Asexual (mis)Representation

MacInnis and Hodson (2012) found that asexuals generally receive prejudice, are viewed negatively, or seen as less human than others. Butler (1990, 1993, 2004) introduced the concept of intelligibility. This is the notion that those beyond the standard categories or discourse are culturally unintelligible and therefore deprived of a subject position. Butler argues against the simple creation of more categories (such as is seen with the burgeoning categories found in asexual and aromantic communities such as AVEN) and purports that staying unintelligible is key to social action. It could be argued that this is a heavy burden, to expect people to do this challenging work with their self/life, foregoing a sense of visibility and validity.

One co-creator shared about how a lack of asexual representation led to her trying unnecessarily to 'fix' herself and being diagnosed with Female Sexual Disfunction, and the relief when she found out about asexuality and attended a nonsexual intimacy event, realizing that physical pleasure and intimacy did not have to be sexual in nature. This experience is represented in the following poem.

*　*　*

The Boyfriend Jumper

She spent so much time

Trying to be a sexual

Not knowing about

Asexuals

So many times

Painfully penetrated

In exchange

For a cuddle

Enduring prodding

By medics

In search of

A cure

So much time

Trying to be

Something fake

Wanting love

Performing orgasm

For his pleasure

Just so he'd cum

And it would be over

Invested in externals

Like his big jumper

That embraced her

Once he'd left

She has her own

'Big Jumper' now

Embracing herself

Completely

All that time

Not knowing

How to ask

For non-sexual touch

Tears of delight

As her capacity

To feel pleasure

Reawakens

Now she knows

About Asexuals

She doesn't have

To be a sexual

*   *   *

This propensity for trying to fix oneself sexually rather than simply accepting (or even celebrating) being nonsexual, is the product of there being very little representation of asexuality in popular culture and the representation that exists being rather negative; often feeding into the 'something to be fixed', 'something lacking' discourse, alongside the idea that this 'fixing' will be achieved by finding a romantic/sexual relationship. The media portrays hypersexuality as the societal standard meaning that asexuality has started to become a challenge as it becomes more visible, leading to it becoming 'the latest stigma'.

An example of this is Sheldon Cooper in *The Big Bang Theory* (Chuck and Brady 2018), who for most of the first three seasons is portrayed as having no interest in relationships or sex whatsoever (and is represented as sex repulsed). In the third season, he is 'fixed up' by his friends with a fellow scientist, Amy, with whom he forms a friendship. The story line focuses on her trying to manipulate him to make their relationship a romantic and sexual one. This coercion is both applauded and encouraged. The storyline regarding their relationship feeds into the mainstream discourse of 'sexusociety' (Przybylo 2011) and couple culture (Budgeon 2008). It also feeds into the discourse that those who do not want sexual or romantic relationships are cold and unfeeling (MacInnis and Hodson 2012), due to Sheldon being portrayed as having little emotion, social intelligence, or regard for others' feelings.

Even more perturbing is the association of asexuality with pathology, as represented by the protagonist of the show *Dexter* (Cuesta 2006), who works for the police by day and is a serial killer by night. He is represented as asexual, emotionally illiterate, highly intelligent, and amoral (Sinwell, 2014).

The number of explicit references to asexuality in popular media is, however, growing, with examples such as the character, Tom Chavez, 'coming out' as asexual in season 4 of *BoJack Horseman* (Bob-Waksberg 2020) and developing a relationship with another asexual character in season 5. Another example, is a brief reference to asexuality in season 4 of *Cobra Kai* (Heald et al 2021), where one of the main characters is represented as ignorant when he misunderstands what another character means when she says she is asexual.

In print there are many young adult titles where the protagonists are asexual and romantic such as, *Let's Talk About Love* (Kann 2019) in which the protagonist is black, biromantic and asexual. There is also a novel where the protagonist is both asexual and aromantic, *Loveless* (Oseman 2020). These novels raise awareness, educate readers about asexuality, and give examples of how to navigate relating as an asexual. They include detailed accounts of how the lead characters discover their asexual identity and their coming out process. These characters give a much more balanced view of asexual people, who are warm, emotionally aware, and interested in relationships and understanding how to navigate these as an asexual.

There are also mainstream, readable books available regarding asexuality (Chen 2020, Decker 2015), which make the topic more accessible to a non-academic audience, and I was surprised to find that there is book of *Asexual Fairy Tales* (Hopkinson 2019), one that I wish had been available when I was a child.

In the quest for visibility, understanding, and sense making, the asexual community has constructed the 'gold star' asexual (Chasin 2013), also known as the 'real' asexual. This person's asexual identity is 'bulletproof' (i.e. they do not have any trauma or medical issues that are likely to be unearthed and linked to their asexuality). According to Chasin (2013) they are also white, educated, middle class, well adjusted, happy, socially confident, physically fit, old enough to be seen to understand themselves and their orientation, sex positive, attractive, and either straight or aromantic. David Jay (AVEN's highly charismatic founder) demonstrates all these qualities and has become the 'poster boy' (Swash 2012) for asexuality. The documentary *(A)sexual* also has appearances by David Jay and many other 'ideal' asexuals (Chevigny and Davenport 2012). This is problematic as it potentially excludes those who do not have such characteristics or perhaps have past trauma, do not fit the ideal age bracket, or have mental or physical disabilities.[77]

Despite the attempt to create an 'ideal asexual', Hills (2012) tells us that comments on online blogs and social media indicate that asexuality is far from becoming a socially acceptable orientation. One such remark that she offers as an example is a comment on a sex columnist's blog saying, "The idea of there being NOTHING inside,

---

[77] This research does not help with this bias due to the demographic of the co-creators and also due to the fact, that due to ethical concerns, most of the narratives that contained stories of past trauma (apart from my own) have not been included.

no juice, no drives at all ... well, to my mind that is the ULTIMATE FREAKINESS, the one eternally unfathomable kink."

David Jay counters this in an interview with Hills (2012). He explains that, "For a lot of people, sexuality serves as an essential metaphor for that desire to live or desire to connect. Those who believe that asexual people are lacking in some essential life force clearly haven't hung out with me and my friends!" (Hills 2012).

3.4 'May the Force be with you'[78]

One of the tasks of sociology is to determine how the social world constitutes the biological libido, an undifferentiated impulse, as a specific social libido.
Bourdieu 1994: 77

David Jay's comment at the end of the last section may have raised some questions in the reader of the article. Questions such as - What is this life force if it is not the feeling of sexual longing or desire that

---

[78] This is a famous line throughout the *Star Wars* films, written by George Lucas and distributed by Disney. It is referring to 'The Force', which in the films, is described as a binding, universal energy field that has both a light side and a dark side. Those who are Force-sensitive can harness and manipulate this energy to achieve various extraordinary abilities. Jedi and Sith, who manipulate the Force, often express their desires, passions, and emotions through their use of this energy. In Star Wars, the Force is often described as the life force that surrounds all living things. This concept has parallels with the idea of the human life force or life energy in various philosophical and spiritual traditions. The concept of "ki" or "chi" in East Asian traditions, "prana" in yoga, or "vital force" in vitalism or the 'breath of life' in Christianity all relate to the idea of a life energy that sustains living beings. Beyond the human or individual context, the Force is an allegory for a broader universal life force. This notion aligns with various spiritual and philosophical traditions that propose the existence of a universal, interconnected energy or consciousness that binds everything in the cosmos. In this sense, the Force represents a life energy that can be harnessed by individuals with the appropriate training and sensitivity, reflecting a belief in the interconnectedness of all things in the universe. I use it here as a title, in a jocular way, to point towards the notion that it is possible that asexuals simply channel a vital energy in a different way to other people and that, like 'Jedis', they should not be seen as 'lacking' because they do this differently to most.

builds up in order to be released in the sexual act? What is the vitality that most people think is sexual in nature and that asexual people therefore lack, but David Jay assures us he and his asexual friends have in 'bucket loads'? This section aims to find some answers to these questions. These answers help with one of the aims of this book, the aim to articulate an expanded erotic, of which the sexual is only one limited expression, and to further the concept of the libido or lifeforce as the energetic expression of eros, which can be directed to sexual activity, but can also be directed towards vitalizing any other activity that one chooses[79]. These answers help to deconstruct the concept that the libido is a sexual energy, or drive, and develop the concept of the nonsexual libido by exploring how this raw vitalizing, energizing pulse of life is socially shaped, structured, and given specific meanings within a particular cultural context. This section aims to offer an understanding of how social norms, values, and institutions influence and channel individual fundamental drives into specific social patterns and behaviors.

One of the key concepts within Freud's psychoanalytic theory is the libido, which he considered the most important motivator of both personality and behavior. Libido is commonly regarded as linked to the human sex drive. In Freud's early writing, he associates the libido predominantly with desire for sex (Fairholm and Lench 2014). Freud (1905) said that he defines 'the concept of libido as a quantitatively variable force ... occurring in the field of sexual excitation.' (p.217)

However, this changed in later work, with Freud expanding the definition of libido as a lust for life, not simply sexual desire. In Freud's essay *Beyond the Pleasure Principle* (1920) he explains that 'critical and other far-seeing minds had indeed for a long-time raised objections to the narrowing of the libido concept down to the energy of the sexual instinct as directed to the object' (p.43). In response to

---

[79] As explained in the Introduction: page 1, and in the aims and objectives in section 3.9 *'Questions and directions'*.

this Freud had re-evaluated his concept and libido became a representation of a 'general life instinct', which encompassed other motivators but still included sex (Schultz and Schultz 2004, cited in Fairholm and Lench 2014). Freud explicitly reframes his concept of libido as being a part of eros through an:

> [E]xtension of the libido-concept ... the sexual instinct became for us transformed into the Eros that endeavors to impel the separate parts of living matter to one another and to hold them together; what is commonly called the sexual instinct appears as that part of the Eros that is turned towards the object. Our speculation then supposes that this Eros is at work from the beginnings of life, manifesting itself as the 'life-instinct'. (1920: 55)

Freud, who was largely responsible, within Western culture, for conflating the life energy or life force with only being sexual, had realized his error and could see that this 'life-instinct' was in fact not simply a sexual drive. Within *Beyond the Pleasure Principle* he explains that whilst libido encompasses sexual desires, it also includes the general life energy that drives various pursuits, including creative, intellectual, and social deeds. In this way, Freud acknowledged that the life instinct (which he indicates *is* eros) is not limited to sexual and emotional desires but is a more encompassing force that drives human activity in multiple aspects of life. He also recognized the full poetic and expansive nature of eros saying, 'Thus the Libido of our sexual instincts would coincide with the eros of poets and philosophers, which holds together all things living.' (p.41)

Unfortunately, this is not a widely known aspect of Freud's work and thus the libido is still conflated with the sexual in common discourse. Freud had recognized that the sexual drive is a 'part of' eros, the eros that compels the desire for 'separate parts of living matter' to join together, to become intimate, to create collaboratively.

Richard von Krafft-Ebing published the first edition an encyclopedia of sexual pathologies, *Psychopathia Sexualis,* in 1886. He explains that he studied sexual life because he believed it is the foundation of society. He begins the book by telling us that the continuation of the human race is 'enforced by a mighty, irresistible impulse' and that without sexual impulse 'all poetry and probably all moral tendency would be eliminated from [man's] life'. He believed that this 'mighty impulse' gave rise to the power for all activities, 'acquiring property, establishing a home... awakening altruistic sentiments towards a person of the opposite sex, towards ... the whole human race' (Krafft-Ebing 1906:1). This is quite a broad definition of the 'sexual impulse', similar to Freud's expanded definition of 'libido'.

Within his manual he did not use the term asexual, he utilized the term 'anesthesia sexualis' to define a lack of this 'sexual impulse'. According to Krafft-Ebing's definitions, this would render the asexual person as fundamentally lifeless. He distinguished between this and celibacy, with this being a practice of utilizing the will forces to redirect this sexual impulse rather than a lack of it. His view fails to recognize that perhaps asexual people experience this energy impulse in ways other than the sexual **naturally**, with no need for the use of will forces to redirect it. Could it perhaps be that there is simply a 'life impulse'/creative impulse or 'life energy'/creative energy that can be directed to any area of life, with sex being *only one*, and perhaps the *most basic way*, to direct that powerful force?[80]

If this is the case, then perhaps asexuals simply naturally experience this force in other ways and direct it to outputs other than sexual intercourse, such as creativity, athletic pursuits, work, or other sensory pleasures (Marcuse 1955, Lorde 1978, hooks 2010, Sovatsky 2000, 2009, 2018, Smith 2017). A graysexual artist in the documentary

---

[80] This question is explored and answered by much of the following theoretical discussion and the subsequent creative outputs from the co-creators' narratives. It is one of the prime focuses of this research — i.e. that the sexual is only one basic potential of erotic expression and that the libido, the energetic expression and movement of eros within the bodymind, can be directed to any activity, and that the pleasure of this energy is not only sexual in nature, but can be felt throughout the body during everyday activities.

(*A)Sexual* (Chevigny and Davenport 2012) identifies as being asexual most of the time because she is directing all of her energies towards her creativity, and simply does not feel any sexual attraction or desire at all when she is being creative. This natural sublimation of 'sexual' energy has been articulated by many of the co-creators. Some of them started with this as a practice (such as Taoist energy exercises or Tantra) and after some time it became a natural sublimation of the energy, and they experienced themselves as asexual once this natural sublimation had occurred .

Carrigan (2011) explains that assumptions about sex are so embedded within our society that, if a person is sexually inclined, they would not necessarily notice them. However, asexual people notice these assumptions acutely because their experiences do not match with them. Sometimes it is useful to look outside of Western culture for an explanation of phenomena that we cannot understand with a Western lens. Foucault (1978) talks of *scientia sexualis*, the western view, which encompasses the church's moral-confessional view of right and wrong sexuality, sexological and sexual liberation encouragement, and practices based in the fields of medicine and psychoanalysis. He contrasts this with an *ars erotica* which he says originates from many societies; 'China, Japan, India, Rome, the Arabo-Moslem'. He goes on to say that:

> The effects of this masterful art, which are considerably more generous than the spareness of its prescriptions would lead one to imagine, are said to transfigure the one fortunate enough to receive its privileges: an absolute mastery of the body, a singular bliss, obliviousness to time and limits, the elixir of life. (p.58)

This *ars erotica* is almost impossible to understand through the western *scientia sexualis* lens. This is because the *scientia sexualis* knowledge-power about sex is obtained by scientists observing others' behaviors, whereas *ars erotica*'s knowledge is embodied and mystical, gained through experience and practice (Foucault 1978,

Sovatsky 2018). Sovatsky's paper focuses attention on the *Indic Ars Erotica*, in particular Tantra and Hatha Yoga, the practice of which 'infuses profound *ars erotica* bliss, creativity and passion within one's own body.' This practice can include sacred sexuality, but this is only one facet of the practice and is not essential to it.

Many scholars (White 2000, Smith 2018, Bishop 2019, Venkatesh 2010, Shri Shashikumar 2003, Sovatsky 2009, Ferrer 2008, Sadlier 2017) have written about the *ars erotica* life force (or 'life impulse'). They write about how the libido or sexual energy is simply one expression of this force that can be directed to or away from sexual expression at will by a spiritual practitioner. This can occur through the practice of 'the drawing of breath' or a natural/spontaneous opening or clearing of blocks in 'the channels and centers of the body' (Sauthoff 2019). The experience of this movement of energy or life force 'causes the energy and hormone enriched blood to swell more deeply into the spine, throat and head as a life-enhancing, quasi-erotic tumescence of love and beauty' (Sovatsky 2009).

The West has appropriated these *Indic Ars Eroticas* and created new modalities which are based in *scientia sexualis*, those of 'neo-tantra' and 'neo-yoga'. The first of which, takes and singles out the sexual part of Tantra. The second of which takes and singles out the *asana* or physical postures of Hatha Yoga. Sovatsky tells us that:

> Westernized 'neo' tantra barely ever goes beyond sex-desire and scientia sexualis understandings of 'the body' into the so-different ars erotica body of [energy body] maturation. (2018: 6)

A Tantra teacher shared that her experiences of practicing Tantra and Yoga were very different to most of the Western teachings. This may be because she already had a propensity towards becoming asexual (unknown to her during most of her years of practice) and, because of this, she researched, studied, and touched the other 'non-sexual' dimensions of the practice. She was so averse to the western viewpoint and appropriation of Tantra that she wrote this Facebook post in a private group she was a member of[81]:

> Facebook post – 2018
>
> I have been responding to other people's posts here with my views. I feel such passion about this that I now feel the need to express it all as an individual post in this group:
>
> Conscious sexuality is only a very small part of the total path of Tantra.
>
> The whole western way of selling tantra as a sexual practice has warped the view of the beautiful and complete life changing path of Tantra. Saying you are following the tantric path and getting stuck at conscious sexuality is like going on the most amazing, vast, adventurous journey of your life, stopping at the first motel and thinking you have arrived.
>
> It seems to me that some female facilitators have co-created this 'sex sells' warped view of what tantra is and then rather than owning this shadow have scapegoated male facilitators for being predatory with participants or behaving inappropriately.

Sovatsky expands on non-sexual erotics in his book *Passions of Innocence: Tantric Celibacy and the Mysteries of Eros* (Sovatsky 1994). He utilizes the term 'celibacy' in the title (I imagine with the aim of making it more accessible to a western audience), however the book in fact describes *brahmacharya*[82] which has been at the core of yoga for over 5,000 years. In a later paper (2018), he tells us that this 'so-different eroticism' has been kept hidden from Western readers and scholars through the distortion caused by the 'mistranslation from the *tantric* Sanskrit term, *brahmacharya,* to the hyper-loaded and de-eroticized English, *scientia sexualis* term, 'celibacy''. He argues that *bramacharya* is not a state of self-repression, it is a blissful inner state,

---

[81] Shared with permission.

[82] Brahmacharya differs from celibacy, which simply refers to abstinence from sexual activity. It generally refers to a lifestyle of complete abstinence and asceticism, where the individual gains complete control of their body and mind, not simply the sexual function (Lochtefeld 2001).

a process of loving your spiritual practice so much that you 'marry' it 'as an erotic life-partner' and that in this state there is no debate about where you direct your energy (Sovatsky 2018).

The misunderstanding of this state of brahmacharya or continence is described in the book *The Sermon on the Mount according to Vedanta*:

> Continence is *not* repression; it stores up energy and applies that energy to better uses. It is not an end in itself but an indispensable means of freeing the mind from distracting passions and keeping it in the consciousness of God. Sex-energy controlled becomes spiritual energy. To one who is continent, spiritual growth comes quickly and easily. Many people think that by being continent they will lose the greatest pleasure the world has to offer: but the strange fact is that they will not really lose anything. As the sex energy is conserved and as it becomes transformed, they will find a new and much more intense pleasure growing inside themselves. (Prabhavananda 1963:55)

This blissful inner state is not limited to the redirection of energy through yoga and meditation. Sadlier (2017)'s research into the ecstatic group dance practices of women describes how 'people channel their energies in different ways and may actually find the flow of their (a)sexualities in activities, which are not necessarily 'sexual' in a traditional sense.' (p.74) Sadlier observed a 'threefold process' that women navigate when engaging in ecstatic dance 'from vulnerability to inner ecstasy and [finally] collective ecstatic motion' and describes the bonds of passionate friendship that women in these dance groups experience, but that these bonds are considered less than those of monogamous couples, or ties based in 'genital sexual relationships'. This theme of individual and communal ecstatically embodied states through dance and music mirror those described by other researchers. These researchers use the term 'jouissance', introduced by Lacan[83] (1959), to describe the almost orgasmic

---

[83] Lacan referred to the coloring of jouissance with sexuality as "the color of emptiness, suspended in the light of a gap" (1966: 851-852).

nonsexual pleasure and union experienced by those in the 1990s dance scene (Gilbert and Pearson 1999, Gilbert 1999, Green 2016)[84.]

Gilbert and Pearson's account of the jouissance of moving in unison to dance music resonates with the experiences of co-creators within this research. I recognize this experience of the jouissance of dance and music and there are poems attempting to articulate this, based on co-creators' experiences in Chapter 7. Gilbert and Pearson's experiences correspond with the co-creators' experience of this jouissance. The jouissance that is a magnetic charge that fills the air between the dancers as the rising melodic rush of synthesizers cascade in electric streams, caressing the skin that is a canvas for the music's touch. The bass feels like a seismic kiss, creating blissful vibrations throughout the body as the beat resonates through muscles and bone. As the bass reverberates it creates a sense of a unified heartbeat and the heart becomes a vessel for the music's magic. Strangers become kin, linked by a shared cadence that transcends words.

---

[84] See Chapter 7 for many poems which describe co-creators' experiences of this type of pleasure experienced through dance and music.

3.5 Having our cake and eating it too[85]

They who dance are thought mad by those
who hear not the music.
Anon

In searching for literature regarding this nonsexual, erotic bliss I found Ela Przybylo's (2019) book *Asexual Erotics*, which explores non-sexual erotic bonding and practices, adding another dimension to asexuality studies. Przybylo references Audre Lorde's (1978) paper *The Uses of the Erotic* to introduce a new language to discuss intimacy and intimate practices that are not reducible to sexuality or sex.

In her earlier (2013) paper she remarks on how 'scientific research on asexuality, while providing asexuality with a sense of credibility, is also shaping the possibilities and impossibilities of what counts as asexuality and how it operates.' (p.224) She also states that a crucial feminist examination of these texts had become imperative as it disrupts interpretations of empirical research as unequivocal and unbiased truths. It prompts us 'to remember the story-telling aspect of scientific fact-production', emphasizing that science itself is a collection of representations 'allied to specific cultural discourses' (Ibid: 225). She suggests that this is particularly pressing in the current nascent phase of asexuality studies, as frequently these empirical depictions of asexuality are unquestioningly accepted as factual records, obscuring the fact that they are part of the uncovering of a long-overlooked sexual orientation (Ibid.)

Although Przybylo's (2019) book offers this 'urgently needed' feminist critique in opposition to scientific views and is based on Lorde's freeing of the erotic from the sexual, for me, it did not help to

---

[85] AVEN made cake an unofficial symbol of asexual-ness, because apparently 'cake is better than sex'. My use of it is also a 'nod' to Julie Parsons' utilizing of food apothegms, such as 'a piece of cake' in her PhD thesis titles (2014).

answer the key focus of this research—describing what it means and feels like to be an erotically embodied asexual. It falls into the category of political rather than embodied experiential asexual literature (Dawson, Scott and McDonnell 2018).

Dawson, Scott and McDonnell (2018) describe political asexual literature as suggesting 'that asexuality has the potential to: redefine the nature of intimate relationships; overcome the dominance of 'sexusociety'; resist neoliberal conceptions of citizenship; and aid anarchist politics.' (p375). They critique this stance for stating what 'asexuality ought to be and, ipso facto, how asexual people ought to behave rather than exploring the beliefs and actions of asexual people.'(Ibid). They go on to say that 'this has been part of a wider trend where 'asexuality' comes to be treated as a disembodied entity which challenges 'contemporary society.' Which is counter to the views of the asexual individuals whom they interviewed who 'saw large scale political action as irrelevant.' (p.374).

Although many asexuals may see 'political action as irrelevant', the definition of asexuality and protection from harm for asexual people is important. Recently, I was watching an episode of *Would I Lie to You* on BBC1, whilst staying with my parents. In response to a female contestant who had said she did not feel sexually threatened by him, one of the panel leaders said, 'Aside from you referring to me as an 'asexual lump'...' (Copeland 2022).

I felt like I had been punched in the gut. Asexuality becoming a politicized identity with a definition would offer protection to those who identify as or 'just are' asexual from having to hear such comments.

However, it is important for the definition of asexuality not to be limited. A limited definition could perhaps lead to the view that asexuals are 'lifeless lumps' (even if this view could no longer be expressed on television because it had become politically incorrect). I understand the value of the protection that such political action has given other marginalized groups of people from hearing slanderous comments whilst they are feeling safe, open, relaxed, and perhaps enjoying a pleasant evening with family.

Viewing the experience of the erotic through the lens of asexuality moves a study away from the political and towards embodied experience. It not only assists with the description of asexuality as a flourishing, and a fulfilling experience rather than a lack, but it also offers a spectrum of non-sexual erotic possibility to anyone, wherever they are on the sexual spectrum between allosexual and asexual. It moves the discussion of asexuality away from the macro political and into the realm of the experiential (Smith 2017, Dawson, Scott and McDonnell 2018) and the philosophical (Foucault 1978, Marcuse 1955, 1974, Smith 2017). In doing so it facilitates the potential of asexuality to facilitate micro social change via giving individuals choice and insight regarding alternative ways of self-understanding, being and becoming. This could of course filter out and cause wider macro societal changes, but the aim of this exploration of erotically embodied asexuality is the liberation of individuals caught within the constraints of 'sexusociety' and 'couples' culture', and the liberation of 'asexuality' from its current locus in lack.

*　*　*

(Journal entry, 22 June 2023)

Although my aim is not to further a political movement, and I do not wish to claim any identity label for myself, the positioning of Asexuality as a lack still creates a sense of resistance within me. (I'm glad I have found Mark Smith's thesis as he also seemed to feel this).

There's that question that Carol asked me ~ 'why challenge the definition of asexuality?' However, if AVEN are going to link asexuality with the definition of not feeling sexual attraction and desire and then tally this definition with it not being anything to do with celibacy, choice, changing circumstances, trauma, or life pathways, they are inviting a challenge. I am concerned that 'not feeling sexual attraction and desire' has been claimed by asexual communities and at once limited by them.

This means that those searching for information on 'not feeling sexual attraction and desire' may (alongside sexological treatises on sexual healing and medical terms like 'FSD') find the term 'asexuality' which leads to AVEN and associated communities. Currently, they will not find a wider scope of literature in which to understand and base their experiences. Those tired of hypersexualized society may not find a 'route out' of limitation and lack, towards discovering all the possibility of becoming erotically embodied as an asexual person and enjoying either non-sexual intimacy or satisfying solitude. They may waste time trying to 'fix themselves' to be sexual only to later find that there are alternatives, like the experience expressed in The Boyfriend Jumper poem.*

*   *   *

Not finding what I was looking for in Przybylo's book I located Lorde's (1978) original work. My first reading of Lorde's essay called to mind a book I had read some years ago, *A Return to Eros*, by Marc Gafini and Kristina Kincaid (2017); a book that explores the nature of eros. Although it includes sexuality as a part of eros (its lens being 'sacred sexuality') the dimension of sex is far from the fullness of the erotic that they describe. The book's central theme is living an 'erotic life', and the central premise is that people can experience great satisfaction, personal effectiveness, and wellbeing 'when we embrace the full beauty of our embodied eros, not merely in the sexual but in every dimension of our lives.' (p.8)

Gafini and Kincaid's rather poetic exposition of the erotic life is similar to that of Lorde. Lorde describes how she finds the erotic …

> In the way my body stretches to music and opens into response, hearkening to its deepest rhythms, so every level upon which I sense also opens to the erotically satisfying experience, whether it is dancing, building a bookcase, writing a poem, examining an idea (1978: 89).

She goes on to explain that there is a hierarchy of activities and the flow of joy they offer; 'there is a difference between painting a back fence and writing a poem' (p.90). However, she tells us that, 'there is no difference between writing a poem and moving into sunlight against the body of a woman I love.' (p.90)

I discovered other scholars who wrote about this expanded view of the erotic, such as bell hooks, who in her 2010 essay *Touch* speaks of the eros in the broader sense, discussing the 'sensuality of eros in the classroom'. She goes on to say that when this 'moves in the direction of sexuality, it creates chaos and dissent' (2010:154). She then goes on to encourage teachers to harness the powerful energy of eros to enliven the classroom setting saying, 'Eros as the passionate life instinct triggered by libido is what makes us able to experience the ecstatic in our bodies. The experience of learning can be intensified when a teacher is able to garner the energy of eros' (hooks 2010:155). In her book *The Eros of Everyday Life* Susan Griffin shares the view that embodiment in connection with nature infuses 'even the most daily acts, with an eros, a palpable love, that is also sacred' (1996:15).

Having seen this link, and feeling my embodied resonance with these descriptions of the non-sexual erotic, and how the sexual is just one part of the erotic, I was left with the inspiration that the key to describing the experience of asexuality as something other than a lack was utilizing Lorde's and Gafini and Kincaid's notion of sexuality being only a small part of eros, and elucidating my experience of the erotic as an energy, a force, a jouissance, an embodied poetic experience, rather than stopping short at using asexuality as a rational tool of analysis or political rhetoric.

On further exploration I discovered that this concept of sexuality as merely a small and basic expression of the erotic is not new within social theory. In Marcuse's talk 'Marxism and Feminism' delivered in 1974 he defines this as:

EROS, as distinguished from SEXUALITY

-- **Sexuality**: a partial drive, libidinal energy confined and concentrated in the erotogenic zones of the body, mainly: genital sexuality.

--**Eros**: libidinal energy, in the struggle with aggressive energy, striving for the intensification, gratification, and unification of life and of the life environment.

(Marcuse 1974:280)

Marcuse (1955) envisioned that liberation would occur through the re-eroticization of the de-eroticized capitalist body. In his chapter *The Transformation of Sexuality into Eros*, he argued that the modern body is suppressed and de-eroticized in order to perform 'alienated labor' and he predicted that once this repression was alleviated through the advancement of society, and the lessening need for alienated production, the whole body would become infused with a libidinal quality. This, he said, would not simply lead to sexual freedom, as there would be a 'natural sublimation' of these erotic energies away from genital supremacy and into a new type of sensual, libidinal gratification in the form of socially useful work, playfulness, and artistic and cultural pursuits[86].

Following this trail of the erotic perhaps being a tool of emancipation led me to Soelle (2001), who points to the erotic as a form of mysticism that can lead to social resistance.

She describes a process, in which regular individuals (as opposed to saints and gurus) may have a mystical experience. This entails first engendering a sense of wonder at the simple things in life (such as nature and community), followed by letting go of all the superficial desire that is stimulated by consumer culture, and finally a sense of wholeness and healing, which recognizes the vibrantly spiritual connected nature of all things. Soelle argues that this spiritually erotic sense of connection naturally leads to resistance towards injustice and feeling compassion for all. The re-eroticizing of the body, she argues, is necessary for resistance, as dulling the senses leads to a lack of feeling, and when we are numb, there is no motivation to create change. I could clearly see the trajectory of my experiences[87] fitting neatly into the process Soelle describes.

Rifkin (2012) also speaks of the expanded view of the erotic saying that it:

> ... speaks to a sense of embodied and emotional wholeness that includes but extends beyond the scenes and practices of sexual pleasure and gratification usually termed sexual. (p.27)

---

[86] Marcuse's utopian vision will be discussed in more depth in Chapter 4, 5 and 6.

[87] Detailed in Chapter 2.

I wrote about my experience of this expanded state in the introduction to a previous paper, submitted as part of my PhD (July 2021):

> My current internal experience of my gender is often binary (consisting of two); both male and female distinct within. Sometimes one is more prevalent and at these times it feels like the other is standing behind, supporting quietly, with a hand placed gently on my back. In very limited situations, they are both present in equal measure but feel separate and noticeable as individual qualities.
>
> When the two aspects of myself are merged it feels like an erotic coupling within me. It is a feeling of total bliss, energy pulsing, no external need outside of the moment; a state that perhaps could be described as the rapture that many people go into at the moment of orgasm.
>
> There is nothing to do, nowhere to go, nothing to add. It is not the most productive mode of being; it is deeply replenishing and allows a great focus and flow in any work that follows, but is not a state that I can maintain whilst navigating worldly tasks... I therefore do not describe myself as 'non-binary' (not consisting of two). To me the non-binary experience is a deeply erotic, spiritual state of oneness that I enter, but in which I do not remain. (p.4-5)

Although I now recognize my process with my 'internal gender' as part of my moving away from romantic addiction, it does not take away from the embodied spiritually erotic experience it engendered. I still have similar experiences, but my need to describe it in internal romantic Jungian terms has changed. It is more grounded and less mythological. I now recognize that this Jungian construct was useful in my process to liberating myself from an unhealthy addiction to romance and to ridding myself of an 'internal misogynist'.[88] This process allowed me to liberate the erotic from the romantic and the sexual and to experience my erotic energy as a pleasurable, vitalizing life force.

---

[88] See Chapter 4 for a full discussion of this.

Lorde further liberates the erotic from the sexual and gives a glimpse of how the erotic may appear within a non-sexual relationship. She describes how:

> The erotic functions for me in several ways and the first is in providing the power which comes from sharing deeply *any* [my emphasis] pursuit with another person. The sharing of joy, whether physical, emotional, psychic, or intellectual, forms a bridge between the sharers, which can be the basis for understanding much of what is not shared between them, and lessens the threat of their difference (p.91).

This erotic bridge allows us a deeper understanding or a feeling of being on the 'inside' of another's experience (Gafini and Kincaid 2017). Gafini and Kincaid speak of this longing to be on the inside, to merge with something other than ourselves, be it an intellectual idea, nature, a piece of music, or even Divinity itself. In the context of this 'longing to be on the inside', it is easy to see why there is a conflation of the erotic with the sexual, especially within limited and hypersexualized Western discourse (Smith 2017). Of course, the physical penetration and merging that occurs within genital sex is one form of the erotic, but it is just *one way* in which the erotic can be expressed (Gafini and Kincaid 2017, Kripal 2007, Lorde 1978, hooks 2010, Marcuse 1955, Sovatsky 2018).

For example, I have found the production of this research to be a highly erotic process of getting on the inside of others' intellectual theories, and trying to get to the inside of co-creators' experiences through interpretation and collaboration, including the negotiation of meaning and language. David Carless and Kitrina Douglas describe this merging in terms of sharing songs:

> Before he had even finished the song it had lodged in the folds of her story, and like an addict she had to have it. She had to sing it. She took ages working out the chords so that she could possess it, so it could become her. And she sang it, over and over again. Something in *his* song had mainlined into *her* being. (2022: 158)

They go on to ponder what it is that drives the 'deep desire to be *in* the song?' They go on to ask a series of questions: 'What does it bring us to? What are we *connected to* in the process of singing, playing music, or accepting the invitation to a lyrical journey? And where does it come from?' (Ibid.) They explain how music offers them a 'literal and a metaphorical way to collaborate' and that within the collaboration each retains their individuality whilst creating a unified whole.

I have experienced this 'inside' connection through music. When I hold my singing and chanting groups, where we sing non-denominational songs of love, peace and unity, there is a feeling of communion. The vibration created by the voices in harmony with the harmonium points to the vibratory life force, a fundamental life force which we all share. Sitting in circle, each person expressing their unique sound, voices merging as one, connecting to the reverberating waves of sound in a heartful, visceral way is an erotic experience. It is an experience of being on the inside, the inside of the sound, the group, and the heart.

Before I came to the state of being that fits the definition of 'asexuality', I first had to heal my relationship addiction[89] to allow me any freedom to find what I truly want and who I can be without a significant other. I then discovered different spiritual practices such as mindful movement and meditation, which led to greater embodiment and connection to the lifeforce energy.

Alongside this, my connection to nature grew, heightened by my time at Embercombe near Exeter and the Animism taught by Tim

---

[89] Please see Chapter 2 for the 'story' of this. Please also note that relationship addiction is recognized as an addiction and there are 12 step groups, similar to Alcoholics Anonymous, who specialize in supporting individuals with this addiction. Many individuals are influenced by Western social conditioning that romantic relationships are the main focus of life and manipulated into consuming 'romantic experiences' (Illouz 1997, hooks 2001). This generalized social conditioning regarding romance is distinct from a romantic addiction in that it is not an obsession and the focus on romantic relationships is not having severe adverse effects on their wellbeing, safety, and other relationships (Peele and Brodsky 1975).

(Mac) McCartney (2007), Embercombe's founder. Thoreau (1854) cherished nature, its seasons and its elements and found it a place of mystical experiences and insights. In his book *Walden* (1854) he writes about a period of his life where he built a log cabin in a forest and lived away from society, immersing himself in nature. He says that this was an 'experiment in simple living' and a quest for spiritual knowledge. Soelle (2001) also identifies nature as one of the key sites in which to connect with mystical experiences. Griffin (1996) goes as far as to postulate that 'if human consciousness can be rejoined not only with the human body but with the body of earth, what seems incipient in the reunion is the recovery of meaning within existence' (p.15).

My connection to nature was, and continues to be, a spiritual and erotic connection, sullied for me by the term 'ecosexual' (Sprinkle et al. 2021). It is not a *sexual* experience; it is an *erotic* experience born of a deep longing to connect as fully as possible. It is not a sexual act when I lean into the strong holding of a tree, stroking its soft moss and feeling my skin tingle. It is not a sexual act when I dive into the river delighting in the water caressing my skin and the sparkling sunlight penetrating my eyes as it bounces off the water.

Before I allow myself to become angry about this, I remember that it is only a semantic difference, describing a similar experience. The confutation of anything erotic, unless tied to the sexual, is dictated by the dominant discourse in Western society (Sadlier 2017, Smith 2017). I myself have been guilty of this to some extent, limited by the available language and framework with which to describe my erotic experience:

Figure 4- Facebook post illustrating an eco-erotic experience.

In this post I use the words 'making love' to try to describe my erotic connection with the flower, thus linking it to the 'sexual' rather than the purely 'erotic'. I also wrote a poem during my time at

Embercombe, entitled *'Earth as my Lover'*, which is a very similar title to the subtitle of the book on 'ecosexuality'. Mark Smith's research into the history of asexuality also discovered this issue with the sexualization of erotic language:

> Pre-modern Christian erotic language describes not sexuality in a modern sense but rather the feeling and intensity of desubjectification, which is achieved, in part, through practices of sexual and self-renunciation. Pre-modern Christian *eros* is, in other words, the process of desubjectivating dissolution into divine limitlessness, otherwise known as "mystical union" with God. (2017: 188)

This language of the nonsexual erotic to describe the pleasure found in religious desubjectification is also found in other writings, such as Bataille who wrote extensively about eroticism's relationship to religion, illustrating how the erotic should not be conflated with only the sexual. He explains that:

> ... the whole business of eroticism is to destroy the self-contained character of the participators as they are in their normal lives ... Erotic activity, by dissolving the separate beings that participate in it, reveals their fundamental continuity, like waves of a stormy sea. (Bataille cited in Brintnall 2012:12).

Following this pertinent quote from Bataille, Brintall goes on to explain that 'the meaning of eroticism also escapes anyone who equates it with the sexual act itself.' His view is that sexual acts have reproduction as their goal whereas the erotic is a desire to merge, to lose oneself, free oneself of everyday identity, and feel the fundamental energy as a continuous flow. He describes this in the following way:

> Desire for and identification with the erotic object culminates in dissolution of the self's physical and psychological boundaries, giving rise to an experience of intimacy through and with the other ... an ecstatic terror accompanies the slipping away of one's self and the dissolution of the other in one's presence. But the 'warmth of pleasure and sensuality'

accompanies this anguish, both suspending and intensifying it. (Brintnall 2012:13)

Here, it is possible to see the difficulty in describing the erotic in sexualized and secular society. For many, sexual orgasm is the only fleeting moment of this 'loss of self into an intimacy with the other' that has ever been experienced, and therefore anything that describes this type of pleasure is thought to be sexual. Kripal (2007) offers some answers regarding why it is that although the erotic can permeate any activity it is often only found in sexual terms. He explains that sacred sexuality serves as a gateway to eros. In French, for instance, the phrase *'La petit mort'* (meaning 'little death') is an often utilized as a synonym for orgasm, pointing to the erotic pleasure of desubjectification (Foucault 1978). In an interview Foucault formulates this link between pleasure and death:

> I must say that's my dream—I would like and hope I'll die of an overdose [Laughs] of pleasure of any kind. Because I think it's really difficult and I always have the feeling that I do not feel the pleasure, the complete total pleasure and, for me, it's related to death. (1996: 378)

He goes on to describe how a near death experience of being knocked down by a car was a beautiful, pleasurable experience and that 'it still is now, one of my best memories' (1996: 378). The fact that Foucault expresses his difficulty in letting go into experiencing the fullness of pleasure, seems to relate to Brintnall's (2012: 13) expression of this experience as 'an ecstatic terror' that accompanies the sense of losing the self and the 'dissolution of the other in one's presence.' This description does seem to describe an experience that could be described as a 'little death'. It seems that the key to being able to experience this pleasure without fear is to keep the connection to one's individuality whilst dissolving into the other (which sounds like another paradox). However, if we go back to Carless and

Douglas' example of music as a way to become unified yet unique, it is easier to understand how this may be possible:

> We make our own noise, retain our individuality yet create some kind of unified whole, within which what makes us unique is not diminished in the process. Rather (perhaps) what we are, or may become, is enhanced and amplified (2022: 156).

In Foucault's writings and interviews (Foucault 1978, 1996, 2011) the erotic pleasure of desubjectification was a sexual one. According to Gautam (2016) Foucault purported that:

> two kinds of sexual pleasure exist: one in which an individual is able to break out of the prison of subjectivity and identity and experience pleasure as an event of desubjectification; and the other a more regular form of sexual pleasure in which an individual experiences pleasure without losing the sovereignty of identity (p.30).

Speaking in a 1978 interview (published 2011) Foucault said that 'the intensities of pleasure are indeed linked to the fact that you desubjugate yourself, that you cease being a subject, an identity.' (p.400). It is possible to postulate, in the context of the expanded erotic and the non-sexual libido, that Foucault's self-professed inability to experience the full pleasure of desubjectification was because he had sexualized the concept and thus limited it. In order to surrender into the full experience of desubjectification there needs to be a trust in something beyond the physical, something that was lacking in Foucault's 'God-less' worldview.[90]

Foucault's limited experience of desubjectification was in the context of gay bathhouses and their supply of strangers for 'identity-less' sex. However, Kripal (2007) and Gafini and Kincaid (2017) tell

---

[90] It is interesting to me that whilst reading many of Foucault's writings I experienced similar bodily sensations of subtle energetic tremoring as I experience when endeavoring to decipher ancient spiritual texts. It made me wonder if Foucault, through his philosophical musings and writing, was searching for a spiritual experience within a self-created prison of 'Godlessness'.

us that, although sex is one expression of the erotic, if sex is not sacred in nature that it only offers an unfulfilling substitute for eros. Marcuse (1955) also supports this notion that sex is a lesser expression of eros, one that becomes shadowed when one experiences the fullness of eros.

It is interesting to find that Foucault ended up having his moment of 'enlightenment' and intense erotic desubjectification in relation to nature rather than within the sexual; perhaps he was able to 'let go' into the transpersonal within the physical representation of the infinite – the expanse of stars in the space of the night sky. Gautam (2016) relates a passage from Miller's biography of Foucault, which speaks of the non-sexual erotic as the fullness of the erotic experience. In the passage it describes how Foucault experienced:

> ... a night in the Mojave Desert, which Foucault, with two other friends, spent looking at the dark sky luminous with stars. Foucault is reported to have said during this experience, "The skies have exploded and the stars are raining down upon me." (2016: 39)

Gautam (2016) goes on say that the significance of this event lies in Foucault's subsequent revelation that he 'now understood his sexuality, likening this experience to sexual experience between two strangers' (2016: 39)[91]. He goes on to say that Foucault's statement that he now understood his sexuality after his experience in the Mojave Desert is extremely puzzling because this experience had absolutely nothing to do with sex or sexuality. The only thing that connects this experience with sexual experience, therefore, is the experience of pleasure itself; In stating that he understood his sexuality in this experience, Foucault acknowledged that he finally comprehended

---

[91] It is important to note that it has been said that Foucault may have been under the influence of narcotics on this occasion. However, in a similar way that the 1990's dance scene opened up some of the co-creators to the experience of non-sexual pleasure – something they then sought in more natural, clean and 'conscious' ways, the experience and its effect is not diminished by its means.

what pleasure, including sexual pleasure, as an event of desubjectification, really was. (2016: 40). This episode clearly reveals Foucault's precise understanding of pleasure as holding the key to an understanding of sexuality, and not the other way around. It was not the anatomical aspect of sex that was important. The domain of pleasure, therefore, is much larger than that of sex.

This experience of the pleasure of desubjectification within nature resonates with my own experience of *jouissance*, of nonsexual pleasure through letting go of any need to perform any identity and connecting deeply with nature[92]; letting go into the sensations of the elements and the sensations within my body. I captured such an experience within a journal entry:

(Journal entry, 21 June 2021)

When Nobody is Watching

I am the uninhibited shudder of joy
moving through the body

I am innocence
splashing in the bubbling stream

I am freedom
catching the air
with outstretched limbs

I am open sensuous awareness
drinking, delighting, in-joying

*   *   *

---

[92] Further experiences of the pleasure of desubjectification, shared by the co-creators from within different contexts, are shared in Chapter 4, 5, 6 and 7.

This was one of the 'rhizomatic' (Deleuze and Guattari 1980) pathways I kept finding myself in as I explored the literature, with strands reaching out and touching other strands and then circling back on themselves. Foucault's experience in nature then closely reflects Lorde's extended definition of the erotic, which ties together with that of Gafini and Kincaid (2017), hooks (2010), and Griffin (1996). This expanded sense of the erotic is founded on the liberation of the libidinal lifeforce (Marcuse 1955, hooks 2010, Sovatsky 2018, Kripal 2017) and also ties in with the life force that is the focus of Taoism and Tantra, which is the focus of Foucault's *ars erotica* (1978). Lorde (1978) sums it up nicely by also linking the erotic with love 'in all its aspects'[93]:

> The very word erotic comes from the Greek word eros, the personification of love in all its aspects ... and personifying creative power and harmony. When I speak of the erotic, then, I speak of it as an assertion of the *lifeforce* [my emphasis] ... of that creative energy empowered." (p89)

The lived experience of how it feels when the lifeforce (or libido) is liberated, spoken of in tantric literature, also finds its place in Lorde's essay:

> I find the erotic such a kernel within myself. When released from its intense and constrained pellet, it flows through and colors my life with a kind of energy that heightens and sensitizes and strengthens all of my experience. (p.90)

Asexual individuals and their partners 'navigate the limits, edges, and boundaries around culturally normative frameworks' (Scott and Dawson 2015) such as sex drive / libido, desire, the erotic and sexual intimacy. Influenced, and perhaps limited, by the (mis)representation available to them they may engage in 'life experiments' (Scott and Dawson 2015) that expand or challenge these frameworks, which is a

---

[93] This is discussed in Chapter 4.

prevalent strategy for those who have been 'consigned to the margins of cultural life' (Weeks et al 2001:1, cited in Scott and Dawson 2015: 12).

Carrigan tells us that the majority of his participants faced the 'sexual assumption', which views sex as 'a culmination of and prerequisite for human flourishing'. He concludes that it is of the upmost importance to 'negotiate understandings of human flourishing which do not hinge on sexual expression and sexual fulfilment.' (2011: 474)

The challenges to assumptions about the libido, desire, the nature of intimacy, and the nature of the erotic explored within the literature in the previous two sections, and the examples of my and co-creators' embodied lived experiences, are an important contribution to the understanding of this non-sexual 'human flourishing' and the expanding of the definitions of asexuality to include erotically embodied asexuality and the possibility of this being a choice – something that one can become. Listening to and telling more asexual stories of 'life experiments', and experiences of flourishing in non-sexual ways, will offer further understanding and representation of this alternative way of blooming and thriving as a non-sexual person. The understanding of the expanded and liberated nonsexual erotic (Marcuse 1955, Lorde 1978, hooks 2010, Przybylo 2019) is key to this process of understanding asexuality as something other than a lack (Smith 2017).

3.6 Let's (not) talk about sex[94]

*Since these things have been made, they can be unmade, as
long as we know how it was that they were made.*
Foucault 1983:453

The problem with endeavoring to tell the story of asexual erotic
embodiment, is the milieu in which the story is being told. In order
for asexuals to be conceived of as erotically embodied, eros first needs
to be revived, replaced in its position as the purveyor of joy and
pleasure in all areas of life (Marcuse 1955, 1974, Lorde 1978, Gafini
and Kincaid 2017, Przybylo 2019). This entails destabilizing sexuality
and its current hold over the term 'erotic'.[95] This relocating of the
sexual as only a small part of the fullness of eros enables a study of
asexuality that does not conceive of it as a sexual orientation or as a
'new addition to 'benign sexual variation'' (Rubin 1984, cited in Smith
2017:27). Przybylo (2013) states that 'asexuality, as a sexual identity,
is entirely specific to our current cultural moment – that it is in this
sense culturally contingent' (p224). Smith (2017) argues that:

> sexuality is so pervasive today that even a *lack* of sexuality is now
> interpreted paradoxically as a form of sexual identity; a vast majority of
> self-identified asexuals define asexuality in this way, oftentimes without
> seeing any contradiction (p.7 emphasis in original).

In their research entitled *Stories of Non-Becoming* Scott, McDonnell
and Dawson found 'accounts of non-identification and non-

---

[94] "Let's Talk About Sex" was the title of a song by American hip hop trio Salt-n-Pepa, released
in August 1991 as the fourth single from their third studio album, Blacks' Magic (1990). It
was written and co-produced by Hurby Azor.

[95] Although loving and sacred sex can be a pointer towards the fullness of eros, transactional,
commodified sex is in fact lacking in eros (Gafini and Kincaid 2017, Sovatsky 2018, Kripal
2007).

becoming' (2016:268). They go on to explain that these individuals 'recognized, engaged with, communicated and managed the term 'asexual', but ultimately rejected it as a central basis of identity' (Ibid.). Many of the co-creators in this research also rejected using asexual as an identity label because of its interpretation as a form of sexual identity and a lack. These were some of the comments made within initial communications regarding participation in the research[96]:

> "I have a problem of defining myself as something I am not. For example vegans and vegetarians do not define themselves as acarnivorous (and for that matter carnivores do not define themselves by which type of meat they prefer!)."

> "What is it? What makes it different and exciting? What are the benefits of it? Are you going to define it as something and give it a name that does not insinuate that it is simply *not* something?"

> "It seems that asexuality has become an identity because society is so oversexed that you have to say 'Oh no! I'm not that!' Whereas before you wouldn't have said anything unless you felt it was FSD and wanted to be fixed."

Downing (2013) affirms that 'we are witness to an extraordinary and often gleeful proliferation of discourses and debates about sex in our present moment' (p.528). It is therefore important to examine the problem of sexual saturation or hypersexualization that we are currently faced with, and to understand asexuality outside of this moment. This sexual saturation can be observed within the field of asexuality studies. Although, as already described, many studies of asexuality now recognize the problem of 'compulsory sexuality' there are many that simply conform to the reinforcement of the normativity of sex. Psychological and sexological studies (such as Bogaert 2012,

---

[96] These quotes have been modified to disguise the co-creators' voices whilst retaining the intended meaning. This is to keep in line with the ethical parameters of this research including no direct quotations or verbatim sharing from the data collected and the fictionalization of all findings in order to ensure anonymity.

Brotto and Yule 2011) treat asexuality as a sexual category and use it as a lens for scientists to gain further understanding of sexuality. Their work also aims to further the acceptance of asexuality as a sexual orientation. Smith tells us that these studies:

> [U]ltimately illustrate the deployment of sexuality in action, as well as the compulsion to attribute a sexual identity to each and every person. Missing from these publications is any consideration of the paradox of lack of sexual attraction as a form of sexuality. By assuming sexual orientation to be universal, these studies have covered over the paradoxical elements of asexuality's current construction (2017:24).

This 'compulsion to attribute a sexual identity to each and every person' that Smith articulates is indicative of the commodification of sex, romance, and love within capitalist society (Illouz 1997, 2007, 2017, 2021, hooks 2001). The very term 'identity label' brings a picture to my mind of lines of people stacked on supermarket shelves, each with their label attached so that they can be easily categorized into sections to be browsed, enabling their easy consumption by time starved others who do not have the time, or wish to take the time, to get to know someone (which is what a physical version of Tinder and Grindr might look like). Masters and Johnson (1970) warned against the growing trend of sexual commodification and the sexualization of intimate touch, in an era when sex was becoming more liberated:

> Preoccupation with manipulative technique turns people into objects; and touching is turned into the science of stimulation for the purpose of reaching a climax … Sex then becomes perilously close to being an exchange of impersonal services, which weakens the bond between a man and a woman. Since neither one prizes the uniqueness of the other, all that each partner must do to find a replacement is to choose a person who can perform the necessary functions (p.238).

Sexual identity labels serve both as a time saving device for those browsing and a way for us to 'sell ourselves' (Ewen 2001). bell hooks (1992) utilizes the metaphor of 'eating the other'[97] to describe the consumption of identities. During her time teaching at Yale university, she found that 'it was commonly accepted that one 'shopped' for sexual partners in the same way one 'shopped' for courses at Yale'. She goes on to say that identity labels such as race, gender and sexuality were categories 'on which selections were based' with 'the body of the other … seen as existing to serve the ends' of the desires of those doing the 'shopping' (hooks 1992: 368). In their book *Channels of Desire* Stuart and Elizabeth Ewen stress that 'consumption is a social relationship, the dominant relationship in our society – one that makes it harder and harder for people to hold together, to create community' (Ewen and Ewen 1992, cited in hooks 1992:376). I reflected on this in my research journal:

---

[97] An ancient religious practice 'among so called 'primitive' people' where the heart of a person that has special characteristics that were desired was ripped out and eaten (hooks 1992:374).

(Journal entry, 7 April 2023)

Why when asexual do we define ourselves by the sexual?

Why do we want sexual identity labels? So that you can browse the goods, have a quick glance to see if the product might fulfil your desires? Make life more pleasurable for you? Fill you up?

Surely whether you may decide to rub genitals with someone is something you can decide once you've taken the time to get to know, to see, understand and appreciate the person. By then you'd know, from intimate conversations, what kind of physical intimacy they like. Surely it would be a natural progression from that either in playfulness, or in a more sexually committed 'let's have babies together' kind of way.

Our identities are so tied up with our sexual orientation, that even asexual people seem keen to establish who they are attracted to (aesthetic attraction) so we have the ridiculous categories of asexual people identifying as homosexual. What happened to people being human beings worthy of getting to know regardless of their sexual or attraction orientation. With relationships being based on love and commitment, not ownership, prestige and self image.

Why are 'sexual' or 'we're attracted to each other in a kind of non sexual romantic way' relationships seen as primary? Why do people even need to qualify their non sexual primary relationships as 'Queer platonic' in an attempt to establish that 'we are romantically attracted to each other and there is a kind of erotic energy between us, but we're not having sex because our sexual orientations do not match.' Why is it anyone else's business? Why do we judge the status of relationships?

*   *   *

The feeling of not resonating with the asexual identity as it is currently defined was one that was shared by all of the co-creators. In the following poem, we endeavor to capture the reason that erotically embodied asexuals do not want to claim the identity label of 'asexual' due to its current representation:

Into the wine not the label

On the outside
She is seen as
Frigid
Cold
Shut down
Dried up
Abnormal

On the inside
She feels
Open
Warm
Fluid
Juicy
Unique

The outside label
Asexual
A boundary
To the ignorant
Investigating no further

The inside substance
Amorous
A blessing
To the loving
Interested in Intimacy

*　　*　　*

This phenomena of an obsession with sexual identity and the pervasiveness of sexuality are also discussed by Eric Olund in his essay *When Has Sexuality Ever Been About Sex?* He talks about the prevalence of sexuality saying that it is 'imbricated in every other social relation' and that the literature regarding sexuality is 'dispersed across subdisciplines. In such a disparate body of work, 'it' is usually 'about' something other than sexuality'. He goes on to say that sexuality 'does not simply refer to erotic desire per se, but also to its production, identification, experience, and regulation. And these phenomena are not simply individual, but they circulate in material, affective, and representational economies that exist in every conceivable spatialization' (2015:107). He explains that added to the challenge of navigating this pervasiveness is the fact that it changes over time and has 'multiple histories and temporalities' (Ibid).

Foucault (1978) argues that sex has become such a pervasive discourse, and has become so deeply entrenched in our ideas and beliefs, that it is now a key criterion in our ability to be intelligible to ourselves that 'sexuality is the crux of modern subjectivity' (Foucault 1976:155-6, cited in Smith 2017: 178). However, Downing observes that although 'sex saturates the worldview of our contemporary moment' that 'simply refusing to talk about it does not constitute an appropriate or efficacious intervention' (2013:528)

It is fascinating how something that is essentially about the act of rubbing genitals together for the sake of the reproduction of the species or a short moment of intense pleasure has become central to our notions of identity and the definitions of pleasure, love, and fulfilment (Marcuse 1955). Steven Seidman, the author of the book *The Social Construction of Sexuality* explores the moment in the 1960s and 70s when discourses appeared that 'defended sex for its pleasurable and expressive qualities apart from it functioning as a medium of love or procreation' (1989: 293). He goes on to describe how this was countered in the 80s with backlash against sexual freedom in the light of the AIDS epidemic saying that 'this must not be allowed to pass into an ethic of repression in the name of health or order. We need to continue to defend a construction of sex that values it for its pleasurable and expressive qualities while not *over-investing it with personal and social significance* or neglecting its dangers' (Seidman: 1989:295, my emphasis). This is a healthy view of keeping sex in its rightful place, where it is seen as a pleasurable part of life, but not the chief element of a fulfilling life, the only means of bodily pleasure, or as the only expression of the erotic (Kripal 2017, Gafini and Kincaid 2017).

Marcuse however, argues that genital sexuality has become the only source of pleasure in capitalist society and that the liberation of eros from the sexual is necessary, so that 'the primacy of the genital function is broken … the instinct's objective is no longer absorbed by a specialized function - namely, that of bringing one's own genitals into contact with those of someone of the opposite sex' (1955: 205). Deleuze and Guattari (1972) describe how capitalism maintains its control through harnessing and commodifying desire. They argue that capitalism's ability to manipulate and redirect desire is a key aspect of its power. The manipulative tactics within this system include the commodification of sexuality and the creation of artificial desires through advertising and marketing, a view also expressed by Naomi Klein in her book *No Logo* (1999). Deleuze and Guattari (1972) challenge the view of desire as merely sexual, emphasizing its multifaceted nature as a dynamic and productive force that operates in various domains of life—that it can be harnessed for multiple expressions of production and creativity.

This liberation from the commodification of desire has been fundamental to my journey to becoming an erotically embodied asexual. I found that once I was enabled to connect with the eros available in every moment, and as the flow of erotic desire moved throughout my body, that it became directed towards connection, service, and the expression of creativity and love. The experiences of co-creators also substantiate the ideas of Marcuse and Deleuze and Guattari. This will be discussed in detail within Chapter 4, which focuses on describing the co-creators' journeys and worldviews.

The manipulation of desire, centered on sexuality, is also discussed by Downing, who raises the question of how to study asexuality from within the current Western milieu 'without simply contributing to this endless proliferation of discourse, this parade of truth claims about a ubiquitous and centered 'sexuality' (2013: 528). She suggests that it is essential that there are scholarly works 'issuing from a history of [a]sexuality perspective'. She explains that these works 'sit between the agendas of corrective historical scholarship and 'queer' political resistance and are necessary reading for those scholars of [a]sexuality whose principal remit is the present.' (p.527). She goes on to say that 'histories of sexuality have been rather silent on the subject of asexuality, understood in the current sense of an 'identity' or 'orientation,' rather than historically as a projection onto certain groups and classes of an 'innate nature' or a mode of practice' (p.530). She argues that an investigation into the history of asexuality could challenge dominant narratives regarding sexual identities and compulsory sexuality. Mark Smith (2017) has produced such a genealogy of asexuality in *Bypassing the Asexual Paradox: A Strategic Retelling of the History of Asexuality*, which challenges 'ahistorical assumptions about the universality of sexuality' (p.4). His historically focused work offers 'a valuable corrective to the inward-looking and present-centered nature of some current thinking on sexual cultures' (Downing 2013: 527).

Smith's (2017) work offers a history of how erotic language came to be purloined by sexual discourse, thus making the nonsexual erotic unintelligible. By examining 'how sexual language became crucial to the rise of modern-day psychological interiority (upon the death of God)' he has endeavored to 'make us skeptical of the assumption that sexuality is intrinsically at the core of human identity'. He hopes that his work 'allows us to conceive of sexuality as an object to be shaped, transformed, and even overcome through ascetic practices'. And that it will allow us 'to think of asexuality not as a lack of experience (or an experience of lacking sexuality) but rather as a pathway to the presence of the divine' (2017:200). This is an important addition to the asexuality literature as it allows a view into an asexuality outside of the current moment, and it explains how the erotic language utilized by Christian mystics to describe their experiences of desubjectification, union with God and ecstatic embodied states, was appropriated by sexual discourse and relegated merely to the sexual.

In addition to the encouragement and insight that Mark Smith's work offered me, it has been essential to my understanding of my own journey, to developing my confidence to challenge the conflation of the sexual with the fullness of the erotic, and encouraged me to read theorists such as Foucault, Marcuse and Deleuze and Guattari, utilizing the lens of erotically embodied asexuality. In doing this, a new perspective on eros, libido, pleasure and desire can be found. Through this lens it can be seen clearly that these philosophers have already spoken of the liberating force of eros and *particularly non sexual eros* (Marcuse 1955, 1974), *Ars Erotica* and its expansive definition of libidinal forces and pleasure (Foucault 1978), and emancipating desire from basic romantic and sexual constraints that suit the goals of capitalist consumption, so that it can flow freely and productively to producing new ideas, connections, and forms of life (not limited to sexual reproduction) (Deleuze and Guattari 1972).

3.7 Hypersexualization and the suppression of Eros

Marcuse (1974) suggests that the full potential of eros must be suppressed in order for the capitalist system to function effectively 'for capitalism cannot possibly allow the ascent of the libidinal qualities which would endanger the repressive work ethic' (p.285). He explains that 'these liberating tendencies' are in fact utilized to reproduce the established system and are commodified. He explains that the 'exchange society comes to completion with the commercialization of sex : the female body not only a commodity, but also a vital factor in the realization of surplus value' (Ibid.). This means that capitalism not only suppresses the 'ascent' of eros into its fullness and liberating potential, but also resells us a quasi-eros in the form of the commercialization of sex, an encouragement to objectify the self, and the promotion of the pornographic (Illouz 2007, 2021, 2022).

There were many points in my research, where I had to pause due to the emotional impact and my need to take care of myself. My search for literature that would highlight this exploitation of the quasi-erotic was one of the points where I had to pause in my research. On searching for literature, which would point to the hypersexualization of society and its negative impacts, I was slightly overwhelmed by how much information I found within only a preliminary search.

*　　*　　*

Resistance

I search

For corroboration

of observation:

Hypersexuality

At first

Excitement

A wealth!

Expansive literature

I read

Interested

Then

Horrified

At The Expanse

What it

means

In reality

I feel

Body slumping

Piercing bilious

heat rising

I Surrender

to sadness

Allowing

Its flow

I think

'I can't do

This

Anymore'

My heart

objects

This

Is Necessary

*   *   *   *

The most disturbing article I found was an example of the impact of hypersexualization on young people. Przybylo (2011) argues that the constant exposure to sexual content prevalent in 'sexusociety' can affect the development of healthy attitudes towards sex and relationships, and may contribute to early sexualization, self-objectification and an unrealistic perception of what a healthy sexual relationship entails (including those who do not have a natural inclination for sex experimenting sexually in order to feel 'normal'). In the first article I discovered regarding young people, Schrader (2020) explains that a song by Cardi B called WAP was number one in the UK charts for three weeks in the previous year. The acronym of the song stands for 'Wet Ass Pussy'. The lyrics to this song start with:

> Yeah, you f*cking with some wet-ass pussy
>
> Bring a bucket and a mop for this wet-ass pussy
>
> Give me everything you got for this wet-ass pussy.

Disturbing as it is imagining children singing these lyrics, Schrader (2020) also reports that there is a trend involving children video recording themselves dancing to WAP, a dance which involves humping the floor, and then posting these videos on TikTok.

Illouz (1997, 2007, 2021, 2022) points towards how consumer society fosters the objectification of individuals, particularly women, reducing them to mere sexual objects for the gratification of others. She gives numerous examples of how advertising and media, such as films and TV shows, often portray women as hypersexualized beings whose value is derived solely from their physical appearance and sexual appeal. Illouz argues that this objectification perpetuates gender inequalities, as women are primarily valued for their desirability rather than their intellect, talents, or personal qualities. More importantly, this societal objectification and encouragement to purchase products to enhance desirability, is now leading individuals to engage in self-objectifying behaviors. Both women and men strive to meet unrealistic beauty and sexual standards, taking to Instagram and Facebook to post highly posed and often filtered images of themselves and ultimately eroding their sense of authenticity and self-worth (Jiotsa *et al* 2021, Pedalino and Camerini 2022).

Candice Dawn (2018) discusses how the commercialization of sexuality leads to the demise of eros. She argues that when someone is reduced to merely being or owning an erotic commodity, they are objectified, with their entire essence transformed into a product available for purchase. Dawn explains that in this process, the individual is no longer seen as an embodiment of personal expression but rather as a tool for achieving an objective. The cohesive nature of eros is destroyed within the commercial system that thrives on maintaining separation. The reasoning often follows: 'You are one individual, and I am another. You possess this commodity, and I possess that one. If I give you mine, I expect yours in return. Alternatively, if you offer yours, I cannot accept it without giving something in exchange.' Her conclusion is that, while such logic may work in material transactions, like buying a car, applying it to our sexual and erotic lives is doomed to fail. This failure occurs because, firstly, commodification fosters division, leading to the death of eros, and secondly, sexuality cannot encompass the entirety of the beauty that eros represents.

This self-objectification and the pursuit of the erotic, in the only form available to most, sex, has led to the increase in popularity of dating apps such as Tinder and Grindr. Turban (2018), a therapist, describes how he conducted an informal survey (including 50 participants) on Grindr to question men regarding why they use the app so frequently, and the impacts it is having on their relationships and mental health. He explains that Neuroscientists have discovered that orgasms trigger activation in pleasure-related brain areas, such as the ventral tegmental area, simultaneously deactivating regions associated with self-control. The brain activation patterns observed during orgasm in men resemble those seen in individuals using heroin or cocaine. When a neutral action, like clicking on Grindr, becomes associated with a pleasurable response (orgasm), humans tend to repeat that action. This repetition can either be a typical pleasure response or may potentially lead to addiction, depending on the context and individual involved.

This objectification of others as a source of pleasure or a 'high' was not the only allure of Grindr. Turban (2018) found that for some users 'the allure of Grindr was not just the rush to feel good. It was to stop feeling bad. Users told me they log on when they feel sad, anxious, or lonely. Grindr can make those feelings go away. The attention and potential for sex distract from painful emotions' (p.1). A gay friend recently told me that he had noticed an increase in the number of profiles on Grindr that were starting to say that they 'wanted cuddles'. He explained to me that his constant search on Grindr was largely his desire for nonsexual intimacy, but that it was challenging to find it. An article written by *Women's Health* (2016) described how one woman is charging $80 to go to a client's house and cuddle them for an hour, usually spooning on the bed, and suggests that this is a new 'profession'. The article also discusses the phenomena of 'cuddle parties', where participants pay to attend an event where they meet and share supervised nonsexual intimacy with other attendees, who are usually strangers.

Illouz (1997, 2007, 2021) argues that love and romance have become increasingly commodified, reduced to consumer-driven experiences. Dating apps such as Grindr reinforce the notion that sex is the primary and most essential component of intimate relationships, overshadowing other crucial aspects such as emotional connection, trust, and compatibility. This can lead to individuals developing unrealistic expectations and prioritizing sexual gratification over deeper emotional bonds, which can not only lead to dissatisfaction and relational instability, but also to low self-worth and self-esteem. The commodification of sex and romantic connection, and the instant availability to be able to swipe and click to obtain such experiences from an objectified 'other', does not lead to a feeling of greater connection, but to feelings of isolation and loneliness (Turban 2018).

I found a wealth of literature regarding the negative impacts of this commodified sexual environment of social media and dating apps. It is beyond the scope of this book (or the researcher) to investigate this in any depth. My brief initial results included Jiotsa *et al* (2021) discussing the correlation of *Social Media Use and Body Image Disorders*, Pedalino and Camerini (2022) correlating *Instagram Use and Body Dissatisfaction*, Plieger *et al* (2021) finding *The Association Between Sexism, Self-Sexualization, and the Evaluation of Sexy Photos on Instagram.* Breslow *et al's* (2020) research with 'sexual minority men' and the number of apps they use, found that there was a positive correlation between the number of apps utilized and hypervigilance with regard to body image and the level of self-objectification, and a negative correlation with levels of body satisfaction and self-esteem. Choi *et al* (2016 & 2017) found that the use of dating apps increased casual and unprotected sex, and that there was an association between the use of recreational drug use in conjunction with sexual activities. Coduto *et al* (2020) found the compulsive use of dating apps was significant among those who had a preference for online social interaction, and who were experiencing high levels of loneliness. Hart *et al* (2016) found that a quarter of the respondents (taken from a sample of heterosexual attendees of genito-urinary medicine (GUM) clinics) use dating apps, and that there was a high rate of sexually transmitted infections, unprotected sex and recreational drug use among these respondents.

Although I am viewing this hypersexualization of society through the lens of asexuality, I cannot imagine how this commodification and self-commodification of human beings, with children being 'sexualized' at young ages, could be seen as a healthy or desired situation. If the suppression of eros has led us to this dark place, perhaps the liberation of the nonsexual erotic and the return of the fullness of eros (rather than the quasi-erotic or pornographic) within the sexual, could have positive effects on society.

3.8 Eros as an agent for social change

The master's tools will never dismantle
the master's house
Lorde 1980: 16

My story and those of the co-creators illustrate how, once we had experienced a connection to the nonsexual erotic, we became satisfied with the simple pleasures of life, and the allure of material excess lost its grip. Erotic embodiment, for us, has become a shield against the insidious tactics of capitalism, as predicted by Marcuse (1955). Although in Marcuse's work he predicted that it would be a change in the system that led to the transformation of eros, the co-creators have found this alchemy on a micro level, both within themselves and the erotically embodied communities they have explored, deterritorializing themselves from a consumerist prison (Deleuze and Guattari 1972). Griffin (1996) explains that in order to 'change a habit of mind that has become destructive we must revise the social architecture of our thought' (p.173).

The co-creators shared how practices such as mindfulness and the exploration of alternative 'social architectures', can facilitate changing habits of mind. Our experiences illustrate how, when an individual is no longer prey to the siren call of consumerist manipulation and the commodification of desire loses its power, it is possible to be liberated from the shackles of insatiable consumption and become a harbinger of social change.

This is not to say that the process to becoming erotically embodied is easy. A metamorphosis is a painful and long process, not a quick fix change that can be bought and consumed (Illouz 2008). Stripping away one's identity, reprogramming one's mind, and changing a way of life and social context is not a quick process[98] that fits with consumerist ideal of being able to buy an experience to fix yourself or make yourself feel better (Illouz 2008). Griffin (1996) explains that this type of 'metamorphosis is required' and that for 'consciousness to migrate further towards the eros embedded in daily and practical life, certain histories must be told and habits of mind revealed' (p.36). She lists the many things that are at stake in order for such a metamorphosis to take place: 'identity, years of study, of training, of experience, economic sustenance, social acceptance, a way of life.' (Ibid.) This list of potential losses on the road to change resonates with both my experience and those of the co-creators.

Marcuse (1955) predicted that the liberation of eros into an eros that permeates all of life, with sexual drives being naturally sublimated and relegated to their procreational position, would only occur once the whole capitalist system was overcome. He postulated that it was impossible that this could occur on an individual level within such a system. However, perhaps he did not envision our current situation, with the rise of globalization and information sharing, ideas from other systems are permeating ours. The affluent individual now has greater capacity (financial and time) to examine alternative cultures and worldviews and embark on a journey to change themselves. I recognize that the social privilege that I and most of the co-creators have may have contributed to this, as we have the financial and time resources to explore trainings, practices and

---

[98] See Chapter 4, 5 and 6 for more discussion regarding the processes and practices of the co-creators.

pursuits which lead to this expanded sense of the erotic. This, in a sense, does match with Marcuse's prediction; that as people started to have more time and resources that they would discover the fullness of eros. It is possible that the micro change of liberating oneself from becoming a unit of consumption can lead to a rippling out of change into society.

An example of the power of consumption, or rather non consumption, can be found in Erica Chenoweth and Maria Stephan's (2012) research into '*The Strategic Logic of Nonviolent Conflict*', in which they examined incidences where local populations took back their power, and mitigated change through their strength as consumers, for example boycotting white businesses in apartheid Africa. Nonviolent resistance, and the power of changing oneself rather than trying to change society, was promoted by Mahatma Gandhi who made a famous statement that our greatness as human beings is not in being able to directly exert resistance on those in power to change the system, but in being able to remake ourselves. As individuals, if we become erotically embodied, there is a pleasure in *all* activities, we gain satisfaction from the simple; *that which cannot be sold to us as products of consumption.*

This erotic embodiment (whether as a sexual or a nonsexual individual) therefore becomes a passive form of resistance that, with growing numbers, could become an agent for change within capitalist society. When the 'everyday' brings great pleasure, one is no longer interested in the products of capitalist society. When you feel the commonality and love with and for all, a natural 'care taking' of others and the environment occurs, there is a propulsion to create and serve – not for monetary reward but for creation and community's sake, a process Deleuze and Guattari term 'desiring production'.[99]

---

[99] See Chapter 4 for more discussion of this natural move away from consumption that occurs with an increase in nonsexual erotic pleasure and Chapters 2, 3, 4, 5, 6 and 7 for more discussion of the theory and articulation of experiences of this non-sexual erotic pleasure.

When individuals no longer become a target for consumption of unnecessary products, services and dreams it disrupts the capitalist system; it is no longer necessary to spend so much time being a unit of production in order to have the money to buy products, because you no longer wish to buy the outputs of capitalist production (Deleuze and Guattari 1972).

It only takes a small percentage of resistant consumers to disrupt the capitalist system. Chenoweth (2013) states that for consumer resistance to be effective only 3.5% of the population need to be committed to the process. This could indicate that a change initiated from micro-societal change, at the level of the individual discovering the fullness of eros, might lead to a macro societal realization of Marcuse's (1955) vision of the *'transformation of eros'*, and the potential for a more fully erotic society, not focused on consumption. Lorde also shares a view of the political power of the erotic, positing that this power is the reason that the erotic is feared and 'relegated to the bedroom alone, when it is recognized at all' (1978: 11). Lorde suggests that embracing deep emotions, in all aspects of life, leads to a demand for fulfilment and joy. Erotic knowledge, in this context, serves as a powerful tool to assess and scrutinize various aspects of our lives, compelling us to honestly evaluate their significance. The power of the erotic encourages us to take responsibility and avoid settling for convenience, mediocrity, or societal expectations, urging individuals to pursue what genuinely brings meaning and satisfaction to their lives (Ibid.).This, in conjunction with Lorde's famous quote 'the master's tools will never dismantle the master's house' (1980: 11), could be interpreted as meaning that the erotic, banished entirely or relegated to the pornographic/sexual by the Master (Corpocracy) is a tool that, once liberated, can dismantle the Master's House (Capitalism/Consumerism).

3.9 Questions and directions

This book aims to *add to the area of asexuality studies by offering a modern day, erotic, mystic, embodied and experiential narrative of asexuality*. Mark Smith (2017) tried to accomplish this with his original (shelved) ethnographic research and his 'botched autoethnography', and redirected his focus into the historical study of asexuality (described in section 1.1). He offered a genealogy of asexuality, which examined erotic, ecstatic asexuality from the viewpoint of Christian mystics. My research *aims to further Smith's aim to describe asexuality as something other than a lack,* utilizing autoethnographic research. It aims to offer some insight into Scott and Dawson's (2015) question of *how asexual individuals negotiate intimate relationships (especially with sexual people)*, to challenge sexual discourse, and to further the work done to disrupt the notion of universal compulsory sexuality and the resistance of sexual norms that has been achieved by Przybylo (2013, 2019), Gupta (2013, 2015) and Carrigan (2011, 2012).

I aim to go some way to answering the question 'what is the *experience* of asexuality?' as opposed to it being defined on a *lack* of experience. I also wrangle with the problem of 'how can we *define* and describe an erotically embodied *asexuality without utilizing terminology that refers to the sexual?'*. I attempt to offer new ways of imagining asexuality, via *the displacement of sexuality* from its current position at center stage in Western society's modern-day performances of identity. I will endeavor to articulate *experiences of the expanded erotic,* of which the sexual is only one limited expression, and to *describe the experience of the nonsexual libido*. I hope that by revealing experiences of other ways of being, new possibilities will be opened for non-sexual individuals to emerge and flourish in unique ways.

4. Love, Romantic Liberation, Erotic Capital and Asexual Pleasure

Introducing the co-creators and their worldviews

> *Stories change, fragment, multiply, disperse. There are*
> *many differences of forms and structures; there are always*
> *differences contained within the story; and there are always*
> *different audiences in the outer world who make very*
> *different senses of the stories.*
> Plummer 2013: 211

This chapter articulates the process of finding, communicating, creating with, and caring for the co-creators in this research. It also discusses the ethical stance of the research, with methods and measures to ensure increased anonymity, and provides some reflections on future ethical considerations for qualitative research. I also reflect on the experience of interacting and creating with the co-creators.

Although this is a 'methodology' chapter, which includes reflections on the research process, including ethical issues, and sensitively presented descriptions of the co-creators and their selection, this also seemed to be the place where I needed to include the influences perceived as contributing to their asexual 'becomings', and worldviews. This discussion of worldviews and influences means that this 'methodology' chapter also, unconventionally, includes theoretical and conceptional analysis, and experiential creative outputs (or 'findings').[100]

It was essential to the main aim of this research – to articulate the lived experience of erotically embodied asexuality – that I locate co-creators who could describe this alternative narrative of asexuality.

Mark Smith (2017) expressed his challenge in locating an alternative narrative of asexuality. He became disillusioned when attempting his autoethnographic research into the experience of asexuality. During conversations with asexual individuals, he found that they simply described asexuality in reference to sexuality—as a *lack*; a lack of a drive or experience that is considered normative rather than an experience within its own right. He redirected his study to creating a genealogy of asexuality, and the asexual erotic found within ancient Christianity, and found descriptions of religious ecstasy described by Christian mystics who practiced celibacy. The descriptions of the experiences he gathered could be perceived as 'sexual' by the limited Western view of the erotic as sexual, rather than the sexual as a small part of the erotic[101].

Smith (2017) suggests that this language was limited with the 'death of God' moment (Foucault 1963), when human experience came to be defined in psychological terms, and became contained within the limits of the individual rather than a religious/spiritual

---

[100] This is in line with the alternative structure outlined in the Introduction. This alternative structure attempts to create a sense of 'narrative development' where the reader is taken along the same journey of understanding as I undertook. The material regarding romance as eros in motion and erotic capital/becoming woman was not apparent to me from either my original narrative or the literature review. These insights came directly from my interaction with co-creators. I then reviewed my journals with this new 'lens' and found some interesting experiences that I simply had not acknowledged previously and I searched for further literature to try to understand these themes. I could not include them within the literature review as this would not have been true to the temporal way in which they arose within the research process.

[101] See section 3.5 for examples of this and discussion of similar modern-day experiences in this Chapter and Chapters 5, 6 and 7.

connection to limitlessness or the divine. This suggests that the loss of divine connection limited the experience of eros to the sexual, and, in turn, restricted our expression and perception of eros to that of the sexually erotic.

Other researchers (Gupta 2015, Przybylo 2019, Scott and Dawson 2015, 2018) also found their attempts to understand the asexual experience limited by the discourse of AVEN, and other similar communities, which rather than exploring the lived embodied experience of asexuality, constantly refer to sexuality and societal norms. Gupta (2015) expressed her concern that much asexual research is biased by being located with the AVEN community, and that research should be done outside of this limited frame. My initial explorations of these communities confirmed that it was going to be challenging to locate an alternative narrative with this sampling population. The issues these other scholars encountered, and my own initial search, inspired me to locate my research participants within a specific population.

I was a member of an online group[102] with members who previously spent much time within new age/neo tantric communities and still practice some of the modalities that they found there, such as mindful movement (such as somatic awareness and conscious dance) and spiritual and/or religious practices (such as meditation, prayer, chanting or mindfulness).[103] I found that the asexual

---

[102] This is a private group where members with therapeutic skills offer free support and signposting to those who may have been traumatized by their experiences within the new age or neo tantra communities. Members also share positive experiences that have emerged from their participation and recommend legitimate, reliable, and regulated classes, groups and teachers to each other.

[103] It is important to note that the researcher and the co-creators within this research project no longer participate in these communities. Although many of the associated practices have been an essential catalyst within their life journeys and experiences and they still have some elements of 'spiritual or religious' practice (see Chapter 1 for a definition of these terms) as an essential part of their lifestyle, this is not to be taken as a recommendation for these practices or the communities. The information given about these communities and details of some of the practices, is included to frame and offer background to the experience of erotically embodied asexuality that this research aims to articulate. Berger (1965:31): 'The

individuals I encountered there tended to have heightened awareness of both body and mind, and a discourse about non-sexuality (and sexuality) that differed from that of the AVEN community and Western society. The co-creators that I found within this community offered the opportunity to develop and write an alternative narrative of asexuality, a narrative that resonated with, and yet deepened and expanded the personal narrative that I have shared within the research.

4.1 Locating the Co-creators

The co-creators all participated in the group for those who have navigated the joys and the pitfalls of participating in new age and neo-tantra communities. Within this group, members share their experiences within, and critiques of, these communities and offer support to those traumatized within such communities. I utilized this particular group to find participants, as I thought that it was possible that there would be asexuals who had followed a similar trajectory to me – discovering practices from other cultures and then trying to find groups within the UK where they would find like-minded people to socialize and practice with. I did this with the aim of finding participants who could articulate an *experience* of asexuality rather than following the same 'dead-end' that Mark Smith encountered when he endeavored to find those who could articulate an experience of asexuality. I thought it was more likely, within the group selected, that I would find asexuals who already shared an alternative discourse of the erotic in which to frame their experiences; in order to offer an ***alternative narrative of asexuality*** and ***a perspective outside of 'sexusociety'***.

---

sociologist, qua sociologist' cannot help with the choice of 'healing cults' or 'the religious or quasi-religious' available today.

It is important to note here that it is not the purpose of this book to discuss the validity or evaluate the worth of the practices[104] that co-creators have articulated as fundamental to their asexual becoming and/or flourishing. I am interested in the states that these practices induced within their bodies, and the *effects this had on their embodied experience of being asexual,* either as someone who already considered themselves asexual or as someone who became asexual whilst partaking in particular practices.

Although the worldviews of the co-creators may not be that of the reader or the researcher, I endeavor to write with respect for the co-creators' beliefs and experiences. In order to facilitate this, the spiritual and/or religious beliefs of the co-creators, and the critiques of the new religious communities within which they have participated, have to be bracketed. This bracketing opens the possibility of this research meeting its aims of *offering some insight into the embodied experience itself;* how the co-creators interpret that experience and how it feels to them on a visceral level.

I aim to offer the reader an experiential reading of an *alternative asexuality as nonsexual erotic experience.* This includes some incidences of ecstatic and mystical states of being. It is hoped that sharing these experiences will offer more understanding and appreciation of a marginalized group of people. David Hodge has written extensively on the importance of such bracketing as a way to achieve 'spiritual competence' within social work, in which he aims to deconstruct 'religious stereotypes and spiritual prejudices' (Hodge 2006: 213). Plummer gives the following advice regarding the process of appreciating others' stories and worlds with an open and active imagination:

---

[104] Experiential accounts of the practices which co-creators attribute to influencing their asexual becoming and/or flourishing are woven throughout the book, both in the more theoretical Chapters (3 and 4), within my own narrative piece (Chapter 2) and within the chapters that focus on presenting the research findings (Chapters 5, 6 and 7).

> Thus we also need a sense of the beauty of stories: 'truth is beauty'. We need a sense of how stories are put to use – their practical and lived realities. We need an imaginative flare – the excitement of moving creatively towards new and unexpected horizons. We need our own self-reflections alongside the selfreflections [sic] of others. We need a sense of amazement at where the story fits into the wider cosmos. And we need ultimately an understanding of all our understandings ... *We need to ask how we can create story bridges to truth, beauty, practice, imagination, reflexivity, spirituality and wisdom.* (2013: 213, my emphasis)

It is important to articulate that the co-creators are aware of the critiques of the new age and neo-tantra movements.[105] I will use similar words here, that are used to describe the previously mentioned group[106]:

> We have experience of and support others through some of the downsides of these disparate and unregulated communities. We are aware of the potential for spiritual commodification and exploitation, sexual predation, self-promotion, victim blaming and cultural appropriation within these communities. Although we appreciate some of the experiences and life developments we experienced within these groups, and still utilize some of the practices, we fully recognized the problems, limits, and dangers that are potentials within such communities.

---

[105] For those who would like a more detailed discussion of these communities and their practices I recommend Samantha Bishop's (2019) doctoral thesis where she discusses the new age and neo-tantra communities, their history, and practices (including a balanced discussion of the benefits and pitfalls). For a detailed history of asexuality, including the ecstatic erotic experiences of asexuality in ancient times, I recommend Mark Smith's (2017) doctoral thesis on asexuality and erotic asexual ecstasy in ancient Christianity. For detailed analysis of Tantra and neo-tantra please see Urban (2000, 2003, 2022) and the new age/new religious movement see Johnston (2000), Heelas and Woodhead (2005), Hodge (2006), Illouz (2008), Gleig (2010), Masters (2010) and Wexler (2013). There are many critiques of the new age movement and neo-tantra communities. It is beyond the scope or focus of this book to offer a thorough critique of these communities/ new religious movements. It is hoped that by following this approach of signposting the reader to these studies, that I will not waste the available space in this book, that could potentially make a contribution to knowledge, by simply regurgitating background knowledge that has already been produced.

[106] Paraphrased to maintain anonymity.

Within this book there are some personal observations from an 'insider' perspective which, of course, add to the critique of these communities. These are included where they are needed to add context, but it is not the purpose of this book to offer an in-depth analysis or critique of new age spiritualities and/or neo-tantra.

The eleven co-creators were found and selected utilizing opportunity/ purposive sampling. The group of co-creators included four men and seven women. According to the self-defined socio-economic status of the co-creators: one was upper class, eight were middle class and two were working class, all were white and of European descent. One was graysexual, two demisexual, two had always felt asexual, although they did not have the terminology to articulate this, one thought she had FSD and tried to fix this, but now realizes she was asexual all along, and the remaining five had been 'sexual' at some point or for a long period of their lives and had 'become' asexual. This is the only place in this book where any demographic data will be shared, in line with the heightened ethical strategy of this research.

4.2 Layers of safety

Due to the sensitive nature of the data, collaborative creative methods such as poetry, art and sociological fiction have been utilized to share co-creators' narratives. Many of these creative outputs were developed utilizing a composite of stories that share similar themes, to add another level of anonymity (Renzetti and Lee 1993). Potential participants were assured that the information would be copied (or transcribed), anonymized and kept in a password protected document on a university, password protected laptop. The original texts and any associated audio files and photographs were deleted once the 'data' had been copied.

Another layer of safety was added by the anonymized data, in its raw format, being kept confidential and I assured potential participants that the anonymized data, prior to its transformation into creative outputs, would not be shared at any time. This is due to the relatively small population of asexual people, and the likelihood of recognition even without common identifiers. Individuals within sexual and gender minority communities are more inclined to share sensitive information with researchers when they perceive the researchers as professional, competent, and considerate of their privacy concerns (Dillman *et al* 2009, Villarroel *et al* 2006).

This creative and fictionalized method of portraying experiences through sociological fiction, dramaturgical texts and poetry enabled me to maintain a high level of ethics and safety within this project. Through fictionalizing the experiences and compositing stories with similar themes, another layer of anonymity was added to the traditional qualitative research procedure of anonymizing data by changing the participant's name. The co-creators were therefore reassured that they would not be recognizable to those who may know them by their 'voice' or events from their lives being portrayed within verbatim quotes. To reassure those who participated that they would not be recognized or 'exposed' in a more formal way, I included a clause stipulating that the raw data, although anonymized before storing it, would not be shared at any point either during or after the research ended.

The collaborative creation of these 'fictions' enabled the co-creators to confirm, within an iterative process, that they were content with the way their experience was being presented, and that they were unrecognizable. Co-creators confirmed that the reassurance offered by the collaborative creative outputs encouraged them to share experiences that they would not have considered sharing if they were simply to be quoted. Denzin (2001) instructed that writers of interpretation must undertake experiments to find alternative modes of presenting these interpretations through 'true fictions' (p.10) and he includes 'novels, plays, songs, music, poems, dance' (Ibid.) amongst the many possible creative ways this could be done.

This collaborative element of the research process, inspired by Arvay's collaborative narrative approach, aimed to ensure that the research attends 'to power relations within research' and dealt 'with issues around voice and representation'; allowing the negotiation of 'multiple and shifting meanings', and allowing 'both parties to be able to voice their understandings equitably' (2003:163). Collaborating in this way also allowed us to form a 'shared voice' and find commonalities, many of which are explored through the theoretical analysis within this research. Carless and Douglas (2022) say that 'when it comes to collaboration, therefore, many of us share Marcelo Diversi and Claudio Moreira's (2010) recognition that 'words, meanings, intentions, and emotions reside not in me but in *us*' (p.13, emphasis in original)' (p.158). It was this collaboration that allowed us to form our own personal definition of our unique shared experience of asexuality as 'erotically embodied asexuality'.

This sensitivity to handling others' narratives is expressed by Gayle Letherby, who speaks of her PhD research and how she is 'conscious that I "took away their words" and then analyzed the data from my own political, personal and intellectual perspective', she goes on to say that 'with this in mind I attempted to be sensitive to issues of power and control throughout the whole research process' (2002: para 3.7). I feel particularly sensitive to this aspect of representing participants respectfully, and with consideration of these issues. During the first year of my PhD, I found myself utilizing my own story as 'data' to carve 'out pieces of narrative evidence [to] select, edit and deploy to border' my arguments (Fine 1994: 22, cited in Letherby 2002: 3.7). This felt uncomfortable to me. Although I was 'doing it' to myself it did not feel honoring or respectful. I certainly did not wish to do the same to others in this research. I wanted to treat their life experiences sensitively and hold them with care. I wrote the following poem in my journal, expressing the strong feelings I had about not being treated as 'data':

(Journal entry, 18 September 2021)

I am not data

I am an unfolding story
Multilayered
Unfathomable

I am an irregular shape
I do not fit in boxes
Forms
Spreadsheets

I am multidimensional
I cannot be analyzed
Categorized
Themed

I am not to be viewed through one lens
To be understood by one -ologist
Psych-
Sociol-
Biol-

I am not uniform
I am unique, as a fingerprint
Straight
Bent
Spiraling

* * *

This personal experience made me particularly conscious of not 'over analyzing' either my own or others' experiences, and the stories of these experiences. Plummer (2013) echoes my concern, with the emphatic statement that 'we should stay grounded with the people and their stories not the methodologies and their abstractions. Be careful of dehumanizing theory and method!' By presenting the experiences, framed with pertinent theory, rather than over analyzing, critiquing, or explaining the poetry, stories and plays, I could ensure that I was not treating myself or the co-creators as 'data' or negating or trivializing their experiences as a means to 'make a point'. This strategy of not 'over analyzing' their stories, and presenting them within a layered arrangement of the creative aspects and the theoretical discussion, also offers a more open experience for the reader; allowing the reader to absorb the creative pieces and interpret them through their own worldview, rather than telling them how to read them, and therefore negating their unique and personal experience of the text.

I have taken care to address the five ethical principles, outlined by Plummer, when presenting research based on 'documents of life'. These are:

1. The principle of respect, recognition and tolerance for persons and their differences.

2. The principle of promoting the caring of others, what has been called ... 'an ethic of care'.

3. The principles of expanding equalities, fairness and justice.

4. The principle of enlarging spheres of autonomy, freedom and choice.

5. The principle of minimizing harm. (2001: 228)

Through layers of anonymity, collaboration and not overanalyzing personal narratives, my research offers an ethical approach towards myself as researcher and participant, the co-creators, and the readers of this work who may be co-creating their own narrative whilst reading the narratives of others.

4.3 Creating Collaboratively

The co-creators' biographical narratives were gathered through in-depth, asynchronous e-conversations. Burns (2010) describes how the asynchronous online interview permits a lengthy delay between communications, giving the interviewee time to construct a response to a particular question. He explains how asynchronicity also enables interviewees to reflect and then supply a considered reply, and that the time to consider their response might reduce the pressure felt by nervous interviewees. This seemed appropriate considering the depth of reflection that I encouraged and the time span of their life that they were reflecting on. They were encouraged to share photographs, artwork, poetry, songs, films, timelines and 'letters to my younger self' to enable multi-layered and richly creative ways to reflect on and share their perspectives on asexuality. It may seem strange to conduct an embodied inquiry in a virtual way. Leigh and Brown (2021) reassure us that this method does not require that the research is done in person, the requirement is that the researcher and/or the participants are practicing embodied self-awareness during the process.

The dialogues were collaborative in nature, with co-creators being encouraged to choose themes they were interested in exploring, the interpretations and meanings sent after the analysis stage for further reflection, comment and feedback, and the creative outputs offered to them for their comments and input. Although some sense of intimacy can be lost in e-mail interviews versus face-to-face interviews, there are other positive factors such as that:

> ... the iteration of email interaction that allows time to both parties to construct a productive next response. Certainly, email interviews are heir to all the positioning, emplotment [sic], and other narrative and discursive issues that apply to other interview narratives. Emails lose the lived moment wherein sound, gesture and spatial setting form part of the exchange, on the one hand. On the other side, however, this form of interview allows analysis and reflection, extension for both parties. (Gibson 2010: 3).

To address the problem of the likelihood that certain respondents may not be confident with writing or spelling, other methods for interviewing can be utilized. I considered that perhaps phone or face-to-face interviewing would not be an appropriate alternative, as it would change the structure and time delay/reflection elements present in e-mail interviews. I considered a variant of the form of self-interviewing utilized by Allet et al (2011) in their *Media of Remembering* project to be more suitable. This method utilizes a digital voice recorder to record responses, whenever is convenient for the respondent. Rather than sending all of the questions in advance, it follows the same dialogue format of the e-mail interviews to preserve the flow of this communication, as Burns (2010: 8) describes:

> An email interview is interactive on an individual basis, in that the researcher in turn responds to the interests and responses of an individual participant. This may be formal or casual interaction, and it may involve more or fewer iterations. Just as some spoken interviews are long and some are short, parallel variation occurs with emails conversations.

With recent advances in technology, it is possible for an audio version of e-mail interviewing to be utilized with those who do not wish to write. The audio answers are sent in the same way as text answers, utilizing a mobile phone voice recorder.

My personal experience and journey with asexuality and androgyny was an advantage when approaching participants. Graham *et al* (2011) state that 'a primary strategy to foster disclosure and reduce non-response is for researchers to establish a bond of trust with members of the target population'. It is also explained that 'sexual and gender minority participants are more likely to trust researchers who evidence knowledge and sensitivity about their community and culture, characteristics commonly understood to be components of cultural competence' (Catania *et al*, 1996: 43). I had a strong resonance with the co-creators; it was as if we were weaving a shared tapestry from compatible and yet multihued thread, facilitated by the shared ground in terms of our experience of being asexual and also the sub-cultures in which our experiences had been formed.

4.4 Witnessing and weaving

As the principal investigator for research of a collaborative nature, I felt a sense of responsibility to create not only knowledge, but a sensitive, honoring, and artistic representation of the experiences shared by others. At times it felt expansive and liberating, as if I were a competent conductor of an orchestra, drawing out layers of harmonies, both aurally stimulating crescendos and gentle melodic interludes, to create a symphony of coherent experiences. At other times, I felt like the chief artist creating a group impressionist portrait, with other artists making unexpected brush strokes in lurid colors across a section I had considered complete. I constantly had the sense of being a patient gardener, lovingly tending to the soil, planting seeds, watching the stems of the narratives grow, and then feeling the joy as the well rooted plants began to unfurl and offer me a sensuous experience of flourishing inner worlds.

Whilst acknowledging and trying to meet the need for a certain standard in the presentation of my research, I have prioritized writing for the reader to whom this research may *mean* something, for example, the co-creators and asexual people that I met during the course of this research, such as 'Nadia' who is mentioned in the introduction, and for other doctoral students and academic researchers who may feel encouraged to experiment in similar ways should they find this book. I have also written with the intention that this book will be accessible to a wider readership than just academics. Therefore, endeavoring to make this work accessible was a key concern for me.

This has not been an easy process. In her essay regarding writing a doctoral thesis differently, Weatherall accurately describes the writing of a doctoral thesis as 'a testament to years of anxiety, excitement, confusion, terror and passion' (2019: 100). I resonated with this as I struggled to balance my feeling of care and my desire to express creatively, with the requirement for convention, which Weatherall refers to as 'pressures surrounding doctoral writing such as the demands of writing an 'acceptable' thesis in order to pass and in order to lay the foundation for future careers' (p.104). I was spurred on by a desire to not be suppressed by 'hegemonic masculine conventions … which marginalize alternative ways of writing, researching and being' (Phillips et al. 2014, Pullen and Rhodes 2015, cited in Ibid.)[107]. By adopting a more 'feminine' style of writing I have been able to honor voices which can 'become marginalized or erased in academia' and hope, like Weatherall, to 'open up new possibilities of identity and embodiment' (2019: 104). Weatherall also states how she also decided to 'explicitly write in, rather than out, my passionate attachments'(p.102). This is a strategy I have also adopted, in an effort to accurately represent my own voice and those of the co-creators. I hope that the inclusion of these passionate tones also adds vibrancy and transparency to the writing and mitigates the fallacy created by a veil of objectivity.

Asynchronous interviews offer benefits and challenges. Some need to be gently encouraged to engage with the communication

---

[107] This desire was heightened by my challenging journey to 'becoming woman', a narrative articulated in section 4.8.1.

process, whereas others are very 'immediate' and demanding, expecting equally instant responses, which necessitates clear boundary settings and managing expectations. Generally, I found it offered space, for me to respond with sensitivity and for them to take time to formulate a response they were happy with. I was surprised by the level of connection found within typed words and pixels on a screen, a rapport that transcended the boundaries of physical presence. The asynchronous nature of the dialogue allowed for reflection, for responses to be crafted with somatic awareness and mindfulness, and for me to navigate the nuances of the unfolding stories with patience and care.

This was a more challenging aspect at times though, with time to reflect on their responses, whilst still engaged in the research process, leading to changes of perspective, segments being retracted or alternate meanings being uncovered, sometimes after the analysis, or even the write up of the creative pieces had felt 'complete'. I enjoyed the flexibility that this method allowed. The time lapse gave space for me to adapt my approach and questions based on the unfolding conversation, delve deeper into unexpected topics, and explore new avenues, which led to a dynamic and open research process.

In a similar way, the stage of collaborative creating was equally rewarding and demanding. Sometimes I would get feedback that they did not like a poem, for instance, with little guidance as to what they did not like or any suggestion regarding words or phrases that they would be happy with. The pieces which were made up of composite experiences were even more difficult as I needed to share them with multiple co-creators and try to incorporate their views without offending one of the others. However, I found that the process added richness and depth, and it felt to me like a process of creatively mutual metamorphosis.

I also experienced disappointment that two of the co-creators had to discontinue the research due to unprocessed traumatic material.

One of the themes I had decided to explore in more depth, following the analysis of my own narrative, was asexuality in relation to traumatic experiences, and that asexuality can be a valid life choice for someone who is traumatized; rather than colluding with the assumption that not wanting sex is something that has to be 'fixed'. They suggested that I could use the responses they had already offered, but I decided not to use them as the use of 'unprocessed' and potentially triggering material did not feel ethical to me. Although this was disappointing at first, it did help to focus and clarify the direction of the research purely towards the life trajectories, practices and experiences that led to erotically embodied asexuality.

4.5 Exploring meaning

In order to develop a 'tentative statement about or definition of the phenomenon' (Denzin 2001: 4) of the experiences of asexuality that the co-creators and I had, experiences that did not seem to fit with the standard definition of asexuality, it was necessary to analyze the experiences shared in order to find meanings and inspect them for 'what they reveal about the essential, recurring features of the phenomenon being studied' (Ibid.). The common theme within all of these experiences was nonsexual erotic embodiment and ecstatic states. The definition or 'tentative statement' (Ibid.) that we collaboratively came to through the iterative process of cooperative creation was 'erotically embodied asexuality'. The process to interpret the phenomena of this alternative narrative of asexuality, that we now term erotically embodied asexuality, endeavored to follow the steps given by Denzin (2001) who outlined six phases in the interpretive process:

1. Framing the research question.

2. Deconstructing and analyzing critically prior conceptions of the phenomenon.

3. Capturing the phenomenon, including locating and situating it in the natural world and obtaining multiple instances of it.

4. Bracketing the phenomenon, or reducing it to its essential elements and cutting it loose from the natural world so that its essential structures and features may be uncovered.

5. Constructing the phenomenon, or putting the phenomenon back together in terms of its essential parts, pieces, and structures.

6. Contextualizing the phenomenon, or relocating the phenomenon back in the natural social world (Denzin 2001: 4).

Experientially, this has not been a linear process. Step two was necessary in order to complete step one. Having completed an initial phase two based on my initial literature review (and lightly on some themes from my own narrative, chosen because they related the themes arising in the literature review), phase two required repetition after phase three, for the themes regarding prior conceptions arising in each co-creator's narrative (including my own).

The exploration of meaning occurs within, stage 4, the 'bracketing' phase of interpretive interactionism, the steps of which are:

1. Locating within the personal experience story or self-story key phrases and statements that speak directly to the phenomenon in question.

2. Interpreting the meanings of these phrases, as an informed reader.

3. Obtaining the subject's interpretations of these phrases, if possible.

4. Inspecting these meanings for what they reveal about the essential, recurring features of the phenomenon being studied.

5. Offering a tentative statement about or definition of the phenomenon in terms of the essential recurring features identified in Step 4 (Denzin 2001: 7).

The search for meaning has been a key theme in my own narrative, and I endeavored also to understand the meanings inherent in the co-creators' narratives:

> Human beings, are by our nature, seekers of meaning. We find or make meanings from our experiences of life. We incorporate those meanings into our identities: our sense of who we are, what we are to do and how we are to be. These senses of identity derive primarily from some combination of our own past experiences; our relationships; the assumptions often unspoken of our social and cultural world; the expectations of others; perhaps for some, a religious tradition (Howell 2013: 4, cited in Letherby 2015: 136).

Peterson (2008) identified three classes of meaning; the first class being about things we are sure of in the world, such as our *motivations, emotions, and social identity*. These meanings are based on instincts and can sometimes be a bit rigid or ideological. The second class is made of those things that are more uncertain, for instance when things do not fit our usual expectations or when we ignore complexities, they are 'meanings based on the *emergence of anomaly, or ignored complexity*' (p.1, my emphasis). These meanings also come from instincts but lean more towards being revolutionary. The third class is about the connection between the certain and uncertain aspects of the world. These meanings come about when firstly we actively explore and engage with things voluntarily and 'second as a consequence of *identifying with the process of voluntary exploration*'. (Ibid.). These meanings can be abstract, are often represented in rituals and myths, and often lean towards the spiritual or religious.

Asexuality provides a rich site in which to explore these three levels of meaning. The co-creators' narratives contained meanings from each of these 'classes'. This is because within the first class they contain explorations of emotion and personal and social identity. Within the second class, the emergence of asexuality as an identity is the emergence of an 'anomaly', which it could be argued is due to 'ignored complexity' (the ignored complexity of the variation in relationships, erotic expression and levels of desire). With reference to the third class, because the co-creators were interested in the process of this research, they both voluntarily engaged in exploratory activity, and identified with the process of voluntary exploration. The meanings have been explored utilizing the 'thick interpretation' within interpretive interactionism:

> Thick interpretation attempts to uncover the meanings that inform and structure the subject's experiences. It is the interpretation of thick description. It takes the reader to the heart of the experience that is being interpreted. It assumes that all meaning is symbolic and operates at both the surface and the depths, at both the micro and the macro levels. It turns on thick description, which always joins biography to lived experience (Denzin 2001:.27).

I found the collaborative production of poems particularly effective, both in explicating meaning and condensing stories, whilst still offering this 'thick description'. Often over four pages of text would be utilized to create one short poem. The use of creative methods such as poetry, fiction and dramaturgical texts allowed us to express experiences, meaning, and interpretation of meaning in artistic ways, rather than following the traditional format of quoting raw 'data' and then producing a prosaic discussion of the meaning. Whilst offering a 'thick description', this method also leaves the interpretation more open than traditional analysis, so that the reader can have their own experience and find their own meaning in relation to their individual life experiences. I hope the tapestry woven within this book is not just a product of inquiry but a living artifact of connection, which continues to generate new layers of meaning and understanding within each person who engages with it, perhaps from within different temporal realities.

During the analysis of the transcripts, I did not simply rationally try to find themes and interpret meanings, I was attentive to my bodily responses such as gut feelings, rushes of energy, or a feeling of warmth or expansion in the heart, and I utilized these somatic clues to direct the process. The sensations were like subtle whispers filling the asynchronous space, each pause pregnant with the potential for deeper understanding. The connection did not seem to be hindered by working in cyberspace, the distance between us measured not in miles but in the silent echoes of shared experiences. I equally utilized somatic clues to alert me to feelings of discomfort within responses, which would lead to me checking in regarding their wellbeing and whether certain experiences should be included.

4.6 A blurring of boundaries

Prior to embarking on the research, I wanted to practice the style of interviewing with someone who would give me honest feedback on the process. Therefore, before commencing the in-depth dialogues with co-creators, I conducted a 'test interview' with a close family member, utilizing the type of questions and trajectory that I planned to use within my interviews. This family member enjoyed the process, but they found it challenging. They had to reflect deeply to answer the questions. They took a long time to respond because they had quite a lot of unmet personal material to traverse before they could write a response. Their reflection on completion was that it had been a worthwhile process but was quite grueling and 'felt like therapy'. This 'rang alarm bells' for me. I am a therapist and a life coach, which means that I am used to asking the type of questions that create an open space for self-exploration and insight. I decided to make it a caveat that participants had some experience of therapy or were therapists themselves. I kept hypervigilant for any signs of mental health issues and signposted where necessary. This means I am only sharing the findings from eleven of the co-creators as two explorations were not completed due to me guiding the participants to share the unprocessed elements of their experiences within a therapeutic setting.

This left me with some concerns about qualitative interviewing, and the training that is required in order for this to be safe for both the researcher and the researched. Researchers are not routinely taught how to navigate issues such as 'transference, burn-out and knowing when and how to end a relationship with a participant' which 'are beyond the scope of many researchers' (Leigh and Brown 2021: 89).

An awful image came to mind of researchers possibly being like a miner, mining for gold, chipping away with questions, in order to reach the 'golden nugget' that would add some sparkle to their research. I know this is a hyped-up image, with the ethic of care being strongly promoted by the research community, and that most researchers would prioritize care over insight. However, the researcher is looking for the data they want, within perhaps a limited time frame, through asking probing questions. The therapist or coach may be able to sense or see the answer to the question already, and may even gently point towards it, but they hold space softly and with ease around how much time it may take to emerge.

This is a concern shared by Leigh and Brown (2021) who say that 'similarly, a participant may not expect to enter into such a personal and vulnerable space within the bounds of a research project, and without a qualified and experienced person holding the boundaries of that experience to ensure that they are contained, they may be left re-traumatized' (p.89). I noted that although doctoral students receive academic supervision, they do not have supervision with an expert in a therapeutic discipline, in order to process the emotional content of their work, in the way that therapists do.

Writing as therapy has been well documented, with Gillean McDougall's doctoral thesis *Madness to Memoir: The Creative Cure* (2021) offering an insightful example of this, and I too found that the process of writing within this research has been therapeutic both for myself and the co-creators. The fact that the writing of autoethnographic works is therapeutic for the writer, but that this is not the intention of the writing—it is a welcome side-effect—has already been discussed in Chapter 1. However, what is less well documented, is the nature of the strong likelihood that the in-depth interviews, focus groups or creative groups within qualitative research will cross the boundaries into the therapeutic space.

Leigh and Brown (2021) warn that 'if, by using Embodied Inquiry, we are touching our own and our participants' emotional and embodied experiences, we need to be conscious about holding space for them' (p.19) They go on to say that:

> In these contexts, Embodied Inquiry becomes particularly delicate requiring the researcher to find sensitivity and strike the balance between gathering data and not forcing individuals to open themselves up to vulnerabilities that may usually remain hidden and risking harm to them. The majority of researchers are not trained therapists. However, just like a therapist, a researcher needs to be aware of the effects on participants when they share their stories, on themselves as researchers when they hear, process and analyze this kind of work, and on audiences when the findings are disseminated. Researchers need to be mindful of boundaries and limitations particularly when dealing with vulnerable groups. (2021:77)

My decision not to publish the findings from the two incomplete explorations, despite being given permission to do so, was due to the 'unprocessed' nature of this material and the potential harm the publishing of this could be for the co-creator. I also had concern regarding the potentially traumatizing aspect to the unprepared reader of this material. The only references to this that I could find are the Leigh and Brown (2021) book referenced above, an abstract from a 2018 presentation given by Jennifer Leigh and an upcoming book by Leigh (2023) which is currently in press with Bristol University Press. It could be a useful future research project to investigate this blurring of boundaries, and the possible therapeutic training needed for qualitative researchers.

4.7 Co-creators experiences of love

As discussed previously, in addition to having backgrounds of receiving and/or offering therapy, all of the co-creators had previous experiences within the sub-culture communities of new age and neo-tantra, often staying at retreat centers and communities of this ilk. Despite the drawbacks of these environments (discussed previously), one common benefit we all found was an expanded sense of love and the non-sexual erotic that we discovered there. The practices[108], some of which were discovered within these communities, and some of which the co-creators had found through their spiritual or religious discipline, that were identified and described as expanding their sense of love, and nonsexual and non-romantic erotic feelings, were as follows:

Breath

The co-creators all had experience of deep and conscious breathing to enhance awareness and relaxation. They found that when this is practiced in pairs, synchronizing the breath, it creates a feeling of connection and unity, which many had only previously felt within sexual or romantic relationships.

Meditation

Co-creators all found that mindfulness and meditation techniques, not only helped to quiet and focus the mind, but also facilitated a deeper connection with the self and others. Feelings of love and

---

[108] The inclusion of these practices is not a form of endorsement. They are included to enhance the understanding of how these practices influenced me and the Co-creators 'becoming' erotically embodied asexual and aromantic.

compassion were particularly heightened by practicing loving-kindness meditation or sitting in stillness, focusing on the heart.

Nonsexual Intimacy

Although neo-tantra often focuses on sexuality, during workshops, exercises which focused on intimacy had to be taught in the context of nonsexual intimacy (i.e. clothes on and focusing on the energy, connection of breath, eye gazing etc.). This therefore led the co-creators to feelings of connection, love and eros that they had only previously experienced during connecting with sexual and/or romantic partners. This desexualized the experience of the libido for the co-creators and gave them a different view of what these energies are or mean—that the energy we label as 'sexual' is not necessarily sexual at all—and gave them a feeling of being 'in love' with multiple people, some of whom they did not even know personally.

Mindful intimacy

Co-creators found that practices such as full consent, presence and awareness, during workshops that focused on nonsexual mindful intimacy, fostered a deeper connection with oneself, their partners and the wider community. Witnessing and experiencing groups of people connecting in nonsexual and non-attached intimacy expanded co-creators' sense of the type of intimacy they really wanted and facilitated a 'letting go' of patterns of attachment and jealousy.

Working with Energy

Many of the co-creators had explored the practice of somatic awareness of the body's energy. They said that, not only did this facilitate a more harmonious flow of energy throughout the body, but that focusing on the 'heart center', and meditating on the heart center and the energy of love, led to feelings of 'heart expansion' and 'unconditional love'.

Nature Connection

All of the co-creators had explored the practice of sensory awareness and presence in nature (sometimes now referred to by the commercialized name - *'Forest Bathing'*).

Mindful Communication

All the co-creators had some experience of 'mindful communication', which some described as 'nonviolent communication'[109], some described as 'heart-centered communication' and some as 'authentic communication'. They said that these practices helped them to express themselves authentically and listen with empathy, which fostered deeper connections and understanding, leading them to re-evaluate their priorities in relationships and be able to express their genuine needs, including the need for nonsexual intimacy. The co-creators also generally expressed that the practice of expressing emotions 'from the heart' cultivated compassion and generated a sense of unity.

Somatic Awareness, Ecstatic Dance and Mindful Movement

All the co-creators had experience, and a regular practice of, dance and movement. These practices helped them to release emotional and physical blockages, feel free in their self-expression, increase the flow of energy within the body, and connect with others in a nonverbal way; expanding their sense of possibilities within nonsexual intimacy and how they experience erotic ecstasy. Many co-creators cited 'contact improvisation'[110] as a movement practice that redefined their

---

[109] A system of empathic, non-judgmental communication and connection techniques developed by Marshall B. Rosenberg.

[110] Contact improvisation is a form of dance improvisation where points of physical contact serve as the starting point for exploration and movement. Dancers use touch, weight-sharing, and momentum to create spontaneous movement sequences. It's characterized by a sense of collaboration, responsiveness, and fluidity between dancers, often performed without set choreography. Contact improvisation encourages exploration of balance, trust, and connection with others through movement.

perception of the experience of bodies in intimate connection and movement—that this could be a non-sexual experience.

Mind-Body Integration

All co-creators had some experience of mind-body integration through exploring mindful movement, body-centered or movement therapy, or therapeutic bodywork modalities such as Pulsing Rhythmic Bodywork, Bodymind Attunement, Rhythmic Healing, Bioenergetics, Hakomi Method and Somatic Experiencing.[111]

Non-sexual Touch

All of the co-creators had many experiences of nonsexual touch and had received regular massage therapy, and/or participated in massage swaps with friends of various genders. They connected that this had helped them to understand the difference between sexual and nonsexual touch and pleasure. These experiences had also increased their capacity to articulate boundaries, needs, and desires regarding nonsexual touch and intimacy.

Spiritual Exploration

The co-creators still had various disciplined practices from spiritual or religious traditions and the practices that they had felt beneficial, and retained, from the spiritual sub-communities. They reported that the exploration of concepts such as 'interconnectedness' and 'connecting to the divine' had expanded their sense of love and had further expanded their sense of the nonsexual erotic to the 'spiritual realm', and the nonsexual pleasurable experience of 'sacred connection' and 'spiritual energy'. They also found that practices such as meditation and mindfulness allowed an expansion of their

---

[111] Many of these offer a unique approach to psychotherapy that emphasizes the integration of mind and body, with a focus on releasing blocked energy, promoting emotional expression, and addressing underlying psychological issues.

perception of reality, and allowed them to consider alternate ways of being.

Despite the (previously discussed) drawbacks of the new age and neo-tantra communities, the co-creators did recognize that the group practices were an important part of their journey to redefining love and the erotic. Participation in group workshops, which often ended with hugging many of the other participants, enabled a sense of community and shared experience. This increased their sense of love for others with whom they were not in a personal relationship or did not feel a particular affinity with. Co-creators reported that through this sense of non-discriminate love, it was possible to feel love, affection, and nonsexual erotic connection with people just because they happened to be there, not because they were 'known' on a personal level or there was some benefit to be had from them. It was possible to feel love and connection with a common sense of humanity, rather than because of certain characteristics that suited the co-creators' particular preferences, or any sense of attachment.

This expanded sense of love is discussed in the next section, which offers a layered empirical and theoretical discussion of alternative perceptions and experiences of love and romance. The co-creators and I all now consider ourselves aromantic in the sense that we do not understand the feeling of 'romantic love' to be anything other than an expression of eros. For most of the co-creators and I this was a 'becoming' aromantic, whereas for two co-creators this was how they had always felt. The co-creators do not endorse relationship hierarchies or limiting the sharing of the nonsexual erotic with only one person, although this does not preclude loving committed partnership, which may include sex for those co-creators who are on the asexual and aromantic spectrum (see Chapter 6). Their relationships do not exclude others, become the prime focus of their lives, or limit connection. Those who are in relationship with a partner still do not label this as a 'romantic relationship' – to the co-creators the feeling of 'romance' is simply eros in motion - an energy to propel us towards creating, connecting, serving, and loving.

4.7.1 Liberation from romantic ideals

*She'd dash her own head if it meant she could
remove these
foolish ideas of true love.*
Jessie Burton, *The Miniaturist*

The more I engaged with the narratives, both co-creators' and in the literature, and then wrote about this eros with full erotic embodied engagement, the more it became clear; once the sexual has been relegated to its position as only one potential expression of erotic, if indeed it is erotic and not transactional or pornographic, and we have the expanded definition of the erotic; as an essential life energy that is 'striving for the intensification, gratification, and unification of life and of the life environment' (Marcuse 1974: 280), a joyful and often somatically ecstatic force which can permeate all activities (Lorde 1978), and 'a palpable love, that is also sacred' (Griffin 1996:15), it is then possible to see how nonsexual, platonic, and even filial love can be erotic.

A love that feels 'romantic' is perhaps just eros at play. The spark, the longing to connect, to create, to be on the 'inside', the feeling of 'energy' between two people. However, that first spark of eros is likely to be only a feeling of erotic connection, guiding one to the possibility of love; the fullness of love takes time, patience, and commitment (Fromm 1956, Peck 1975, Merton 1979, hooks 2001). Susan Griffin tells us that, 'there is an eros present at every meeting' and that, if we become more embodied and reconnect with the nature that we are an intrinsic part of, the eros that perhaps we are currently not even aware of will 'infuse every kind of meeting' (p.15). Tagirov explains that 'eros in love inevitably implies the transcendence of one's own 'me' for the sake of 'you'' (2018: 832), which aptly describes the state of transcendence individuals feel when they are in that first flash of 'romantic' love, which may or may not become 'mature love'[112]. Eric Fromm states that this 'desire for interpersonal fusion is the most powerful striving in man', and that it is therefore dangerous to limit this desire to 'romantic' love alone:

> It is the most fundamental passion, it is the force which keeps the human race together, the clan, the family, society. The failure to achieve it means insanity or destruction—self-destruction or destruction of others. Without love, humanity could not exist for a day. Yet, if we call the achievement of interpersonal union "love," we find ourselves in a serious difficulty. Fusion can be achieved in different ways—and the differences are not less significant than what is common to the various forms of love. Should they all be called love? Or should we reserve the word "love" only for a specific kind of union. (1956: 18)

He goes on to point to a problem with the limited nature of the English language and concept of love, and how we often misplace the word 'love' when really we are talking about immature forms of 'romantic' love or co-dependent 'symbiotic union'[113], saying that:

---

[112] [M]ature love is union *under the condition of preserving one's integrity, one's individuality*. Love is an active power in man; a power which breaks through the walls which separate man from his fellow men, which unites him with others; love makes him overcome the sense of isolation and separateness, yet it permits him to be himself, to retain his integrity. In love the paradox occurs that two beings become one and yet remain two (Fromm 1956: 20-22).

[113] The concept of symbiotic union draws parallels between the biological connection of a pregnant mother and her fetus, where they function as two entities yet share a symbiotic relationship. This relationship is characterized by mutual dependence—they live "together" and rely on each other. The fetus, while physically a part of the mother, receives all necessary sustenance from her, making the mother its world. This biological symbiosis not only benefits the fetus but also enhances the mother's life. In the realm of psychic symbiotic union, two individuals may be psychologically independent, yet a similar kind of emotional attachment exists between them (Fromm 1956: 19). This type of 'psychic symbiotic union' or relationship addiction is discussed further on in this section along with the language utilized to describe love.

as with all semantic difficulties, the answer can only be arbitrary. What matters is that we know what kind of union we are talking about when we speak of love. Do we refer to love as the mature answer to the problem of existence, or do we speak of those immature forms of love which may be called symbiotic union? (Fromm 1956: 18).

When you are 'in love' everything seems more beautiful – that is the power of the erotic – life becomes fuller, more beautiful, when you connect to it, but a romantic partner is not necessary for one to feel this. In secular society physical or 'romantic' attraction to another and that first flush of 'being in love' is often the only way to have an experience of the transpersonal, or a feeling of transcendence (Fromm 1956, Illouz 1997, hooks 2001, Tagirov 2018). In this context, it makes it easier to understand why, for those who identify as aromantic, it can be challenging. In secular society, challenging the notion of 'romance' as a fundamental part of human flourishing is the equivalent of turning up to church on a Sunday morning, going onto the altar, and headbutting the priest. I will include a poem, that is also in Chapter 3, as it illustrates how this 'not being romantic' is even sometimes seen as a problem within the asexual community.

*　　*　　*

Spock

Sex wasn't a problem
Who would?
Want that
Sweaty
Messy
Entangled

Romance was different
Who wouldn't?
Want that
Swoony
Magical
Exciting

The shock
Called 'Spock'[114]
For showing
Love differently
Yet
Fully
Committedly

Not fitting in
It's a sin
To not want
The white dress
A ring
Coercivity
Exclusivity

*   *   *

In her lecture entitled *An Erotic Toolkit: Asexual and Aromantic Critiques of Heteronormativity* (2020), Ela Przybylo explains that she would like to see further studies into romantic love, in relation to asexuality and aromanticism. She makes the link between the critique of sex being the 'glue' that holds relationships together within Asexuality Studies and how aromantics critique the premium placed on romance as the

---

[114] Spock is a character in the long running TV series and multiple motion picture series *Star Trek*, produced by CBS. Spock is a Vulcan, which is an imaginary alien race who do not experience emotions.

'kind of glue' that is supposed to hold relational structures together. She explains that with a/romance there are 'clear parallels with asexuality' and the concept found there that sex is 'the glue' within compulsory sexuality, but that she thinks with romance 'it is a different thing'. From the narratives shared by co-creators and my own narrative, in conjunction with the literature, I can see that perhaps 'the glue' is the same thing, that the link between the two is the erotic.

Within consumerist, secular society the sexual is a way to feel the erotic, the erotic that is challenging to find within such a society. It is a way to partially fulfil the 'desire for interpersonal fusion' (Fromm 1956). Likewise, romance is a way to experience the erotic transcendence that is experienced in spirituality (Kripal 2007, Smith 2017, Tagirov 2018), and allows us to transcend our boundaries and feel at one with another. The co-creators within this research, who became asexual, found that by becoming erotically embodied, they no longer had an interest in the sexual or seeking 'romantic' experiences, because they already felt fulfilled erotically. Those who were already asexual, but felt that they had enhanced this through becoming erotically embodied, said that once they experienced the erotic in everything, they felt 'romantic' feelings were simply an expression of eros.

This is not to say that those who participated in this research are no longer interested in loving relationships and the eros that they feel within these relationships. It is just that they are not limited by this needing it to be a 'romantic' or 'primary' coupled relationship. All of those who participated in the research consider themselves polyamorous, although not in the sexually promiscuous way often prevalent in neo-tantra communities. They refer to this in the sense that they engage in nonsexual erotic and intimate connections with multiple people. We have all found this an important step, and a gateway into discovering more expansive and liberating notions of love.

My time experimenting with polyamory was one of the first stages of me realizing that perhaps an asexual lifestyle would suit me more. The connection that I previously would have labelled as 'romantic', I simply felt as a spiritual connection – the feeling of joy and electric energy, as I connected with another sacred being. I could feel the sensation of 'falling in love' with somebody without it *meaning anything*. C S Lewis describes this eloquently:

> When we meet someone beautiful and clever and sympathetic, of course we ought, in one sense, to admire and love these good qualities. But is it not very largely in our own choice whether this love shall, or shall not, turn into what we call 'being in love'? No doubt, if our minds are full of novels and plays and sentimental songs, and our bodies are full of alcohol, we shall turn any love we feel into that kind of love : just as if you have a rut in your path all the rainwater will run into that rut, and if you wear blue spectacles everything you will see will turn blue. But that will be our own fault (1952: 99).

As I think back, and also look at my diary entries, I can see how often I have been confused when my personal expression has been misconstrued as 'romantic' or 'sexual'. I can now see clearly that this is because of the conflation of the libido with only sexual energy, and feeling an energetic, sparky connection as 'romance'. This was a similar phenomenon experienced by Nadia, the woman that stated that she could now say she is asexual following my presentation regarding erotically embodied asexuality at a conference[115]. I am postulating that the reason that I got confused when people made it all about sex, romance, and ownership, was because of my propensity towards being asexual and aromantic, but having no model to guide me. I therefore went against what I felt in order to have relationships or maintain relationships.

---

[115] This story is related in the Introduction. Nadia is a pseudonym, and the story is shared with permission. Nadia had previously felt that she could not claim to be asexual because others perceived of her as sexy and full of 'sexual energy' and dismissed that notion off hand.

I had not found any narratives in the literature that were similar to mine or the co-creators, until I recently found Michele Morano's book *Like Love* (2020). I found a resonance, particularly in the chapter *Ars Romantica*. Morano describes a relationship that she had, whilst she was also participating in another sexual and romantic relationship. This relationship, however, was not sexual or 'romantic' in the traditional sense, but it did have the spark of 'romance', which led Morano to reflect on what this is.

Morano describes how they would 'agree to meet at his place at six, and from the moment I hung up the phone, the day shimmered. Loneliness evaporated; buoyancy took over. The last hour of work was the most productive of all' (2020: 64). This certainly sounds like how one may feel with a 'romantic' partner before going on a date. She goes on to say that, after an evening sharing intimate conversation, dinner, and drinks:

> The walk home, from the reach of Ben's porch light through darkness to the reach of my porch light, felt magical. Partly it was the drinks and the way Ben conversed as if my life experience were on par with his, but mostly it was the studio, the walls, the sculptures and paintings and sketches, the intimacy of all that expression (Ibid).

She explains her confusion about her feelings saying that 'this was years before researchers at the University of London learned that looking at an appealing work of art stimulates the same areas of the brain as having a crush on a person' (Ibid). When she did find this research, it became clearer to her and she 'began to understand why I'd float home from Ben's house feeling dizzy in love'. She describes how she would 'make a cup of tea and wrap in a blanket, then sit on the porch and look at the stars. Even when the temperature fell below freezing, I wanted to be out in the world, inhaling deeply, enjoying all that craving' (Ibid.). She goes on to say that 'it's the sparks themselves that interest me most ... the constant, low-grade pleasure of attraction.' This is the type of connection reported by many co-creators in this research. They also interpret these 'sparks' as the erotic that is present in aesthetic, intellectual and intimate connection of a nonsexual nature, rather than 'romance'. This experience can be confusing within a society that conflates the erotic only with the sexual, as Morano's grappling with her experience illustrates:

> Were these conversations erotic? I want to say yes, of course, they were intellectually erotic. But isn't the intellect physical, too? Doesn't it live in the body? Didn't my skin tingle as we talked, and didn't my organs seem to enlarge until I could hardly sit still? (2020: 66)

* * *

The following poem offers a window into this experience of the erotic within platonic intimacy that was shared by co-creators:

Platonically Erotic

They embrace
Melding, merging
Bodies melting
Pulse Fluidly
Traversing boundaries

The vehicle
Carries them to Heartsong[116]
Energy rising
Windows steaming
From intellectual heat

---

[116] A group singing event, where musicians lead the singing of uplifting songs with themes of Love and Peace, often with vibratory instruments such as harmonium and harp.

They sit
On luxurious sheepskin
A rug for two
Knees touching
Hearts softening

They sing
Melodiously mingling
Hearts' Harmony
Two as one
In Erotic fusion

*   *   *

4.7.2 Consuming love

> *Religion is the sigh of the oppressed creature,*
> *the heart of a heartless world and the soul of*
> *soulless conditions. It is the opium of the*
> *people.*
> Marx 1844

In order to understand this limiting of eros and love through the concept of 'romance', I examined the historical and societal context of the concept of romance, and found examples of how it can be a quasi-erotic substitute for spirituality and a bypassing of other, perhaps more challenging, forms of love. Following the 'disenchantment' (Weber 1905) of Western society and the loss of the 'sacred canopy' (Berger 1967), romance became the 'opium of the people' (Marx 1844) replacing 'religion as the focus of everyday life … love began to be represented not only as a value in itself but as an important motive in the pursuit of happiness, now defined increasingly in individualistic and private terms' (Illouz 1997: 29-30). Romance as a constructed concept became reified and concurrently deified, with it being one of the only sites for 'liminal' and 'sacred' experiences; an experience which 'projects an aura of transgression and both promises and demands a better world' (Ibid: 9). However, the 'romantic' experience quickly became commodified with 'the modern romantic ideal' being harnessed by corporations to sell products and experiences meaning that 'it is the very act of consumption that constitutes and creates the romantic moment' (Ibid: 76).

Romance, like sex, is another place where the erotic is felt in a potentially liberating, but often limited way. As Illouz tells us:

> [I]n contemporary culture the experience of romance affords a secular access to the experience of the sacred, and without this experience or some analogue of it daily life becomes oppressive in its continuity, regularity, and necessity (1997: 285).

With romance and sex as two of the prime ways in which we experience the erotic within our secular society, it is easy to see how this creates the primacy of the romantic relationship and the potential for commodification of romantic experiences. These experiences can offer a temporary feeling of transcending personal limits, and thus experiencing the quasi-erotic. This temporary 'high' offered by sex and romance can lead to these becoming an addiction for some, in a similar way as many drugs, or unhealthy habits such as obsessive shopping are to others (Peele and Brodsky 1975). Illouz (1997) tells us that the romantic ideal was central in the rise of the ethos of consumerism. The importance of maintaining romantic excitement within long term relationships was actively promoted by 'advertisers' who 'prolonged the couple's need to engage in practices of consumption' (Ibid: 41), which she says, coupled with the rise of psychologism, created the 'hedonistic-therapeutic model' (Ibid: 53) of long-term primary relationships.

Interestingly, within her research Illouz found that individuals who were middle or upper class were most likely to find a 'romantic utopia' in the everyday: 'The more one is objectively distanced from necessity, the more one is likely to say that a mundane or ordinary moment can be romantic'(Ibid: 284). If we are to accept that the romantic experience is an experience of the expanded erotic, this fits with Marcuse's (1955) notion that the fullness of eros would only be realized in society with a general raising of living standards and lessening need for participation in production. Wegner (1999) asks the question of 'how we might work to transform [romance] from an 'opiate' or 'liminal experience' into an integral part of the everyday reality of all peoples' (p.268). I would argue, like Marcuse, Kripal, Gafini and Kincaid, Lorde, hooks, Sovatsky and many others, that the liberation of the erotic—from purely being conceived as a romantic or sexual energy, to being understood as a primary life force accessible within the simplest of everyday activities, tasks and interactions—would facilitate the emergence of a very different 'reality' for 'all peoples'.

bell hooks (2001) speaks extensively about love in her book *All About Love*, explaining that the media offers us a warped view of love. She explains that recognizing knowledge as a crucial component of love is essential in light of pervasive messages suggesting that love thrives on mystery and the unknown. Media often portrays love in ways that lack communication and understanding, emphasizing that ignorance adds allure and excitement to love, such as 'movies in which people are represented as being in love who never talk with one another, who fall into bed without ever discussing their bodies, their sexual needs, their likes and dislikes' (p.94). However, hooks explains, these messages are often delivered by profit-driven producers who lack insight into the true nature of love, relying on mystified depictions because they struggle to authentically portray genuine loving interactions.

Thomas Merton (1979) warns against the type of commodification and misleading messages about love that those in Western society receive on a daily basis. Messages teaching that 'falling in love' is not a choice, it just happens to one, and that 'love is regarded as a deal. The deal presupposes that we all have needs which have to be fulfilled by means of exchange' (p.29) and that 'we unconsciously think of ourselves as objects for sale on the market. We want to be wanted. We want to attract customers' (Ibid.). In this relationship 'marketplace' he suggests that 'we waste a great deal of time modelling ourselves on the images presented to us by an affluent marketing society' and 'in doing this we come to consider ourselves and others not as *persons* but as *products* – as "goods" or in other words as packages.' (Ibid.) His essay was written in the 1960s and posthumously published in 1979. However, his writings about the state of this warped concept of love have become even more evident in current times, with people 'selling' themselves through dating apps and social media. Over sixty years ago Merton had already observed that:

> This concept of love assumes that the machinery of buying and selling of needs and fulfilment is what makes everything run. It regards life as a market and love as a variation on free enterprise. You buy and you sell, and to get somewhere in love is to make a good deal with whatever you happen to have available (1979: 30).

He goes on to say that the problem with the commodified romantic idea of love is that it takes the attention from truly loving another, in the fullness of their being, with depth and commitment, and that individuals in this situation 'become obsessed with the effectiveness of your own package, your own product, your own market value' (p.30). One of the outcomes of the 'marketplace' of this quasi-erotic form of romantic love is that its focus on attraction and being attractive means that 'sexual cravings are kept in a state of high irritation, not by authentic passion' but instead due to the 'need to prove themselves attractive and successful lovers' (p.32) He tells us that people caught in this trap often seek through sexual encounters 'the repeated assurance that they are still marketable, still a worthwhile product' (Ibid.).

*   *   *

The following poem, based on some experiences shared by co-creators, aims to illustrate the sadness of only valuing oneself as a sexual commodity:

Worthless

Thinking he only wants sex
The other intimacy a preamble
For penetration
She declines his visit
Because she bleeds
She is worth less
Than love for loves sake

Thinking she only wants an orgasm
The bleeding stops her quest
For pleasure
He is angered
Her dismissal suggests
They are worth less
Than a spiritual intimacy

*   *   *

According to bell hooks romantic love is 'one of the most destructive ideas in the history of human thought'. She goes on to explain that:

> Its destructiveness resides in the notion that we come to love with no will and no capacity to choose. This illusion, perpetuated by so much romantic lore, stands in the way of our learning how to love. To sustain our fantasy we substitute romance for love (2001: 70).

Peele and Brodsky (1975) describe that this type of romance can become an addiction. It is easy to see how this can happen when we understand Fromm's previously noted concept of the 'powerful striving' human beings feel for 'interpersonal fusion' (1956: 18). Fromm explains how people in this state of romantic attraction can 'take the intensity of the infatuation, this being 'crazy' about each other, for proof of the intensity of their love, while it may only prove the degree of their preceding loneliness' (1956:4). Fromm holds a similar view to Merton (1979) regarding the danger within capitalist society for individuals to potentially regard each other as commodities. He observes that those who become influenced by this 'marketplace' mindset 'fall in love when they feel they have found the best object available on the market, considering the limitations of their own exchange values' (p.3). According to Illouz (1997) they then become the ideal consumers as they will need to keep purchasing 'romantic experiences' in order to maintain that romantic high throughout their relationship, and the ideal appearance in order to remain attractive to their partner.

hooks shares the view of Peele and Brodsky that romantic 'love' can become an addiction:

> Many people want love to function like a drug, giving them an immediate and sustained high. They want to do nothing, just passively receive the good feeling ... When the practice of love invites us to enter a place of potential bliss that is at the same time a place of critical awakening and pain, many of us turn our backs on love ... we [USA] are a nation that normalizes dysfunction (hooks 2001: 114).

hooks shares the same concern that 'addiction is not about true relatedness' (Peele and Brodsky 1975:4), saying that 'addiction makes love impossible' (2001: 114). She goes onto say that 'greed characterizes the nature of this pursuit because it is unending; the desire is ongoing and can never be fully satisfied'. Her concern is that this type of objectification of, and dependence on, the other can never lead to a full flourishing of truly loving. Throughout his book *The Art of Loving*, Fromm stresses the importance to human flourishing of committed, respectful and unselfish love. He tells us that this type of 'mature love' requires the perspective of 'I want the loved person to grow and unfold for his own sake, and in his own ways, and not for the purpose of serving me' (1956: 28). This is simply not possible when a person is addicted to the quasi-fulfilment that idealizing a relationship, or the idea of a person, gives them (Fromm 1956, Peele and Brodksy 1975, Peck, 1978, Merton 1979, hooks 2001).

Peele and Brodksy explain that they encounter 'understandable' resistance to the idea of love as an addiction:

> There is an understandable resistance to the idea that a human relationship can be equivalent psychologically to a drug addiction. Yet it is not unreasonable to look for addiction between lovers when psychologists find the roots of drug addiction in childhood dependency needs and stunted family relationships. Chein, Winick, and other observers interpret drugs to be a kind of substitute for human ties. In this sense, addictive love is even more directly linked to what are recognized to be the sources of addiction than is drug dependency (1975: 86).

However, within my narrative and in Elizabeth Gilbert's (2007) memoir regarding her recovery from relationship addiction through travelling and spiritual practice, we can see the true marks of addiction to romantic love, which Peele and Brodsky state:

> [O]ccurs, as in drug addiction, when a single overwhelming involvement with one thing serves to cut a person off from life, to close him or her off to experience, to debilitate him, to make him less open, free, and positive in dealing with the world (Peele and Brodksy 1975: 98).

Gilbert describes romantic love as taking a hit of a 'heady, hallucinogenic, emotional speedball', and tells us that 'soon you start craving that intense attention, with the hungry obsession of any junkie'. This corresponds with a description shared by Peele and Brodksy written 'by an addict in *The Road to H* of his first shot of heroin [which] can apply equally well to the addicted lover's experience: "I felt I always wanted to feel the same way as I felt then."' (p. 100). They go on to explain that although the addictions to romantic love and heroin are different the consequences are the same:

> Both addicts have discovered something reassuring that they hope will never change. From the turmoil of their inner worlds, they recognize and latch onto the one sensation they have encountered which they feel can bring them peace ... neither feels like a whole person when alone. This is the development of tolerance in a relationship ... As with heroin and its irrecoverable euphoria, or cigarettes smoked in routine excess, something initially sought for pleasure is held more tightly *after* it ceases to provide enjoyment ... The love partner must be there in order to satisfy a deep, aching need, or else the addict begins to feel withdrawal pain (1975: 100-101).

It could be said of both types of addiction that a quasi-erotic experience of consumption has replaced the experience of the fullness of eros. Whenever there is a reliance on the goods of consumption, or unhealthy attachment, to bring fulfilment, rather than the simple 'every day' infused by eros, there is a danger of individuals becoming addicts, on however subtle a level:

> When a constant exposure to something is necessary in order to make life bearable, an addiction has been brought about, however romantic the trappings. The ever-present danger of withdrawal creates an ever-present craving' (Peele and Brodksy 1975:88).

This 'out of control' heady high of romance being conflated with love is not helped by our use of language: 'We speak of "falling in love" as though love were something like water that collects in pools, lakes, rivers and oceans' (Merton 1979:25). Merton explains that 'falling in love' is a phrase that he has been unable to find in any other language. He goes on to say that:

> The expression to 'fall in love' reflects a peculiar attitude toward love and life itself-a mixture of fear, awe, fascination, and confusion. It implies suspicion, doubt, hesitation in the presence of something unavoidable, yet not fully reliable. For love takes you out of yourself. You lose control. You 'fall' (1979: 26).

hooks (2001) explains that 'if you do not know what you feel, then it is difficult to choose love; it is better to fall. Then you do not have to be responsible for your actions' (p.171). She goes on to say that even though psychoanalysts such as Fromm (1956) and Peck (1975) have critiqued the idea that we fall in love, 'we continue to invest in the fantasy of effortless union. We continue to believe we are swept away, caught up in the rapture, that we lack choice and will' (p.171). Fromm (1956) describes how love is not a feeling it is an action 'essentially an act of will' (p.55) and goes on to say that 'to love somebody is not just a strong feeling-it is a decision, it is a judgment, it is a promise. If love were only a feeling, there would be no basis for the promise to love each other forever. A feeling comes and it may go.' (p.56).

Scott (1975) describes love as the desire to grow spiritually and to also facilitate the spiritual growth of one's partner. Scott's work is largely based on the ideas of Fromm, and he also explains that love is an active force, not a passive one: 'The desire to love is not itself love. Love is as love does. Love is an act of will-namely, both an intention and action. Will also implies choice. We do not have to love. We choose to love' (1975: 83). hooks (2001) observes that 'despite these brilliant insights and the wise counsel they offer, most people remain reluctant to embrace the idea that it is more genuine, more real, to think of choosing to love rather than falling in love' (p.172).

As can be seen by the discussion in the literature and also from the co-creator's narratives, it is both possible to recognize and enjoy the 'spark' of romance as an expression of the erotic that leads us to connect whilst recognizing this as an initial meeting that may or may not lead to a deeper longer lasting connection. hooks claims that:

> We are all capable of changing our attitudes about 'falling in love'. We can acknowledge the 'click' we feel when we meet someone new as just that - a mysterious sense of connection ... How different things might be if, rather than saying "I think I'm in love," we were saying "I've connected with someone in a way that makes me think I'm on the way to knowing love." Or if instead of saying "I am in love" we said "I am loving" or "I will love" (2001: 177).

hooks explains that 'much as I enjoy popular new age commentary on love, I am often struck by the dangerous narcissism fostered by spiritual rhetoric that pays so much attention to individual self-improvement and so little to the practice of love within the context of community' (2001: 76). I agree that such 'spiritual rhetoric' is dangerous. However, both the co-creators and I have spent much time in spiritual community, communities which, although considered 'new age', are still a community context, where many practice loving kindness and compassion. We have also spent years dedicated to disciplined spiritual practice.

Disciplined spiritual practice is recognized as essential for spiritual development both by all those who participated in this research and also by hooks who confirms that 'a commitment to a spiritual life requires us to do more than read a good book or go on a restful retreat. It requires conscious practice, a willingness to unite the way we think with the way we act' (p.77). That said, during our time in communities that focused on nonsexual intimacy and love, the co-creators and I discovered that we became more able to express love as 'Spiritual Love', Lokānurāga[117] or Agape[118]. We found that it is possible to open and connect with whoever we are meeting in the

---

[117] Lokānurāga (लोकानुराग) is a Sanskrit word that translates as 'love of mankind', universal love, general benevolence, philanthropy.

[118] Agape is a Greek word that Christians use to describe an indiscriminate love for other persons, corresponding to the Love of God for humankind.

moment with a sense of erotic fusion. In this sense, it is possible to experience the 'feeling of falling in love' very frequently by being open to, and immersed in, the flow of eros.

This experience can enable individuals to break free from the notion that this initial spark 'means something'; that we should pursue a relationship because it is being felt. This reflects the way that the freeing of eros from the sexual allows us to feel our libido aroused in response to another without it meaning that we have to try to have sex with them. Our time in these communities also enabled an appreciation of all types of intimacy, and the importance of not devaluing nonsexual relationships and relegating them further down the 'relationship hierarchy' than sexual relationships. The following poem is based on one co-creator's expanded perception and valuing of various types of intimacy and relationship:

*　*　*

Perceptions of polyamory

She feels special
Enlivened
After their shag in the shower

Going down
To her 'frigid friend'
With the message to meet him

Not knowing
The Beauty
They will share

Heading out
Swimming at the lagoon
Sharing Inner secrets

An ineffable connection
As light bounces on water
Illuminating innocent intimacy

*   *   *

By connecting to the erotic energy of love as a group in gatherings and workshops, co-creators found that they also became less needy of a particular person to facilitate the experience of feeling eros, and that they could also experience eros in the group field rather than it being a personal phenomenon. This is illustrated in much of the poetry in Chapter 7 and is also summed up by a comment made by a participant in one of my singing groups who described it as '*A beautiful sacred space, embodying the theme of love in a pure and real way. It was a poignant experience for me tangibly filled with Love and Spirit.*'[119] There are many practices that the co-creators articulated as facilitating their opening to the nonsexual erotic and an expanded sense of the erotic. The following poem is about one of these practices of nonsexual intimacy.

*   *   *

---

[119] Shared with permission.

Eye Gazing

He looks into her eyes
Softly
Encompassing
Seeing
Deeply

Is it the sparkle
Of her heart that
Arouses
Tingling
Expansion
Appreciation

In his gaze
She becomes
Essential
Beauty
Radiance
All-pervading

A bell chimes
He must move
Placing hand
On Heart
A gesture
Of honor
He moves

He sits

He gazes

Into another

Man's eyes

Glowing

Internal Light

In that moment

This man is

Everything

The focus of

Love

*   *   *

4.7.3 Peril of a Society that Limits Love

Love is not just something that happens to
you: it is a certain special way of being alive.
Love is, in fact, an intensification of life, a
completeness, a fullness, a wholeness of life.
Merton 1979: 26

hooks asserts that 'our patterns around romantic love are unlikely to change if we do not change our language (2001:171). She explains the danger of the unrealistic ideal of romance, thinking that a 'romantic spark' must mean something more, and limiting love to this 'fantasy realm':

> The myth of true love - that fairy-tale vision of two souls who meet, join, and live happily thereafter - is the stuff of childhood fantasy. Yet many of us, female and male, carry these fantasies into adulthood and are unable to cope with the reality of what it means either to have an intense life

altering connection that will not lead to an ongoing relationship or to be in a relationship. True love does not always lead to happily ever after, and even when it does, sustaining love still takes work. (2001: 181)

The prioritizing of the romantic relationship was problematic to many co-creators. This idea that sexual, romantic, long-term relationships are the most important creates a hierarchy that renders committed, nonsexual, and unromantic relationships unintelligible and often undervalued, despite their significance and impact on those involved.

*   *   *

Always the bridesmaid

They jokingly call him
A 'Fag Hag'
His latest 'big thing'
A gay man
Although he's asexual

"Always the Bridesmaid,
Never the Bride!"
He jokes, hiding the pain
As his beau marries a groom
In touching ceremony

They jokingly call them
A 'Throuple'
But it is actually true
No sex for him
But the love is real

"They're just engrossed.

In their Babymoon!"

He explains, feigning flippancy

Dismissed again

As baby makes three

They rudely call him

'Just a friend'

As she lies in isolation

Behind glass screen

His Primary Platonic

"Please let me in!

I'm her Next of Kin!"

He cries, desperate, dejected

As she takes her last breath

Alone

*   *   *

Fromm warns of focusing the direction of 'love' on only one person saying that 'if a person loves only one other person and is indifferent to the rest of his fellow men, his love is not love but a symbiotic attachment, or an enlarged egotism' (1956: 46). King 1967, (cited in hooks 2001: 75) said that: "When I speak of love I am not speaking of some sentimental and weak response. I am speaking of that force which all of the great religions have seen as the supreme unifying principle of life." hooks also points the reader towards the gospel of

St John, which I have expanded here: 'Beloved, let us love one another, because love comes from God. Everyone who loves has been born of God and knows God. Whoever does not love does not know God, because God is love' (4:7-8).

When love is defined in this way, it makes the notion of limiting love to 'romantic love' absurd. Perhaps it does not seem absurd in secular society though, as these views are from religious people; 'religious seekers and thinkers, both men focused attention on the practice of love as a means of spiritual fulfilment' (hooks 2001). The co-creators in this research also experience love in this way, as a 'practice' that leads towards 'spiritual fulfilment'. hooks explains that this view, the view of myself and the co-creators, and also the views of Fromm, King, Merton and Peck, 'differ from much of today's writing. There is always an emphasis in their work on love as an active force that should lead us into greater communion with the world.' (Ibid.) Although Fromm's view is not religious it has the same flavor as the religious teachings on love; he describe this as a 'rational faith' as learning the *art of loving* is essential for human flourishing:

> Indeed, to speak of love is not 'preaching', for the simple reason that it means to speak of the ultimate and real need in every human being. That this need has been obscured does not mean that it does not exist. To analyze the nature of love is to discover its general absence today and to criticize the social conditions which are responsible for this absence. To have faith in the possibility of love as a social and not only exceptional-individual phenomenon, is a rational faith based on the insight into the very nature of man (1956:133).

Merton writes that the wider possibility of love is that instead of 'falling in love' we rise in love:

> Love is, in fact an intensification of life, a completeness, a fullness, a wholeness of life … Life curves upward to a peak of intensity, a high point of value and meaning, at which all its latent creative possibility go into action and the person transcends himself or herself in encounter, response and communion with another. It is for this that we came into the world — this communion and self-transcendence (1979: 26-27).

Wegner (1999) tells us that the problem with romance is not the promise of happiness and fulfilment that it offers, but rather in the fact that it presents such a utopia as an alternative to the contemporary world. This opiate does ease suffering but only provides a compensatory 'illusory happiness' that keeps people from engaging in the hard political struggles that would enable them to transform contemporary social conditions, and thereby perhaps begin to realize for the first time ''real happiness', a heaven on this earth.' (1999: 264)

If the word 'romance' is replaced with eros, it can explain why this 'opiate' can be a vehicle for social action. Eros is an energetic force that both fuels us and enables us to feel the underlying fabric of reality that connects us all, sparking a passion for taking action that benefits the whole. Whether one is a social constructionist, who finds meaning in the context of human beings being connected at their most fundamental nature beyond social constructs, beliefs and identities, who is in love with humanity, or an animist inspired eco-warrior who is in love with nature or a religious mystic who is in love with God and all that was made by God, this type of love is the love that transforms, connects, and includes. By conflating this passion with romantic love our focus is insular, and it limits the power of eros to one relationship rather than to a relationship with many, with a vocation, with the totality of life. The following poem aims to articulate the co-creators' experience of communal erotic intimacy.

*　　*　　*

Erotic Intimacy

Shared Joy ...

Emotional,

Intellectual,

Physical,

Psychic connection

Spiritual bliss

Shared purpose ...

Communion

Creativity

Tee(a)ming with

Vibrancy

Love in action

*　　*　　*

When you replace the word 'romance' for 'eros' any relationship has the possibility to feel 'romantic' including friendships, spiritual connections and even a connection to the divine. In this context relationship hierarchies dissolve and it is also possible to grasp how sometimes intense platonic spiritual relationships are confused with romance and the sexual by onlookers. hooks explains that:

> When we see love as the will to nurture one's own or another's spiritual growth, revealed through acts of care, respect, knowing, and assuming responsibility, the foundation of all love in our life is the same. There is no special love exclusively reserved for romantic partners. Genuine love is the foundation of our engagement with ourselves, with family, with friends, with partners, with everyone we choose to love (2001: 136).

Once the sacred is recognized within everyone, it is easy to treat them like many would only treat a romantic partner. A common view expressed by co-creators was that once you see a person's inner beauty and you want to express that to them, you want to treat them like royalty, like the most special person on the earth. You may express that through serving them, cooking for them, or other gestures to let them know how special they are. However, this can be misconstrued by those who only equate these 'romantic' gestures and erotic intensity with romantic and sexual love. Many great spiritual ecstatic relationships have been sexualized.

There has been much written about the relationship between one of my favorite ecstatic poets and philosophers, Rumi and his relationship with Shams of Tabriz, some of which insinuates that their relationship was sexual. These authors cannot understand the erotic or loving another as a Beloved outside of the sexual and they therefore misunderstand the content of their profound and transformative relationship. This misconception has since been corrected by other scholars.

Harvey (2000) portrays their relationship as a deep spiritual and mystical bond, going beyond traditional understandings of friendship or mentorship. Shams acted as a catalyst for Rumi's spiritual awakening, helping him to move from a life grounded in conventional religious scholarship to a more ecstatic and direct experience of the divine.

Harvey emphasizes that their relationship was characterized by intense love and devotion, but not in a romantic or sexual sense. Instead, it was an expression of divine love, a reflection of Rumi's quest for union with the divine. Shams became the embodiment of God's love for Rumi, and their interaction symbolized the transformative power of such a connection, where the ego is shattered, and the self is opened to the divine. This relationship profoundly influenced Rumi's poetry and his entire spiritual outlook, leading to his creation of some of the most beautiful, poetic expressions of mystical love. Harvey's description of their relationship offers a model of the sacred, eros-filled love that transcends the boundaries of conventional understanding.

I find that the feeling of spiritual love is heightened if the other person is in touch with the sacred within you and within themselves. It is a circling, a reciprocation that intensifies the feeling. I can sometimes even act in 'romantic' ways towards myself, treating myself as I would treat any other person in whom I appreciate an embodied expression of the sacred.

The co-creators and I sought a way to describe that we still want to have physically affectionate relationships with people that are charged with erotic energy. We wanted a way to express this concisely without contributing to the 'asexual paradox' as noted by Smith (2017), of having a sexual orientation to describe an orientation that is not sexual. Those co-creators who were engaged in this process agreed on the term 'platonically erotic'[120]. I decided to search online to see if anyone else had used this term. That is how I found Michele Morano's book *Like Love* (2020), while searching to see if anyone else had used anything similar to this this term only proffered one article; something Morano had written promoting her book. It had the title '*Whoever Said Platonic Love Can't Be Sexy? (Hint: Not Plato)*' (2020).

We hope that 'platonically erotic' conveys a connection that encompasses deep emotional, energetic, or intellectual bonds, characterized by intimacy and intense, passionate feelings, without involving sexual or romantic attraction.

---

[120] Some of the other unusual and seemingly contradictory terms that the co-creators and I played with were "sensual solitude", "poly-amorous, not poly-sexual", "erotic agape".

4.7.3 Loving Solitude

Sing and dance together and be joyous,
but let each one of you be alone.
Even as the strings of a lute are alone
Though they quiver with the same music.
Stand together yet not too near together
For the pillars of the temple stand apart,
And the oak tree and the cypress
Grow not in each other's shadow.
Kahlil Gibran

For both me and the co-creators, learning to love being alone was fundamental to beginning our journeys to becoming erotically embodied asexuals. Once we had become erotically embodied, it added a greater sensuality, joy and pleasure to our solitude. hooks explains that 'knowing how to be solitary is central to the art of loving. When we can be alone, we can be with others without using them as a means of escape.' (2001: 140) Nowen states that 'no friend or lover, no husband or wife, no community or commune will be able to put to rest our deepest cravings for unity and wholeness.' He suggests that in order to meet these cravings for unity and wholeness we need to welcome our solitude and convert:

> loneliness into solitude. Instead of running away from our loneliness and trying to forget or deny it, we have to protect it and turn it into fruitful solitude. ... Loneliness is painful; solitude is peaceful. Loneliness makes us cling to others in desperation; solitude allows us to respect others in their uniqueness and create community. (1986, cited in hooks 2001: 141)

hooks goes on to say that 'individuals young and old striving to overcome fears of being alone often choose meditation practice as a way to embrace solitude. Learning how to 'sit' in stillness and quietude can be the first step toward knowing comfort in aloneness' (p.141). For me and the other co-creators, meditation was crucial to this feeling of loving solitude and as we opened to eros this became infused with energy and pleasurable sensations (see Chapter 7). Connection with nature was also a fundamental part of our erotic embodiment, and spending time alone in nature became a pleasurable active meditation. Nouwen says that 'a man or woman who has developed this solitude of the heart is no longer pulled apart by the most divergent stimuli of the surrounding world but is able to perceive and understand this world from a quiet inner center' (1986: 2).

For all those who participated in this research meditation and mindfulness were essential in finding this 'solitude of the heart' that allowed us to have a 'quiet inner center' and not be influenced by the standard discourse of Western society regarding love, intimacy, and sexuality. We began to develop a sense of being inherently loveable, and, through meditation, started to connect to what we all agree felt like an 'all-pervading sense of love'. As Rilke said, 'what is going on in your innermost being is worthy of your whole love' (cited in Nouwen 1986: 28).

Fromm's conclusion in *The Art of Loving* is that individuals can be truly loving only when they have reached the stage that allows them to be alone and still feel complete and secure. It is only at that point they can offer 'mature love', which 'is *union under the condition of preserving one's integrity,* one's individuality.' (1956: 20) He suggests that it is necessary to have 'a state of intensity, awakeness [sic], enhanced vitality, which can only be the result of a productive and active orientation in many other spheres of life' (Ibid: 129).

Once I started to embrace my solitude and feel the sense of an energy of pervading love, I reflected on how foolish I felt for not realizing it sooner:

(Journal entry, 11 October 2018)

Silly cat, her biscuits are there all the time, but she waits for me, crying and walks to heal looking back at me all down the corridor to the kitchen, then eats them when we're together.

I have often been like this. The love is always there but I waited and cried for someone or that special someone to take me to it so I could eat.

*　*　*

The following poem aims to express the feeling of connection co-creators felt with the Divine, experiencing this as a relationship or an experience that many would label 'romantic':

Walking alone with my Beloved

I walk alone

On moonlit beach

But not Alone

For You are

With Me

My Beloved

Who created

This Beauty

That I may See You

Everywhere

*　*　*

All the co-creators found that by embracing and loving solitude, and discovering within it an erotic, embodied asexuality, they unlocked a key to relating in a way that resonated deeply with them, that felt both liberating and life-enhancing. Daniel Odier confirms that 'becoming free by finding completeness will enable you to have unusual relationships with other people – that is to say, truly warm and sensual relationships that involve the whole body-mind and that escape all classification' (1999: 88), and that 'these relationships will lead you to discover that with each true look, with each profound contact of your relaxed and easeful body, you will receive and transmit the teaching: a peaceful, sensually nourishing, authentic human presence' (Ibid: 89). These 'unusual relationships' can also encompass the inner relationship to self and a transpersonal relationship with the sacred.

As discussed in this chapter, asexuality and aromantic perspectives offer alternatives for intimacy, romance and relationship types. In the case of the asexual and demi-sexual co-creators whose narratives are represented in Chapter 6, approaching a relationship from an erotically embodied asexual perspective offered them a wider choice of intimacy practices within the relationship with their sexual partners and lessened the primacy of sex. The experiences shared by these co-creators also illustrate some of the expressions of the expanded erotic possible within relationship to another and how spirituality adds another dimension to relationships.

4.8. Erotic capital

*The important thing is this: to be able, at any
moment to sacrifice what we are for what
we could become.*
Charles Du Bos 1922

This section explores another process which was fundamental to me
and many of the co-creators in our becoming erotically embodied
asexuals; the process of 'becoming woman' (Deleuze and Guattari
1980). As has been discussed throughout this book, eros is an essence
of life that can infuse even the most mundane tasks with a sense of
connection, joy, love, and pleasure. It is the electric spark that entices
connection and fires creativity (Lorde 1978, Kripal 2007, hooks 2001,
2010). The sexual, in its truly erotic form –rather than its pornographic
quasi-erotic expression– is a part of eros and this expression of the
erotic can be a bridge that leads to the ability to connect to eros in the
seemingly 'everyday' and in non-sexual relationships (Kripal 2007,
hooks 2010, Gafini and Kincaid 2017, Sovatsky 2018). The erotic can
enhance and expand the realm of relationships, both those that are
sexual and non-sexual. The erotic can be a force which propels us
towards a spiritual quest and a mystical connection with something
beyond ourselves.

The suppression and exploitation of the liberating power of eros
within consumer culture was discussed within Chapter 3. However,
once I had started to further digest the theoretical material in
conjunction with starting to communicate with co-creators, I re-
examined my journals. I could see other layers inherent in my
becoming asexual and in the 'becomings' of the co-creators which
related to both Marcuse's (1955, 1974) and Deleuze and Guattari's
(1980) theories. Marcuse (1974) articulated how the suppression and
exploitation of eros within society is achieved through the concurrent

suppression and exploitation of the 'feminine'[121]. True eros has been suppressed in order for humans to be exploited within alienated labor (Marcuse 1955). The quasi-erotic has then been packaged as a product to sell to the hungry masses craving this lost and essential faculty of human existence (Illouz 1997, 2007, 2021, 2022, hooks 2001).

This section explores the concept of 'becoming woman' (Deleuze and Guattari, 1980) and 'androgyny' (Marcuse, 1974), which align with similar ideas in Eastern philosophies, such as Taoism's 'yin and yang.' It examines how cultivating 'feminine' qualities within can lead to a flourishing of eros and a redirection of desire, ultimately generating a new form of 'erotic capital.'

When I say, 'erotic capital', I am not referring to the limited quasi-erotic capital based on sexual attractiveness and allure as posited by Hakim (2010) in her article *Erotic Capital*. I am defining true erotic capital as a profound and holistic appreciation for the beauty of existence. It is a recognition and nurturance of the sacred within the world around us. It is appreciating in full presence the simple sensual pleasures, taking quiet moments of contemplation to appreciate the taste of a delicious meal, or the joy of a simple conversation. The valuing of true erotic capital involves a rejection of the reduction of desires to mere consumption. Erotic embodiment comes from an exploration of the richness of the subtle and profound pleasures to be found in simple things. It is the possibility of creating a more beautiful quality of life by breaking free from the constraints of consumer

---

[121] The 'feminine' here is utilized in the same way that Marcuse (1974) utilized it to describe certain attributes or qualities that have become associated with femininity such as 'receptivity, sensitivity, non-violence, tenderness' (p.283). These are similar to the Taoist category or energy of 'yin', which must be kept in balance with 'yang' the more aggressive, accumulative, directive qualities (which in Western discourse have come to be associated with masculinity). Therefore, when I use 'feminine' and 'masculine' I am using them to refer to a group of qualities which can be developed in anyone, whether they happen to be biologically a man or a woman. Thus, in a similar way to Marcuse, I am using 'feminine' and 'masculine' as a recognition that masculinity and femininity are a spectrum of qualities, that can be displayed and cultivated by anyone regardless of their birth sex.

culture and embracing the eros inherent in everything. This is a form of capital that cannot be bought, sold, or taken from us, and it is unlimited once we have opened our capacity to receive it.

Erotically embodied asexuals offer a living example of Marcuse's (1974) vision of 'a qualitatively different way of life' where individuals 'would not only use the productive forces for the reduction of alienated labor and labor time, but also for making life an end in itself, for the development of the senses and the intellect for pacification of aggressiveness'. He suggested that this liberation of eros would increase 'the enjoyment of being' and facilitate 'the emancipation of the senses and of the intellect from the rationality of domination' and led to the rise of 'creative receptivity versus repressive productivity' (p.286)

Far from seeing the 'feminine characteristics' as submissive or weak, Marcuse saw them as a revolutionary force with 'the feminine characteristics' having the potential to activate a new kind of power, a powerful creative, caring and loving energy as a counter force 'against domination and exploitation'. He articulated that the problem with society's current 'emancipation of the female and the feminine energy' is that although women to some extent have been physically and intellectually emancipated, at the same time 'this emancipation is arrested, manipulated, and exploited by this Society' (Ibid: 285) by the dynamic of 'the working woman [continuing], in ever larger numbers, to suffer the double exploitation as worker and housewife. In this form, the reification of the woman persists in a particularly effective manner' (Ibid.). He postulates that in order for this reification to be dissolved and for the true emancipation of the woman to become a decisive force in building a qualitatively different society, that the fullness of eros, and other 'feminine' qualities will need to be realized and valued.

Kellner (1984) predicted that the realization of Marcuse's vision of 'emancipation' will occur through the re-eroticization of the 'de-eroticized capitalist body, and the binding together of individuals through work, play, art and culture, in a sensuous, libidinally gratifying, new order; one in which reason and happiness converge' (p.104, cited in Williams and Bendelow 1998). Williams and Bendelow reassure us that the 'alienation and aggression, misery and suffering' experienced within a capitalist system are not 'therefore (biologically) inevitable' and that they are 'simply an artefact of socioeconomic restrictions and patriarchal taboos imposed on the 'wisdom of the body' (1998: 102).

The re-eroticization, that Marcuse offered as the key to liberation, may not currently be noticeable on a societal level, but within the world of the researcher and co-creators this reconnection with the 'wisdom of the body' and the fullness of the erotic has led to a reduction in consumption and the view that the most important form of 'capital' is nonsexual erotic capital. Marcuse (1974) argued that to be liberated from commodified lives, both men and women would need to embrace more of the 'feminine' characteristics which are currently suppressed. Marcuse describes eros as a 'feminine' attribute. When he talks of 'the feminine' Marcuse explains that he is describing this as qualities that we label 'feminine attributes' rather than them only being applicable to women. He likewise describes the attributes associated with the 'performance principle'[122] as

---

[122] Marcuse (1974) described defined reality principles as the 'sum total of the norms and values which govern behavior in an established society' (p.279). He then defines the 'performance principle' as 'a 'reality principle' based on the efficiency and prowess in the fulfilment of competitive economic and acquisitive functions' (Ibid.) Marcuse asserts that the 'performance principle' is 'the rule of functional rationality discriminating against emotions, dual morality ... the 'work ethic', which means for the vast majority of the population condemnation to alienated and inhuman labor, and the will to power, the display of strength, virility.' (Ibid: 282) He describes the characteristics, which he considers 'masculine' as 'profitable productivity, assertiveness, efficiency, competitiveness'. (Ibid.) He goes on to speak of a 'value hierarchy' in the capitalist society that values these 'masculine' traits above the 'feminine' traits, both in men and women. He explains that 'according to Freud, this value hierarchy is expressive of a mental structure in which primary aggressive energy tends to reduce and to weaken the life instincts, that is, erotic energy.' (Ibid.)

'masculine' attributes which are also not simply applicable to men. In a similar way to the yin and yang in Taoism, Marcuse is suggesting that the 'feminine' and 'masculine' are ways to describe sets of polarizing characteristics that can be brought into union for a more balanced human being and society.

4.8.1 Becoming woman

Looking back through my journals, with this new lens, I can now see another important theme which did not stand out to me during my first analysis. This was a significant part of my personal development that I can now only name 'becoming woman' (Deleuze and Guattari 1980). On reading this term, I felt my body soften in recognition of an idea embodied. Williams and Bendelow (1998) state that 'all becomings, for Deleuze and Guattari, are 'minoritarian', and must necessarily pass through the process of what they term 'becoming-woman' as an abstract line of flight.' (p.109) Deleuze and Guattari are not talking about physically becoming a woman, in their own words:

> What we term a molar entity is, for example, the woman as defined by her form, endowed with organs and functions, and assigned as a subject. Becoming woman is not imitating this entity or even transforming oneself into it.... All we are saying is that these indissociable aspects of becoming woman must first be understood as a function of something else: not imitating or assuming the female form, but emitting particles that enter the relation of movement and rest, or the zone of proximity, of a microfemininity, in other words, that produce in us a molecular woman, create the molecular woman. We do not mean to say that a creation of this kind is the prerogative of the man, but on the contrary that the woman as a molar entity has to become-woman in order that the man also becomes—or can become-woman. (1980:275–6)

I felt their articulation of a journey I had wrestled with throughout numerous journal entries, relationships and conversations (both therapeutic and personal). My journey was one of 'deterritorialization' and 'reterritorialization'. I had to move away from a culture dominated by the masculine qualities or as Marcuse named it the 'Performance Principle' (1974), in order to embody other qualities which would serve me better. This reflects Marcuse's statement that 'the social basis for the antithesis to the Performance Principle is the emancipation of female and feminine energy' (1974:285).

My first introduction to the notions of masculine and feminine principles was through Jungian psychology[123] during my *Bodymind Attunement* therapist training (a somatic awareness and psychodynamic therapy). The principles of the anima and animus[124] and reclaiming this lost part of myself in a form of inner 'romantic relationship', was a wonderful imaginal tool for my romantically focused mind at that time. However, what became apparent was that I did not feel like I was reclaiming a 'masculine' lost part of myself, even though I am a woman. I felt very masculine 'inside', I could not find many 'feminine' qualities, and those that I did have I tried to suppress. I realized that I was always the 'knight in shining armor' in my relationships. I had a tendency to have relationships with men who needed support, and I would 'rescue' them. I was without deviation, the main breadwinner in all my relationships. In this position I can see now that I had power and control. The means to keep my objectified supply of romantic highs close and dependent.

---

[123] Jung's gender ideology and theory of archetypes has been taken up by a number of movements in the holistic milieu and further afield. Robert A Johnston (1985) explores this in relation to the notion of romantic love and how it represents and inner journey to wholeness that we should not project outwards onto an idealized 'other'. Johnston postulates that Jung's various archetypes can help one to self-reflect and come to wholeness; he focuses on Jung's concepts of the female's *animus* (the inner male aspect of a woman) and the male's *anima* (the inner female aspect of a man). He tells us that until we claim and develop these aspects or essential qualities of ourselves, we will constantly project them outwards and find them in external 'others' who we will have unrealistic, idealized romantic relationships with.

[124] See the footnote above for a description of the anima and animus.

When I started to self-reflect, I was horrified to realize I was also dominating myself with this ambitious, insensitive, aggressive, achieving 'masculine' aspect. I realized that in order to find some kind of inner balance, I would first need to work on my 'masculine' attributes and ensure that these were healthy. I thought that then, my 'feminine' aspects may be able to flourish in a safe inner environment, held by a strong, directive, supportive, protective masculine, thus developing strengths from traits that I already had (or as Jung would poetically say I went on a quest to 'find the gold in my shadow').

During this process I started to notice the imbalance in the society around me and how I reflected this. Another thing I noticed, as I focused on the 'feminine' aspects that I longed to welcome home, was the sometimes insidious and often blatant misogyny in Western culture. This started to bother me, irritate me, almost to obsession. With horror I realized that my unhealthy inner 'masculine' was a misogynist, and I had been actively suppressing my 'feminine' qualities and equally despised and denigrated them in others.

I worked on this throughout my four-year therapist training. Once I was able to welcome my vulnerability and become more receptive, I found a growing pleasure in being in my body and I felt less like a disembodied and directing 'head'. I felt able to honor my creative energies, simply for the sake of the joy of being creative, rather than for financial reward. I started to honor and celebrate my role of 'mother' and 'homemaker' as an expression of love infused with the erotic, and I started to ponder how the 'emancipation' of women as being freed from their caretaking duties, was actually a double bind.

My primary focus became my children (although, as a single mother, in order to have this focus, I did have to get up at 4am to work for 4 hours before they got up every day[125]) and, as the everyday

---

[125] As a single mother, I had to find ways to bring both the feminine and masculine parental aspects to my children and simultaneously offer both mothering and fathering to them. I partially fulfilled this by being fully in my newly reclaimed nurturing, emotionally sensitive

spent in presence was becoming erotically infused, this was the perfect way to spend a life. I considered parenting consciously, with awareness and choice, based on researching alternative ways of being, the ultimate spiritual path. As discussed previously, during this research I discovered that Marcuse had already pondered upon this problem of the emancipation of women in our current social system simply being a 'double exploitation' (1974:285).

At the beginning of the therapist training, I was also completing my training to be a mindful-movement teacher. Due to the introduction to Jungian psychology, I started to become more aware of parallels in Eastern philosophy, where the 'feminine' and 'masculine' qualities are described as moon and sun. These, rather than remaining as imaginal concepts, or 'inner characters', are energies that can be felt within the body. Within the neo-tantra community most participants have some understanding of this non biological 'masculine' and 'feminine', as qualities that can be developed within either sex, whether they are understanding this through the Taoist 'yin' and 'yang' the Jungian 'anima' and 'animus', or just the more vague and idealized new age 'sacred feminine' and 'sacred masculine'. Bishop (2019) describes these characteristics found within 'holistic spirituality' thus:

> The masculine characteristics are thought to include, but not limited to: direction, clarity, pointedness, stability, ambition, rationality, business acumen, strength, consciousness, and decisiveness; while feminine qualities include but are not limited to: sensitivity, sensuality, softness, nurture, maternalism, spontaneity, and receptivity (p.29).

---

and creative femininity whilst offering the masculine elements through puppetry with a 'male' voice, authority and discipline. I also told them 'Grandpa' stories every night before bed. In these improvised stories, two little boys would walk through the forest, a forest alive with all the aspects from the season we were in, to Grandpa's house. He would sit with them by the fire and tell them a wisdom story, based on personal issues they were facing or current social issues that were impacting them. This offered them a daily voice of wisdom and subtle direction from a wise 'male' elder.

Marcuse (1974) describes the idea of developing this inner 'androgynism' as 'the fusion, in the individual, of the mental and somatic characteristics, which in patriarchal civilization were unequally developed in men and women' (p.288). He describes this as 'a fusion in which feminine characteristics, in cancellation of male dominance, would prevail over their repression'. But he goes on to say, 'no degree of androgynous fusion could ever abolish the natural differences between male and female as individuals.' He explains that 'all joy, and all sorrow are rooted in this difference, in this relation to the other, of whom you want to become part, and who you want become part of yourself, and who never can and never will become such a part of yourself.'

Marcuse's view is reflected in neo-tantra, where it said that:

the opposition (or 'polarity') of Feminine and Masculine energies means that when they do come into contact, energy and attraction is created (the analogy of positive and negative ends of a magnet is often used) (Bishop 2019: 29).

Bishop shares that 'a London-based Tantra and Yoga teacher Adrienne' described the following to her:

That polarity between the feminine and the masculine, both inside our own beings and between beings, is what creates the 'zzz' ['electricity' noise], the magic in relationships and love and life and music and art and cooking and everything. Each person is thought to contain both essential principles; however, in each individual, either the feminine or masculine aspect is seen as being expressed more than the other (Ibid.).

A co-creator shared how he found these imaginal and energetic practices useful in his journey. He told me that becoming more 'feminine' or receptive and vulnerable in his sexuality was key to him experiencing full body ecstatic states and eventually becoming asexual. He said for him, it was about overcoming the feeling that opening to the energetic sensation, which felt penetrating at the perineum was sexual and perhaps 'homosexual' in nature. He said that when he experiences surges of life force energy (libido) they start at his perineum. Before he learned to be more vulnerable and receptive, that energy would get stuck at the base and move towards his genitals and cause an erection. However, once he could relax and be receptive, that energy moved backwards towards the base of his spine, moving up his spinal column and then erupting out of his chest in all directions, through his limbs and into his head, and lower torso in waves of ecstasy. 'Becoming woman' was essential to him experiencing ecstatic body states and erotic embodiment. The following co-created poem is based on his experience.

*　*　*

The Routed Root

He always thought

That pulsating

In perineum

Had one direction

Penetration

Now he knows

This life force

His root of Life Energy

Pulse enlivening

Routed by choice

He always thought

That tumescence

Was genital

Uncomfortable

Undesired

He now knows

To direct

Energy swelling up

Through spine, throat, head

Dissolving into Love and Beauty

*   *   *

The co-creators and I found the study of Eastern spiritual practices central to the process of moving out of our habituated understandings of ourselves, finding inner balance and experiencing a redirection of libido. Deleuze and Guattari (1972) spoke of this process as becoming a 'body without organs' with uninterrupted 'flows of desire' and confirmed that in order for this to occur a process of 'deterritorialization' is necessary. Williams and Bendelow (1998) describe how within *Anti-Oedipus* (Deleuze and Guattari 1972) the goal is to rediscover the unbounded flows of desire, those not constrained by Oedipal codes and neurotic territorialities. They explain that this involves a psychopolitical analysis where the interplay between desire, reality, and the capitalist 'machine' provides insights into practical questions. Foucault (1972, cited in Williams and Bendelow, Ibid.) emphasizes this perspective by stating, 'Ars erotica, ars theoretica, ars politica.' As Deleuze and Guattari (1972) assert, 'desire is revolutionary in its essence,' challenging societal structures of exploitation, servitude, and hierarchy. This viewpoint blurs the lines between the personal and the social, the individual and the collective, as both the political and psychological realms are influenced by the same libidinal energy.

For both the men and women co-creators, 'becoming woman' seemed to correlate with the expansion into the fullness of eros, the redirection of the flow of desire, and the ability to experience full body ecstatic states, not just as a philosophical idea, but as a lived, embodied experience. Their experiences correlate with the philosophy of Deleuze and Guattari (1972, 1980), as the co-creators found that when eros or desire is freed, along with the means to produce freely – that they wished to create for, and serve the people whom they love passionately and indiscriminately, voluntarily without direct economic reward. With this lens it is easy to see, in the way that Marcuse (1955, 1974) did, that capitalism suppresses eros both through its mechanisms and the complicit participation of its population, invested in the quasi-erotic. This suppression is beneficial to the maintenance of the system – the fullness of realizing and feeling desire without an object, the flow of the erotic towards spiritual connection, can lead to transcendence and a spiritual satisfaction that no longer leaves an emptiness that needs to be filled with consumption (Deleuze and Guattari 1972, 1980, Odier 1999, Stryker 2011).

Williams and Bendelow question Deleuze and Guattari's work saying:

> This in turn connects up with another 'latent' problem regarding Deleuze's and Guattari's notion of 'becoming'. Despite being shrouded in notions of contingency, unpredictability and abstract lines of flight, their discussion of this process none the less suggests an underlying telos or determinate end-point: a direction in which, judgmentally, they suggest we should all be moving. There may also be an 'implicit' hierarchy lurking within Deleuze's and Guattari's discussion of becoming-woman, child, animal, imperceptible. (1998: 111)

I would argue from the perspective of the narratives collected within this research and the extant literature, that Deleuze and Guattari's 'becoming' and flows of desire lead to desire desiring itself.

Rod Stryker (2011) explains that once we have fulfilled a desire, we feel fulfilled for a while before moving onto the next desire. He describes desire as the erotic energy of the desire for life to exist and evolve. The feeling of desire is energizing and erotic in itself. I have found that the ability to experience this desire without an object, or towards a transpersonal other, is thrilling and that rather than having a sense of 'wanting' anything, I just want to feel the sense of desire coursing through me or over me. All those who participated in this research do not experience this erotic desiring force as a prison as presented by Williams and Bendelow:

> Desire itself, predicated as it is on a fundamental lack, becomes the ultimate metonymy of the 'desire to want to be'. Indeed all our fantasies, according to Lacan, are symbolic representations of this desire for wholeness—something to which we are all condemned from birth. (1998: 96)

The desire that initiated my and the co-creators' liberating 'becomings' could also be described as a 'desire for wholeness'. This is seen as an emancipating flow by Daniel Odier (1999) and Rod Stryker (2011). Odier offers us a view of fully realized desire that offers a liberation from Lacan's prison, he tells us that:

> Dissatisfaction will cease to exist, as will outer demands, because it is the whole of life that brings you this loving tremoring. There is no longer something missing to make up for; it is the unrestrained intensity of your desire that fulfils you now, and no longer the ideas of possessing, of seducing, of filling a void, of feeding your dissatisfaction. (1999: 88)

He goes on to say that 'curiously, you will see that the more incandescent your desire, the less it will turn toward objects of desire, because it no longer needs them to mask incompletion.' He also tells us that this this is what 'tantrikas experience and know, and that this is what is so misunderstood by those who see Tantrism as a quest for ego-tied sexual satisfaction.' Stryker describes this as:

> a complete and enduring fulfilment ... a kind of wealth far beyond the riches and accomplishments found in the material world. It is an indestructible treasure, one that can never be lost or taken away. Throughout the ages it has been described in various ways as the unfolding of the most glorious presence, a contentment that words can never fully convey (2011:10-11).

Some of the descriptions offered by co-creators of this desire flowing without an object, or towards a transcendent 'object', were: 'it is embodied bliss', 'it is life loving life', 'it is life desiring being fully alive' and 'it is life desiring life'. This resonance that the co-creators offered is one I feel in Deleuze and Guattari's writings. However, an important point to note is that although feeling this flow of undirected desire is now often an ecstatic transcendent feeling, or simply a gentle background pleasure during action undertaken in presence, getting to the place where this is an uninterrupted flow was quite painful. The flow of the life force 'pushes against' all that stands in its way, and it was an arduous process of much reflection, mental, physical, and spiritual practice. I am guessing that this is the 'pain' that Lacan refers to when he tells us that when one transgresses a certain level of pleasure, the sensation is experienced as pain (1959:184). I endeavor to capture the experience of this process in the following poem.

* * *

The pain of opening

"How much Beauty can you tolerate?"
My teacher asks me
When I describe the pain of my heart opening
Tears flowing with Grace

How much ecstasy is bearable?
I ask myself
As Life's breath rushes irrepressibly through me
Body shaking, releasing involuntary gasps

* * *

Rod Stryker acknowledges this process and speaks about how the path to fulfilling desire demands that 'you apply skill, sensitivity, insight, courage, compassion, surrender, strength and love' (2011: xvii). He goes on to say that fulfilment 'cannot be achieved merely by thinking about it, nor simply by making a random decision about what you want and then sitting back with an expectation that it will happen.' He is advocating for disciplined practice and facing challenge as the only way to achieve fulfilment, guarding against offerings such as 'new age' workshops, visualization techniques and initiations which promise instant gratification and evolution. As mentioned previously, although the co-creators had all spent much time within new age and neo-tantra communities, they also had disciplined spiritual or religious practices outside of this. However, the ideas that they discovered with these communities were also seen as influential to their 'becoming' erotically embodied asexuals, as discussed earlier in this chapter.

4.9 Asexual pleasure

If the mind remains in women and gold, nothing will happen.
When the vision of The Beloved happens, the bliss is millions of times
greater than sexual pleasure.
Matsyendranath

All the co-creators reported that part of fully flourishing into eros can be an experience of embodied ecstasy. They identified this experience with the redirection of the libido throughout their bodies and described this as an 'ecstatic life force'. hooks (2010) explains that 'eros as the passionate life instinct triggered by libido is what makes us able to experience the ecstatic in our bodies' (hooks 2010: 155). Within Western culture's limited discourse regarding the erotic as sexual, this erotic somatic ecstasy is also limited to the sexual. By limiting the erotic to the sexual it is impossible to understand full body ecstatic states as anything but sexual.

The narratives of the erotically embodied asexual co-creators challenge this misconception as do the ecstatic Christian mystics described by Smith (2017). Both groups of individuals describe the movement of energy, pulsations, tremoring, pleasure and ecstasy, which most people only experience during sexual orgasm, as being something they experience through activities such as art, music, dance or meditation. This section explores this, continuing in the theoretical and empirical layered format, and the conclusion of this book is a gallery of co-produced poetry describing these experiences. The following poem endeavors to describe locating this nonsexual pleasurable lifeforce within the body.

* * *

Become intimately familiar

With the part of you that's alive

How you know that you're alive on a physical level

Get a sense of that

Locate it in your body

Cultivate your awareness

Allow it to expand

To exhilaratingly encompass you

* * *

In discussions regarding my research, the concept of nonsexual orgasm, seemed to be a difficult one to grasp for those who have not experienced it. It seems to be challenging for those who have not experienced such nonsexual pleasure to perceive of such a thing. It is, however, a common occurrence for those who participated in this research. Kripal (2007) tells us that:

> The hermeneutical challenge consists in trying to understand other 'astonishing' ontological conceptions of human sexuality, which are in turn embedded in elaborate webs of cultural practices and emotional fields, and allowing these to define and guide, at least initially, one's own interpretations. Something like erotic forms of mysticism, in other words, cannot be discussed comparatively, as if they were all minor variations on the exact same thing. Behind such a discourse lies the unspoken assumption that every time and culture has more or less agreed on the ontological natures of spiritual and sexual experience and on the manner in which they do or do not intersect (p.164).

For me, the key to this challenge is being open to accepting others' experiences, experiencing similar things myself and/or getting an embodied sense of what is being written about whilst reading. Kripal explains that it is important to acknowledge the cultures and sub-cultures within which individuals have their experiences and the varying experiences these may create:

> Such a discourse also ignores the very real possibility that different cultural systems set their actors up for radically different subjective and emotional experiences of the body and its energies, in effect creating different life-worlds with different social practices and symbolic systems (2007:164).

This would also apply to actors who have traversed various cultural systems in a process of 'deterritorialization', who therefore have 'radically different subjective and emotional experiences of the body and its energies'. A body open to experiences outside of its original cultural understanding can bridge cultural boundaries, as Kripal tells us, 'our bodies at least know that cultural boundaries are fictions, and that physical communion is quite possible between and beyond them' (2007: 164).

Again, we encounter the problem with the limits of language to describe embodied experiences. I love to study languages, to feel the essence of words as they create sensations in my body, and I have an appreciation for how some words cannot be translated, they must be *felt* to be understood. As with love and romance, where I found more resonance with the wealth of words in other languages, I have found the same with describing pleasure, particularly nonsexual pleasure, for which we seem to have no adequate words in English (which possibly could be seen as a reflection of our lack ability to connect to these more subtle embodied pleasures in hypersexualized and commodified cultures).

Jane Gallop explains that 'it is impossible to give an adequate translation of *jouissance* saying that it is a 'word for pleasure which defies translation' (2018: 110). She goes on to say how many writers 'choose not to translate the word *jouissance*, not to assimilate it, but to retain its foreignness'. The translator, Claire Marie Frock, encountered similar problems when translating Daniel Odier's book *Desire: The Tantric Path to Awakening*. Odier uses the term *fremissante* within his original text 'to indicate the idea of *spanda*' (1999: 13), which Frock explains, 'has been translated variously as 'the divine pulsation' or 'vibratory dynamism of the absolute consciousness''. She goes on to say that 'here, *inner/sacred/divine tremor* or *tremoring vibration* will be used in absence of a single English word that adequately conveys this sense of *fremir*[126] and *spanda*'. I in-joy these words; both of these words evoke strong sensations in my body; *jouissance* a thrilling expanding energy moving from toes to head, rushing through me and *fremissante* a gentle, simmering pulsation which energizes me, warming my heart and creating a tingling sensation in the area of my brain (this is not just a physical sensation

---

[126] Fremir is a French verb meaning 'to tremor, to quiver, to shudder, to shiver, to thrill, to simmer (as in water)' (Odier 1999: 13). It is a beautiful word that does an adequate job of pointing towards the background simmering pleasure that I, and others, find in all mindful or present activities, once we had discovered an embodied presence. It aids in the understanding of Lorde's (1978) definition of an expanded erotic that is present in all activities to varying degrees.

in my head, but feels like a more subtle sense of sensation in the broader energy outside of the material 'mind'). As I write about it now, because I am focusing on the sensation in my head, it grows with my attention, I feel it expanding outwards from the area of my head down my neck and into my shoulders, meeting the feeling of warmth in my heart.

Cross cultural understanding is necessary to understand, or perhaps be open to, the experience of nonsexual embodied ecstasy or 'orgasm'. This type of pleasure, in a similar way to eros, cannot simply be conflated with the sexual. Sexuality is a concept; pleasure is an embodied experience. If we are able to drop the concept, perhaps more pleasure would be available to us. Kripal states that 'the category of *sexuality* is usually understood to refer to a biologically driven instinct that, although genetically determined to varying degrees, is nevertheless open to the profound cultural conditioning and influences of the social environment in which it develops' (2007: 165). Marcuse argued that the suppression of eros had resulted in its distorted expression in Western society. He proposed that the liberation or transformation of eros would lead to a 'decline of genital supremacy,' where the entire body becomes an object of cathexis, 'a thing to be enjoyed—an instrument of pleasure' (1955: 201).

Williams and Bendelow explain how it is the intense focus on particular organs that given them their significance, they suggest that body image is shaped by the changing emotional and libidinal intensities assigned by an individual to different bodily zones, organs, and functions. They explain that these emotional investments influence the significance and form of body image, with the dynamics of 'libidinous tendencies' determining the varying value and clarity of different body-image components. They also suggest that body image is likely to differ based on an individual's 'psychosexual tendencies' (1998: 98).

I found a journal entry describing an experience that illustrates Williams and Bendelow's suggestion that 'libidinal intensities' in various organs and body parts are influenced by the individual's awareness and focus. It was written after a 'somatic awareness' class:

(Journal entry, 11 January 2001)

Wow! What a strange but wonderful class today. When Brian said we would be focusing on moving our right arm, particularly the hand and the wrist I thought 'what for over an hour?!' How bizarre.

Oh my ... The RESISTANCE! I was so bored, I really felt like stopping these stupid small movements. The intense focus on my hand was annoying me so much. But then I relaxed, I thought, well if I'm going to be here I may as well get into it. It did still feel weird just focusing on my hand and wrist and doing various movements of the arm.

At the end though ... it was incredible, I'd never experienced anything like it. My right arm and hand, particularly my hand felt huge. I mean HUGE. Almost like my hand was bigger than the rest of me! And the sensations in my hand – it was like my hand was picking up all the energy in the room and buzzing.

* * *

The theoretical discussion offered by Williams and Bendelow and the diary entry illustrate how body zones and sensation grow with awareness and focus. This means that if we are conditioned and stimulated to focus on our genitals as the only source of orgasmic pleasure, and then further encouraged by those who wish to sell us things to focus on our sexual instinct, it becomes a self-fulfilling cycle of constant desire, the focus on how that desire can be fulfilled, and the limitation of the fulfilment of that desire. C S Lewis puts it very eloquently, talking about 'the state into which the sexual instinct has got now':

> There is nothing to be ashamed of in enjoying your food : there would be everything to be ashamed of if half the world made food the main interest of their lives and spent their time looking at pictures of food and dribbling and smacking their lips. I do not say you and I are individually responsible for the present situation. Our ancestors have handed over to us organisms which are warped in this respect : and we grow up surrounded by propaganda in favour of unchastity. There are people who want to keep our sex instinct inflamed in order to make money out of us. Because, of course, a man with an obsession is a man who has very little sales-resistance. (1952: 89)

He also explains that 'the old Christian teachers said that if man had never fallen, sexual pleasure, instead of being less than it is now, would actually have been greater' (Lewis 1952:88). I was very interested in this point, but I have not managed to find any further references. My interpretation of this is that if 'man' had not become so focused on genital sex, full body ecstatic states and pleasure would have been possible.

However, the co-creators' narratives illustrate that this pleasure is available to us, that it is possible to 'rewrite' the body in terms 'quite different' from those which 'currently mark it' (Williams and Bendelow 1998: 97). This 'rewriting' of the body has occurred for all of the co-creators in this research; both for those who already felt 'asexual' and became erotically embodied and for those who moved from being sexual to becoming erotically embodied asexuals. As mentioned before, all the co-creators have a practice of some type of somatic awareness and/or movement practice. All have had massage therapy regularly. All have some acknowledgement of the sense of energy and its 'touch' on both the inside of the body and the epidermis of the body, in addition to the traditional sense of touch in Western culture. The co-creators also have experience of practices that focus on the sensation of the movement of this energy, through dance, embodied meditation, mindful movement, and breath.

In discussions, many have challenged me regarding the possibility of nonsexual orgasm, they argue that orgasm has to be sexual and originate in the genitals. However, there has been recent research published by Pfaus and Tsarski (2022) into *A Case of Female Orgasm Without Genital Stimulation*. They investigated a 33-year-old woman who had developed the ability to attain and control the duration of a subjective orgasmic state without genital stimulation after tantric training. They explain that 'prolactin surges after orgasm are an objective marker of orgasm quality' (p.1) and concluded that the 'increase in prolactin after her Non Genital Stimulated Orgasms indicate that they induce the same physiological changes as Genitally Stimulated Orgasms and result from 'top-down' processing in the brain.' (p.2) Although this is described in clinical terms, rather than embodied experiential terms, it does give some scientific credence, for those who want such a thing, to the fact that non genital orgasms are possible.

All the co-creators had experiences of asexual orgasmic pleasure. For some this was during somatic awareness or movement, an embodied psychospiritual experience, for many it included experiences of the eco-erotic, or the embodied pleasure experienced whilst creating. Many of the co-creators experienced nonsexual orgasmic states during meditation, mindful energetic connection with another, or other nonsexual intimacy practices (described earlier in this chapter). A gallery of poems articulating this experience of asexual erotic embodiment and pleasure is offered in Chapter 7.

5. Stories from the Intermezzo[127]

I am well aware that I have never written anything but fictions. I do not mean to say, however, that truth is therefore absent. It seems to me that the possibility exists for fiction to function in truth, for a fictional discourse to induce effects of truth, and for bringing it about that a true discourse engenders or 'manufactures' something that does not as yet exist, that is, 'fictions' it.
Foucault, 1980: 193

This chapter describes the initial phases of asexual 'becomings'. The place where individuals were on the threshold of becoming erotically embodied asexuals, or in the case of those who were already asexual, were on the threshold of becoming erotically embodied, or discovering erotic nonsexual intimacy. Due to the ethical stance of the research, these experiences are presented as composite fictions. Although these experiences are fictionalized, they retain the meaning and impacts of the types of practices and interactions that led to the

---

127 Deleuze and Guattari (1980) use the term 'intermezzo' to refer to the space between points, concepts, context and content, where there is a pause, a silence, a sense of possibility.

co-creators 'becomings'. They give examples of how nonsexual erotic intimacy enhanced the experiences of asexual co-creators, how experiences of desubjectification can lead to a natural asexual becoming and how asexuality can be an option, a choice, a chosen becoming. It also starts to narrate the challenge of negotiating intimacy between sexual individuals and asexuals, and how the nonsexual erotic can be the bridge that facilitates this connection, allowing these relationships to flourish. The fictions also illuminate the social interaction that was inherent and important to the 'becomings' of the co-creators, and the importance of acknowledging social interaction in the process of identity and lifestyle formation.

This approach was inspired by Kay Inckle (2006, 2007) who utilized a similar approach within the conclusion of her doctoral thesis and her subsequent book, utilizing sociological fiction to enable the articulation of a wider sphere of experience, and achieve a greater level of anonymity. She explains:

> None of the women, as they are constructed here, would be easily recognisable to anyone but myself. I have fictionalised enough of their immediate biographies for the characters who appear on these pages to be entirely distinct from the individuals I have encountered. However, the themes of their original stories remain true—or at least to the way in which I understood and interpreted them. Finally, I hope that, if self-recognition was to occur, then it would arise in a context which is empathic, transformative, generative and hopeful. (2007: 203)

In a similar way, I have veiled immediate biographies in the fabric of fiction, utilizing the interpretations of experiences, ethnographic observations from my journals, and reflexivity. All the co-creators were engaged in the process of interpretation, and most were engaged with influencing the content of the stories. The essence of the original experiences is present in these fictions, resonating true—or, at the very least, to the melody of my understanding and interpretation. As with all of the creative pieces based on experiences, these fictions 'leave open the possibilities of meaning, interpretation and transformation.' (Inckle 2006: 14-15)

These four pieces of sociological fiction are based at a fictionalized Intimacy Festival, based on similar festivals at neo-tantric, new age retreat centers, with the fictional name *The Retreat*. Similar centers were frequented, in the past, by the co-creators. The pieces are subtly interlinked but are separate stories. The third story includes the perspectives of two characters and the switch is indicated by three stars within the text ' * * *'.

5.1 Among the sexuals

You can't stay in your corner of the
Forest waiting for others to come to you.
You have to go to them sometimes.
A.A. Milne, Winnie the Pooh

Arrival

Rach opens the heavy wooden door and steps into a large porch filled with an assortment of muddy boots and wellies. The main entrance door looms before her. Why did she come? Her hand reaches out for the imposing brass doorknob, just as someone sweeps open the door from the inside. A beaming face greets her, "Welcome to *The Retreat!*"

Her eyes flit from the beaming face, long enough to see groups of people sprawled across couches in the large entrance hall; entanglements of legs, bodies slumped in the accommodating gap between open thighs, some enjoying shoulder and neck massages. There are a couple of intimate hugs taking place in inconvenient locations, leading to a queue of patient people waiting to get past. Her question of *Why did I come?* evaporates into a sense of *I need to leave now.*

She feels like a fish out of water and her ability to breathe seems to be synonymous with that scenario. No matter, the breath would have been squeezed out of her in any case, because suddenly the beaming face is resting against her cheek, and she has been pressed into a full body welcome hug.

It is a hug unlike any she has experienced before. The body belonging to the beaming face is pressing against her body in every place it is possible to press. Cheek to cheek, chest to chest, tummy to tummy, genitals to genitals, and even legs somehow adeptly inserted around hers, in one quick move. Beaming Face is breathing so deeply, she wonders if he is breathing for them both and then realizes that she is actually breathing again, but that they are breathing in time. His body is welcoming, soft and passive and she finds she is relaxing. Looking over his shoulder the scene starts to appear less like a sex orgy and more like an enthralling picture of the non-sexual intimacy she has been craving, and yet not quite daring to imagine.

It was a big decision for her to come to the festival, a decision fueled by desperation. As an Aroace[128], finding intimate connections has not been easy. Her Ace friends who are looking for romantic connection find it slightly easier; at least they can date sexual people and navigate that hurdle at some point into the relationship. Not easy, she knows, but it is almost impossible without a romantic inclination.

When a Poly[129] friend of hers first told her about *The Retreat* community, she was intrigued but felt she would be an outsider. Most people there were Poly or Tantric and by default, dead into sex, even if they were breaking the boundaries of traditional romantic

---

[128] The colloquial term for being Aromantic and Asexual in the Asexual Community. Ace is a term for being Asexual and Aro is a term for being Aromantic.

[129] Colloquial term for Polyamorous – having multiple romantic relationships.

relationship structures. Her friend's description of the non-sexual intimacies that abounded at the community intrigued and enticed her though. She loved touch, the thrilling sensation of a hand gliding up her arm, just sleeping cozy together in bed, the warmth of holding hands, a soft kiss on the lips. These things had been easy when she was young, with friends and siblings, but that all changed as they grew up and others' sexual feelings and obsessions got in the way.

She had therefore dared to add her email to their mailing list on the website and had been receiving emails from them for some time. Some of which she did not even open due to the off-putting titles such as *'conscious kink'*, *'union of shiva and shakti'*, and *'tantric sexual liberation'*. The one entitled *'Intimacy Festival'* with a subhead *'Drop into a space of the heart and make connections with new friends'* was the one that had lured her in. It promised so much of what she wanted; non-sexual yet sensual, alive touch and loving, full-hearted friendships with attractive people (yes, she had an eye for cute people of all genders, with a strong propensity for aesthetic attraction[130]).

The addition of a venue beyond the boundaries of the festival site, a shed-like structure called the *'Cock Inn'*, perhaps should have been enough to put her off, but to her, this was a selling point. The fact that, at the *Intimacy Festival,* full sex with penetration is so discouraged that those that cannot refrain have to take themselves to an insalubrious venue, strewn with drape-divided mattresses. A mockingly named venue, seeming to reverse the usual narrative where sex is the goal, and she is left feeling ashamed for not wanting it.

Now as she looks around, a new world of possibility opens up. She focuses in on one of the groups on the sofa; they have name badges sporting *The Retreat* logo, so they must be community members. Their closeness is palpable and enchanting in equal measure. They are

---

[130] Attraction purely based on enjoying the physical appearance of the other rather than sexual attraction linked to sexual desire.

clearly taking pleasure in each other's company. There seems to be an unspoken embodied and emotional understanding between them, a closeness with an almost mystical quality to it. She doesn't consider herself a spiritual person, but if she had to describe it she would say it was like the air around them was glistening, as if they were caught in a glimmering web that captured every movement of their breath, thoughts and emotions, so that these instantly vibrated out in unspoken ways among them, touching all simultaneously.

Beaming Face breaks her out of her reverie. He has apparently been trying to get her attention for a while as he has resorted to waving his hand in front of her face. She hopes that she was not gaping. She realizes that he is asking her if he can show her to her dorm, and she manages to garble an affirmative, stumbling awkwardly over the sprawled bodies as she endeavors to follow him up the sweeping staircase.

The dorm is a grand, high ceilinged, large room, with varnished wooden floors. A bay window covers most of the outward facing wall, with vast floor to ceiling windows, spilling soft late afternoon light across the floorboards. That is where the grandness ends. There are twelve mattresses on the floor in two rows, with small, etched bedside cabinets between them, housing a plethora of cosmetics, earplugs, self-help books, thongs, and dirty mugs. It is like a student house share without doors, and with an equal disregard for personal space as that encountered in the lobby.

She notices two girls laying on a mattress near the window, bathed in the incoming light. They are afternoon napping, spooned together, one laying on her friend's hair, which creates a fan on the pillow. It is a picture of contentment and connection. She thinks, *just maybe … maybe I could feel at home here.*

Her glorified view of the situation is dampened somewhat by a night of interrupted sleep, snoring, door banging, and giggling. As she drags herself off her lumpy mattress to attend the early morning workshop with Akhila, she feels vulnerable and slightly sick. She decides to put on layers of comforting fluffy clothes; it is her way of feeling as if she is having a hug without the need of another human. She is the first to arrive in the entrance lobby and decides to stay there rather than getting a coffee, cramming herself into the relative safety of a corner sofa, hoping that she will become invisible.

~ ~ ~

Posthumous polyamory

Kate stumbles bleary eyed down the carpeted corridor, cursing that the one workshop she came for is so early in the morning, and wishing she had gone for the ensuite option with the private room she booked. Long past the time where she could tolerate dorm living, the thought of the large, shared shower, with multiple naked bodies soaping themselves publicly, was not enticing her. Luckily, she is the only early riser and is pleasantly surprised to find a freshly cleaned and empty shower room.

As she pulls the faucet towards her, she notices a bottle of *Little Green People* body wash in the shower caddy. Instantly transported to thoughts of her children; she wonders what they are doing right now. They are probably both jumping on Nana and Pop's bed or eating their organic, gluten free chocolate stars cereal, with raw gold top milk from the farm near her parent's house. Maybe they would go for a walk to the local beach today. Looking out of the slightly steamy window, she can see that it certainly looks like it is going to be a clear day; here at least, the cerulean sky is pristine with just a hint of hazy amber lining the horizon behind the silhouetted trees. She wishes she could be with them, having a simple day; their early years seem to be slipping through her fingers whilst she tries to sort herself out. She thought she was done with coming to *The Retreat*. She finds the rampant rhetoric, overcompensating for what has become a rehearsed formula, a little old now, although perhaps it is somewhat comforting in its familiarity.

She has come for the workshop *'Taking the Sex out of Tantra'* led by Akhila. She has carefully researched Akhila's work to ensure it has the depth and focus she is looking for, and had tried to get a one-to-one coaching session with her, but according to her website, the wait list had become so ridiculously long that she is no longer adding names to it. She supposes that this is not surprising, considering she is one of the only Tantra teachers whose work genuinely supports trauma (rather than causing trauma), and resembles traditional Tantra, unlike the sex focused and rather flaky neo-tantra that is commonplace in the community.

She is desperate to find something, anything, that can save her marriage. Their time at *The Retreat* was largely responsible for the vitality, freedom, and exquisite connection within their marriage, but introductions made there had ultimately led to its demise. She had been reluctant to go the first time her husband had suggested it. She considered herself spiritual, but it was a secret side to her, not really fitting with her corporate image. She was more a 'crystal in the handbag' type than the sort who filled her home with sparkling rocks from a major archaeological dig.

At the beginning of their relationship, her husband had only tolerated this aspect of her and found it endearing at best. However, the polyamorous community had attracted him. He had always been fascinated with the notion of multiple partners and had read the book *'The Ethical Slut'*, which, although it was quite a good read and did contain a good ethic (if you were into that sort of thing), had made her feel sick at times. The thought of negotiating who would sleep in the bed and who would be on the couch tonight, and then exchanging pleasantries with her husband's lover whilst they retrieved breakfast items from their allocated shelf in the fridge, was not appealing.

What was appealing though, was the freedom to have other nonsexual connections, affectionate, vibrant connections with women, men, whomever she pleased. Connections that, outside of this community, would be perceived as 'romantic' and a cause of jealousy between primary partners. The other thing that hooked her in was the communication side of things. She was enticed by the openness and honesty inherent in negotiating a polyamorous relationship within a community that promoted emancipation through the process of conscious relating. A community that also offered workshops to equip couples to become adept in the process of communicating authentically and processing emotions healthily.

It had been working well. Once they had become proficient 'conscious communicators' their relationship had flourished. Friends outside of the community were equally shocked and inspired by their startling authenticity, and commented about how sickeningly close they seemed. She could never explain the magic formula to them; they would have been horrified. Her husband had other lovers, but she had been fulfilled by intimate connections of a non-sexual nature. In fact, she had been quite glad of the less frequent sexual needs of her partner, especially after the birth of their second child.

Then there was Rob. She had been doing a shift in the coffee shop, bending over to get a cup from a low shelf when he walked in, which meant that as she straightened up, he was instantly there, as if appearing from nowhere, strikingly tall, cheeky, and bombastic. She usually considered herself centered and strong, certainly not romantic, but her legs really did feel like they were going to give way. He said that he had been doing a ridiculously long shift in the tea ceremony tent, and asked if he could have a coffee and a brownie, 'he'd pay later'. She instantly complied with the request, something forbidden within the community coffee shop – serving on credit. Makaresh who was serving with her commented, "Wow, I've never seen you like that before, I wish I could have that impact on a woman."

She felt slightly ashamed to have played the part of the wilting maiden.

His effect on her did not diminish, and they became quite enthralled with each other. She kept her distance as much as she could, although she felt rather magnetically pulled towards him. There was a fear, a fear that she might have an energetic connection with him that may rival that of her connection with her husband, a boundary she did not want to cross, even though her marriage was officially polyamorous. At the end of the festival, they hugged in the lobby, and he asked her, "So, what would it take for me to be a Goddess' tea boy? I would just hide in the cupboard, and you could get me out whenever you wanted!"

She laughed in response, and he said, "Next time I'm in Stroud, I'll let you know, so we can meet up."

She agreed and within two minutes, his Facebook friend request pinged on her phone.

His death was a terrible shock. Not just for her, but for everyone in the community. However, for her it had another dimension, the fact that they had become 'close' in cyber world, but that she had kept him at arm's length due to her fears. When he reached out to see if he could come to stay, he must have been at his most desperate, and she turned him away. Her grief was the type of grief that can engulf us when something longed for, and offered, is snatched away before we have the courage to grasp it. It was the type of grief amplified by guilt and regret. Her grieving affected the whole family and particularly her relationship. The depth of her grief reflected how much she had felt for Rob and strangely, for the first time, her husband was extremely jealous. He was also angry because he said there was no need for it; she should have connected fully with him if she wanted to so much, because their relationship allowed for it.

It was when Rob started to talk to her that things really fell apart. She never understood why she had so many anomalous supernatural experiences. She did not welcome them or share them with others, despite the fact that they would have been ideal material for those spiritual overshares that she often saw on Facebook. She was sure it was Rob rather than her imagination, even though it was essentially a voice in her head, because he 'spoke' in his voice and said things she would not usually think. After a couple of weeks of this talking, it reached a point of desperation where she cried out, "Why are you doing this?"

The next time he dropped in to chat with her, he answered her question. She was having a rare moment of relaxation in the bath. The kids were in bed, and her husband was away on a business trip. Rob dropped in to explain, "I'm trying to resolve all of the things that I left unresolved with people before I died."

Ah, of course, she thought. There was a pause, long enough for her to develop the unsettling sense that she was going insane, before Rob interjected, "And I want to make love with you."

Of course, she thought, *that is normal*; a dead person wants to make love with me! Despite her reticence, she got out of the bath and went to the bedroom, half imagining *that* scene from the movie *Ghost*, but with less clay. She sat on the bed and rationally tried to think about how this was going to work. She decided on a tantric energy meditation, so sat cross-legged on the bed and started to focus on her breath and her spine. But Rob had other ideas instructing, "No, no techniques just lie down on your back."

What? How does this work? She thought but did as he requested. Laying on her back on the bed, she felt rather foolish that she was even expecting something to happen, and then she heard his voice saying, "Breathe in spaciousness."

She took a deep breath and as she exhaled, she felt very calm and pleasantly empty. "Breathe in spaciousness," he said again.

This time she felt full of nothing, which of course is an oxymoron, but nonetheless was the only way she could describe it. The nothing was not empty though it was subtly effervescent, peaceful. His voice continued to say those words 'breathe in spaciousness' over and over. Each time she breathed in, she felt as though the effervescent emptiness grew until it was expanding within her and yet moving across the boundary of her physicality, almost as if her insides were expanding outwards, until her essence was as big as the room. At some point, she fell asleep, an unusual sleep where she was almost conscious of sleeping and of his voice still with her. The spaciousness kept growing until she had no sense of her boundaries.

On waking, she felt unusually refreshed, transformed, into what she could not say, she just felt very different. She had more patience with the children, the grief had dissipated into acceptance, and she felt that her heart could hold so much more. Every time she started to contract her body or feel confined, the words 'breathe in spaciousness' would repeat like a mantra in her mind and she would breathe deeply, open and relax. The words were now a thought in her mind though, his voice had gone, and she never heard him again. Her husband joked when she told him, that he was the first one in their community to have to deal with posthumous polyamory.

The problem was that something that seemed like a joke to her husband had turned into a big problem for them. The experience of 'making love' with Rob had transformed something more than her peace of mind and openness of heart. She now had no sexual desire at all. Literally, overnight it was as if someone had flicked a switch, and that circuit was not in operation. Frustratingly, this was non-negotiable with her husband, despite all of their explorations, conscious communication and non-sexual intimacy; he equated her lack of sexual desire as a lack of love for him. She was hoping that Akhila might be able to help her, or at least explain what had happened to her, and how she could live like this now that it had.

Since that night, physical sex just seemed so animal, basic and disgusting. She wondered if it might pass, but it had been nearly a year now, and her husband had recently moved out.

She snaps out of her thoughts and turns off the shower. She is going to be late. She grabs her yoga clothes and struggles into them, pulling her hoodie over her head as she runs down the stairs to the main workshop room. She need not have rushed, everyone is still milling around in the lobby, most with half eaten toast and cups of tea. She sits down next to a timid looking girl who wears the expression of a startled rabbit and is wearing equally furry attire. She wonders if she would mind if she stroked her, maybe she would ask later. She realizes her presence is disturbing the girl next to her and decides she should introduce herself.

"Hi," she says, "I'm Kate."

The girl jumps to such an extent that she breaks contact with the sofa. "Oh, um, hi! I'm Rach. Is this your first time here?"

Kate laughs, grimacing at the thought of how many times she's been here. Rach looks like she's about to run for the door, so Kate quickly apologizes for being off-putting and explains that it just gets a bit "same-y" when you attend retreats regularly.

Rach's features visibly relax, and she sinks back into the comfort of the sofa. "Phew, that's good to hear. Yes, yes, it is, it's my first time. I, well, I'm kinda interested in being intimate, but not sexually."

"Ah, yes, it's nice to learn that, rather than everything always being about sex," Kate replies.

"Oh no, um, you see, I'm Aroace," Rach explains.

"I thought you said your name was Rach?"

Rach looks equally startled and excited. "Uh, no, um, it's not my name! It's my orientation!"

Kate pauses, her eyes rolling upward, searching for information she's sure she should have accumulated in all her years of relationship work. The information eludes her, and she asks, "You're what? Sorry, I don't…"

"My orientation… I'm Aromantic and Asexual," Rach replies, and Kate notices that Rach's body seems to relax, radiating presence as she settles into a sense of authenticity. Unfortunately, although Rach has dropped into this place of self-assurance, Kate doesn't understand the terminology.

"What does that mean?"

"Oh! I'm so used to it I forget to explain," Rach says. "Aromantic means that I don't have romantic feelings for people, and asexual means I don't feel sexual attraction or desire."

Kate's eyes widen with interest, and she leans toward Rach. "That's certainly not same-y! Wow, that's so interesting—I mean, I'm so interested in you. Sorry, I'm saying it all wrong. I'm just so excited to meet you! Are you going to the workshop in there?" She points to the main workshop room.

Rach nods. "Yeah, it's the only Tantra workshop I'm interested in."

"I am too," says Kate, "and ditto about it being the only Tantra workshop… In fact, I think, I think maybe I'm what you just said. What did you call it?"

"Aroace—Aromantic and Asexual."

The door opens to the group room, signaling the start of the workshop. Kate wishes she could stay here on the sofa with Rach, she asks her if they can grab a cup of tea afterwards and Rach agrees. She feels so disoriented that she almost staggers into the workshop. Maybe that is why she is here. Synchronicities like this seem to happen to her when she finds herself flummoxed by something. Her mind is reeling, spinning with thoughts and questions. She must concentrate, this workshop is the reason she came, but she has a sense that Rach might offer her far more insight than a Tantra workshop.

~ ~ ~

Together in electric dreams

Akhila leaves her workshop feeling inspired. That was quite a sharing circle at the end. That new girl and Kate brought up some interesting insights that resonated with her work. How wonderful that they had found each other, and it was great to see more diverse people showing up to the festival. Kate's story of interacting with something beyond the human and material realm and experiencing a natural state of moving into a fluid and expansive sense of self, rather than experiencing this through a disciplined practice, was enthralling. She had never heard a tale of someone experiencing this naturally and had only heard of it articulated within the context of meditation, breathwork or movement meditation. It had compounded her view that everyone has the possibility of experiencing the mystical, if they open to connecting to something beyond the limited commodified world and the social norms imposed by Western culture. It had also opened her eyes to how this state of transpersonal connection can lead to becoming asexual. It had also offered her a little more understanding of her friend Ben. In fact, she thought, although she had wanted to talk more with them, he was her priority, and she could not be late for the *Dance of Sacred Union* workshop. It was her chance to connect with Ben.

She wonders whether this will be a safe space where they can explore intimacy. She is tired of the ever-looming phantom of sex hovering around every corner, causing the freezing of spontaneous expression. She knows he is asexual, so why is this always such a problem? Does he feel it too? Whose tension is it? Is she picking up on his tension? Is his tension caused by his fear of sex being an issue or does he misinterpret her anxiety as suppressed sexual desire?

She does find him attractive (who wouldn't? She has told him before that he is mythically handsome), and she wonders, if things were different, if she would pursue a relationship with him. She just does not know if her ego, still in place despite all the meditation practice, could tolerate being with someone who did not sexually desire her.

She has told him that she loves him, she even felt like she was falling in love with him at one point. They had been acquaintances for a couple of years, just bumping into each other at festivals or the occasional dance event. That changed when she started to work near his flat, and they had begun to meet regularly.

The intimacy festival might be the opportunity she has been waiting for, to experiment with how it feels to connect with him more deeply, without the pressure of it becoming something, a commitment, or a construct. She had been asked to teach and had then passed on the details to him, when she realized there was a teacher teaching the inner union of the masculine and feminine, a particular interest of his; integrating archetypes was something they had many animated discussions about.

It was a comfortable way to invite him. Not really asking, just opening a doorway. They were not actually going together; they would just be there at the same time.

* * *

The room is dark, with the blinds pulled, and lit with candles. There are yoga mats, placed in pairs, laid beside each other to make doubles. As with all of the workshops, attendees know to enter quietly and place shoes and bags on the racks by the doors. Silent acknowledgements including smiling, soft eye gazes, hands pressed in prayer position against the middle of the chest, and little nods of the head abound.

As he enters, Ben sees her across the room and catches her eye nodding a greeting. For that one moment, it feels as if there is not anyone else in the room. Her beatific smile widens into a joyful grin as she sees him, the ebullience of which travels upwards and seems to light up her eyes (or is that just the candlelight?) He doesn't sit next to her, she is already surrounded by her many friends and admirers, but he sits close enough, close enough to allow the possibility, when the circle breaks up and they all choose someone to work with, that she might choose him.

The breathing and meditation session ends, and the facilitator invites them to choose a partner with whom to practice the dance of sacred union. Frustratingly, he does not feel able to move, and he sees a couple of other women tentatively making their way towards him. He looks around and notices that she is no longer sitting where she had been in the circle. Then, miraculously, she is there, right in front of him. 'Would you like to work together?' she says.

He cannot hide his joy from her, although he would rather have kept his cool, always incredibly concerned about how she may perceive his enthusiasm.

The facilitator instructs them to sit opposite each other and reminds them of the rules of boundaries and consent. They are encouraged to mirror each other in their movements, with the man leading the feminine aspects of the dance, and the woman leading the masculine elements (or to decide what feels right for same sex couples). The facilitator instructs them to start facing each other, about a meter apart, and to breathe in unison, whilst looking with a soft gaze into each other's eyes.

He starts by looking everywhere but her eyes, but she is already looking into his, noticing his discomfort. As their eyes lock, he feels like electricity is passing between them, as if her gaze is gently frying his brain, extinguishing its usual contents, and filling it instead with a joyous buzzing. Her demeanor is serene, taking the practice seriously, and yet her eyes glisten with a sense of merriment. He notices that they are breathing harmoniously, unaware of how it happened, although it was probably her synching in with him like she always did, with her incredible knack for coming into a comfortable symbiosis with him, making him feel he is the most important thing to her, and that he is worthy of her full attention.

The music starts, "And now we will dance the dance of the dark masculine, allow yourself to be guided by the music, embodying the energies and mirroring each other's movements, I suggest you move at a distance to start with to allow yourselves to focus on more than the physical."

The physical, a moment of panic breaks the sublime connection he was feeling. What if their dance does get more physical? What if he gets uncomfortable and she notices? Would that be the end of their friendship? Distance … distance, it is ok. He has to get back in the zone. He doubts she is going to start writhing all over him. The thought makes a bubble of laughter start to rise from his belly, which he dissipates with a strong outbreath. She mirrors with a strong outbreath, interpreting it as him using his breath to ground himself into his body, into the moment.

She is crawling around on their mats, in an animalistic way; he hears a low growling and reciprocates. He imagines they are big cats stalking around each other, heckles rising, will they be friends or foes? The physicality happens naturally, in this cat like way, shoulder and then hips brushing, mimicking the sinuous rubbing that cats will do against a human leg or another feline. He enjoys feeling her warmth, the curvaceous strength of her body. Then, her body is pushing his strongly and their chests come together, she is breathing strongly, and really growling and baring her teeth. There is a passion in her movements, which stirs him energetically, not in his genitals, but he feels pulsating in his hands, arms, legs and spine. He feels alive, in pursuit of more aliveness, just wanting to feel the gravity of her body, the raw expression of her animal vitality, without a goal, just the wrapping motion of two bodies wanting to feel the undeniable, life affirming sense of being warm flesh and blood, wild beings in embodied connection.

As the dance slows, he has some recognition that they danced the other parts of the dance, but it all becomes a bit of a blur; there is just an intense feeling of connection, understanding, full body aliveness, and joy that is slightly overwhelming to his sense of any detail. As he searches for recollection, he remembers that they moved into the dance of the dark feminine, during which he surprised himself by seeming to become an exotic dancer with hips like Shakira, yet more surprised that he felt ok when she matched him, introducing her own style of rotation at the hip level. He could not understand how he was enjoying the sensuality so much without becoming tense or switching off, but he did not really have the capacity to analyze because he was completely in the moment, fully appreciating every part of his body and the flowing way that her body was moving in unison with his.

The dance of the light feminine, he remembers as a moment suspended outside of physicality, they were touching but he felt like it was their hearts touching, not their bodies. He had a sense of 'more than her' enveloping him in a subtle hug, scented with sweetness.

They are now in the final section; the 'dance' of the light masculine, the facilitator tells them to sit in front of each other as close, or far apart as is comfortable. He sits cross-legged and she sits with her legs bent over his thighs, they gently place their hands on each other's knees. He does not need the instruction to look into her eyes, and their breathing seems to be naturally synchronized. They are guided to imagine the energy moving between them from his base across into hers, up to her heart, across into his heart, and back down to his base. Imagine? He is already feeling it, is she? Keeping track of the breathing pattern is impossible but the feeling of the energy between them is there without any forced effort.

To feel this waving of subtle pleasurable energy moving through him, sending it to her, and feeling it from her is sublime connection (and is it love?) He has not experienced this movement of energy with another before; it has only been something he has been open to when he is alone. As the practice finishes, he feels complete, content and full of energy. He feels grateful that Akhila's tantric teachings are obviously not just rehearsed words, and that she seems able to share an energetic connection free of sexual undertones.

He hears the instruction to share their experience of the practice with each other. He looks down and gathers himself. He does not know how to articulate how he is feeling. As he looks up, she is gently gazing at him with tears flowing down her cheeks. She says, "That … That is what I want. That is what I want with you." He is filled with a sense of possibility, the possibility that, perhaps, they could have a relationship without him having to compromise and pay the 'entrance price'.

~ ~ ~

50 shades of A

Her client is late. Ben must be new; she doesn't think she has heard that name before. Most people around here have appropriated Indian names, how refreshing to see a 'Ben' on her list.

She wonders who he is and what he is like. With a name like Ben perhaps he'll be different. She is sick of it. Men who say they are tantric, but they just want a 'happy ending'[131] (and not the type of 'happy ending' found in fairy tales). She tries to offer them something profound, the experience of a sense of love through touch, a movement of energy away from the genitals and into the heart.

---

[131] A 'happy ending' in reference to massage is when the masseuse offers the client an ejaculatory orgasm at the end of the massage.

Instead, they leave her feeling dirty, a glorified sex worker. She remembers the humiliating banishment from Facebook for being a 'sex worker', simply for talking about the movement of 'sexual energy'. The message that she sent to their customer services department, explaining about Tantra being a practice to transmute sexual energy, did not receive a reply.

She ponders, for the millionth time, why she was attracted to this scene in the first place. Was it the possibility of men appreciating her in a different way? Fat chance. Men are men in any scenario. The neo-tantra scene was full of predators in disguise, what was the expression? 'A wolf in sheep's clothing'?

If she had not invested so much time and energy, so much of her identity, into the training with Agropa[132], she would have bailed after the awful experience with Swami Aharmi[133]. She cannot believe that teachers like him can still get away with teaching and practicing, even once their sexual abuse becomes public through their students' testimonies. It still makes her shudder, the thought of him saying, "Oh, you know, the most effective way to massage your yoni is with my lingam."[134]

She had not had sexual intercourse since giving in to his coercion. Nor had she any sense of sexual desire for anyone; only a sense of desire for intimacy with her primary partner who she had been with for many years, and even then, she had mainly been performing the 'giving' role.

---

[132] This is a fictional name.

[133] This is a fictional name. There have been many reported incidents of such things occurring within neo-tantra trainings that focus on 'sacred sexuality' (see Ellis-Petersen 2018 for an article reporting this). None of the co-creators have participated in such trainings. I include this as part of this piece of fiction as a way to acknowledge the 'darker' side of this new religious movement. I feel it is important to acknowledge this. The awful effects of such abuses of power are often reported in the private online support group that me and the co-creators are a part of.

[134] In neo-tantra the female reproductive organs are often referred to as a 'yoni' and a man's is often referred to as a 'lingam'.

She feels the familiar rush of anger as she remembers how she felt completely abused sexually and emotionally. However, she did not feel able to say she had been raped simply because he did not ask for consent. Consent, so important. She wonders if Ben has done the consent workshop[135]. She will ask him and, even if he has, she will go through the principles with him. That might take up a bit of their session. Anything to take up a bit of the session. She only agreed to offer bodywork so she could get a free ticket; she is so hard up now because of the struggle to work, due to her repulsion towards the school she studied with and the perception of her career path, but she wanted to be here to be with her community.

The door opens tentatively, and a striking male face peeks around the small gap between the door and frame.

"Ben?"

"Yes. Sorry I'm late. I got held up at the dance workshop. I, I'm here for... Well, I'm here, I'm not sure for what really, or if I should be!"

"Oh! I see! Or rather, I don't," she laughs gently. "Come in anyway, have a seat, and try to relax. I'm not that scary!"

She gestures toward the chair opposite her, and he sits awkwardly on the edge of the seat. She asks him what motivated him to book the session.

"Well, it's a bit weird, I guess. I don't like sex, I mean I don't want sex. This is awkward," Ben mumbles, twisting his hands in his lap.

"No, no, please carry on. I'm glad you don't want sex because that's not what I offer," she says with a wry smile.

"Oh, oh, no, that's not what I thought!" he exclaims, looking mortified.

---

[135] Consent and consent workshops within the tantric community are often based on the work of Betty Martin, which has now been published in a co-authored book (Martin and Dalzen 2021).

"I'm only kidding," she smiles. "Carry on... so you don't like sex, why did that motivate you to book a tantric bodywork session?"

"Well, I saw what you said on the flyer, about energy orgasm, about feeling love through touch, and I think..." He pauses, leaning back in the chair, closing his eyes, and placing his hands on his chest and belly. He breathes deeply and continues in bursts. "...I'm not sure, but I think that... the energy... is what I feel sometimes when I'm lying on my bed, listening to music, just breathing, or when I'm dancing. I get these rushes of energy in my body..." He continues explaining how he had just experienced this with someone else in the dance workshop for the first time.

"Wow, this sounds great!" she exclaims, slightly over-enthusiastically. He looks startled.

She leans toward him with intense interest. "Do you practice Tantra? I know you said you don't like sex, but has this happened when you've had sex?"

He leans away from her, anxiously blurting, "Oh, no, I mean, I don't, I haven't. I'm asexual."

"Ah, I see!" she says, thinking, *At last, my ideal client!*

She pauses, mentally flicking through all of her disappointing sessions and hardly daring to believe there's another possibility. He takes her distractedness as an opportunity to gather his strength, leaning forward several times as if to speak, then pulling back. She refocuses on him with a gentle, inquiring gaze.

He inhales through his teeth, puffing up his chest, and speaks quickly with his outbreath before he loses courage. "I want to see what it's like to be touched, for my body to be touched, I think. I'm not sure about that. But I have a friend..."

"Akhila? I've seen you with her, I think..." She shakes herself and straightens her spine. "Sorry, I shouldn't ask that!"

Ben softens, her name like a soothing balm. "Yes, Akhila... I, we, have, I mean, we are very close. It's funny because that experience I had while dancing, that was with her... It was like the energy rushes I sometimes get when I'm alone, but it felt like they were going through both of us."

She nods reassuringly, encouraging him to continue.

"Well, I guess that's why I'm here. I'm not interested in sexual touch, but I heard about conscious touch and 'tantra massage', where the focus is on the pleasure of touch and energy, without it having anything to do with genital arousal. I think, if we're going to explore relating more intimately as a nonsexual couple, I'd like affection and touch to be part of our relationship. But it's just an idea. I want to make sure I'm comfortable with it before I suggest it! I want to be more intimate with her, perhaps try massage and snuggling, but I don't want to give her the wrong idea, and I don't even know if I would like it—her touching me in such a sensual way—so I'd like to find out what it's like before I suggest it at all..."

"Wonderful," she smiles. "I'm so honored that you trusted me enough to come here today, and that you've shared all this with me. I want you to know that anything you share here, and that happens here, stays between us and these four walls."

"That's good to know. I just want to know whether it could work with me and Akhila before our relationship changes..."

"I have to say, looking at you together, you seem very much in love."

"Hmmm, that's how it feels, but I'm sure she wants more than I can offer her."

"I think it's always difficult to ascertain what people want without asking and sharing. Moreover, it's very difficult to tell if any relationship will work—it's a complex thing under any circumstances. Have you done the consent workshop?"

"Um, no."

"Perhaps you could go together?"

"She's a teacher; she won't want to do that... she teaches that stuff!" He says defensively.

She replies with soft authority, "It's not just about learning consent—it's practicing it together in a safe environment. I think you'd both learn a lot about how you feel and what you want and need by going together. But it's just a suggestion."

"Hmmm," he says, shaking his head doubtfully.

"Our session today might help. I'm going to talk you through the principles of consent and finding your true 'yes' and 'no,' and how a 'maybe' is always a 'no' until it turns into a heartfelt 'yes.' It should be easier to do that in session, rather than in a real relationship situation, and it will be good practice for out there in the 'real world.'"

"That sounds really good, thank you."

"Great! After that, we can explore some touch, with you giving voice to your needs and directing what happens and how, so you can find out what feels good for you."

As the session ends, she is not sure who received the most healing. She feels blessed to have worked with him, and to have experienced a session rooted purely in the principles of loving touch, consent, and energy work. She had only previously witnessed his energetic capacity and awareness with female clients. She had doubted the teachings that it is possible for a man to experience such pleasure and energy in his body, without an erection or any pressure to move towards sexual interaction. This natural sublimation of 'sexual' energy was why Tantra had appealed to her originally, and she feels re-inspired. She could not help but feel a little jealous of Akhila and the potential of the relationship that might be possible with this extraordinary man. She had always presumed that asexual people were 'wired wrong' or juiceless. She could not believe how mistaken she had been.

~ ~ ~

6. Ars Romantica[136]

I was fortunate in this research to find two couples on the asexual spectrum, whose positions on the spectrum have been transformed through their interactions with each other. This enabled me to offer an answer to Scott and Dawson's (2015) call for research that explored how asexuals navigate intimacy, often with sexual partners. It also enabled me to include additional examples of asexual 'becomings', to further their 2018 research, which concluded that asexuality is not an innate identity, but rather is formed through social interaction.

The couples considered themselves nonsexual polyamorous (i.e. they have connections outside of their partnership that many would consider 'romantic' with other people, but they experience these as nonsexual erotic connections and friendships). They prefer to refer to their relationship as a partnership, rather than a romantic

---

[136] This is the title of a chapter in the book *Like Love* by Michele Morano (2020).

relationship. Their narratives struck me as being examples of 'mature love' (Fromm 1956), and they also offer examples of a 'healthy relationship', as defined by Peele and Brodsky (1975), in counterbalance to their exposition regarding 'addicted' unhealthy 'love' relationships. The co-creators referred to this as a 'conscious relationship'. Peele and Brodsky described the ideal coupled relationship thus:

> The impetus for this exploration is the life instinct of the individuals involved: they were growing beings before they met, and they entered upon their union as a positive choice for continued growth, only this time to be carried out in conjunction with—though not exclusively with—another person. The lovers approach the relationship itself as an opportunity for growth. They want to understand more about it, about themselves, and about each other. For this reason, a love relationship necessarily becomes deeper, out of the experience the lovers share, and out of their constant desire to uncover new facets of their connection and to better understand its old facets. (1975: 102-103)

Exploring love, and experiencing an expanded sense of love, was the most important element of Tantra practice for co-creators who had explored Tantra. Rod Stryker tells us that 'perhaps the least-known meaning of the word *tantra*, is "to be touched," referring specifically to the concept of your heart being touched'. He goes on to say[137]:

> Think of the last time you felt a sense of awe, wonder or profound appreciation for life, when you suddenly saw life as the greatest of all gifts … that moment, when all sense of limitation fell away, is tantra. The vast array of techniques, practices, and teachings that tantric masters developed through the centuries are for the purpose of awakening you to this experience and enabling you to weave it more and more consistently into the tapestry of your life (2011: 17).

---

[137] Here Stryker cleverly integrates the word 'weave' which is another meaning for tantra, without directly articulating it as one of the word's possible meaning. He also explicitly introduces some of the other 'most important meanings of the word *tantra*' which 'is "system", "method" or "technique"' in the text preceding this quote.

Within 'mindful relationship' there can be a constant, natural appreciation of being touched in the heart, which occurs beyond the system, methods or techniques that allowed it to happen. This 'touching of the heart' can be read in the relationships of the co-creators who inspired the dramaturgical text, and within the narratives of the co-creators who did not have a partnership.

Although the co-creators are polyamorous, as discussed previously, this is an openness to intimate, erotic, loving connection with others, but not sexual or romantic connection. Daniel Odier describes eloquently how this works for erotically embodied couples:

> Fidelity, which worries many people is not a problem. The more you fully live, the more desire will find itself in constant tremoring vibration, with or without an object. This tremoring will come from you, from your consciousness, from your heart, and will shower down both on those close to you and on those you meet. Even those sitting near you on the bus will benefit from it... Your desire will therefore pour out in a new, continuous way. There will no longer exist an accumulation of energy that can find calm only in orgasmic release. You will enter into a sphere in which you will be unceasingly in the process of making love, and enjoying immense pleasure, with the whole world – which leaves hardly any room for what we call "affairs". You will live the Great Affair, the one that never ends (Odier 1998: 88-89).

6.1 Stage setting

This dramaturgical text is a fictionalized conversation between two couples. Based on four co-creators' stories, the thematic analysis of these, the ethnographic observations collected within my journals, and the subsequent collaborative production of the script. After a thorough analysis of the stories, the initial script was created by immersing myself in the story of each of the fictionalized characters and their individual personalities, and performing their parts whilst recording this using a voice recorder, to facilitate the production of authentic speech. The dialogue and stage instructions are written in the style of a contemporary play text.

The script illustrates how sexual identities, with a focus on asexual and asexual spectrum identities, are fluid and non-essentialist, often influenced through social interaction. The content further elucidates and expands upon many of the themes arising within the preceding chapters. Asexuals and others with asexual spectrum identities (such as demisexual) often navigate relationships with sexual people (Carrigan 2011, Przybylo 2013, Gupta 2015, Scott and Dawson 2015, Scott and Dawson 2018). Scott and Dawson (2015) called for research that investigated asexual intimacy with sexual people and how it works in practice. This chapter aims to answer this call and add to this body of knowledge.

Interestingly, the previously sexual identified individual within each couple articulated how they had been changed to identify on the asexual spectrum as a result of being in a relationship with an asexual person; that the prevalence of the sexual had been eradicated by the expanded nature of the nonsexual intimacy and the nonsexual erotic. The asexual partners indicated that the focus on the expanded erotic, to which they already felt connected, enabled them to engage in sexual activity that they had not felt interested to participate in before.

The script, therefore, also aims to illustrate how an expanded view of the erotic and intimacy can enrich relationships (asexual or sexual). Despite the need to view the new age and neo-tantra movement with a critical lens, and understand the potential abuses of power and the spiritual commodification that can be rife in such contexts, the new age/neo-tantra movements offer some useful tools for enhanced communication, consent, practices of intimacy, and choice of relationship structures; examples of these are present within the script.

The setting is a fictionalized intimacy festival, based on similar festivals at a neo-tantric, new age retreat center (as presented in Chapter 5) with the fictional name *The Retreat*. Centers such as this one were frequented, in the past, by the co-creators. This conversation takes place after a workshop held by C and D and is a conversation between the couples about how they met, became partners, and navigated their differences in sexuality and needs for intimacy.

The characters in this script are as follows:

C – Was graysexual and aromantic, and now considers herself demisexual as a result of being in a relationship with an asexual man. (Her partner now considers himself demisexual - in the sense that he knows he can be sexual in the context of a loving relationship).

D – Was asexual and aromantic, and now considers himself demisexual as a result of being in a relationship with C (in the sense that he knows he can be sexual in the context of a loving relationship).

A – Was a demisexual and romantic, and now considers herself demisexual and aromantic.

B – Was sexual and aromantic; self-defined as a 'predatory, highly sexually motivated man'. He now considers himself demisexual as a result of being in a relationship and starting a family with A.

6.2 Meeting Mature Love

*All the ecstasy that we feel emerges as this love
nurtures us and challenges us to grow and transform.*
bell hooks

[C and D are sitting on the sofas in the large entrance lobby, which is one of the spaces where participants at The Retreat socialize between workshops and meals. A is sitting with them - they left the workshop together and she wanted to continue her conversation with them to find out more about their relationship and how it works in practice. A's partner, B, sees them talking

animatedly together and saunters over to join them, sitting above them on the arm of the sofa. He arrives after A has asked how C and D met.]

C: Well, we met on a teacher training, and I kinda liked him *[pause]* but it was more of a friend thing *[pause, rolls eyes upwards]*. Although I guess looking back I do remember being jealous of the woman he was *particularly* friendly with, which I kinda guess says quite a lot! *[Places hand gently on D's shoulder and laughs gently.]*

D: For me, I think I always knew I was in love with her. She just shone *[pauses looks up at C and smiles]*. A special quality, I was really attracted to that. *[Quickly]* I didn't think of it in a romantic way necessarily because I wasn't even thinking about romantic relationships *[pause and back to normal pace]*. I never really understood the importance of sex and romance. I mean, I wondered why people couldn't just decide to have a partnership because they like each other more than anyone else and they want to spend most of their free time together, rather than because they fancy each other. And I think my practice of yoga just strengthened that really, I felt very … very self-contained really. I just didn't have room for that in my life, wasn't seeking it.

C: Yeah, we were friends, I would say *friends*, for a long time and we did, we did sort of keep in touch for that seven … seven years *[D: shakes his head, C looks upwards and then speaks quickly]* but it wasn't seven years *[laughs, back to normal pace]*. For about three years *[smiles at D]* after the course we kept in touch regularly, shared our process, or not process, but you know … progress, with our practice, what we're doing with our practices and stuff, our career, and actually we, so then we sort of lost touch.

D: But yes we, we kept in touch and I loved keeping in touch I like, look forward to the emails, and they were often a highlight of my week. I loved to hear what she was doing and be inspired. And you wanted to try, we tried, to arrange a few times for you to stay or something that … yes, never quite, never quite met up, never, you know, timings were never on the same track.

C: Yeah, we did sort of try to arrange coming to stay a couple of times, but then as friendships go, you sort of lose touch a bit. And then we went for another retreat, with the group we graduated with and we reconnected and it was really, *really* strong.

D: I must admit when we went on the retreat, I was a bit scared about seeing her. I didn't know what it would be like, it held a sort of anticipation for me.

C: I can't really explain it, it felt, I guess you might say, divinely guided.

D: Yes. And then when I saw her at the airport, she was still shining. But it did feel slightly, slightly strained and less natural.

C: That didn't last that long though really. As we started to connect more deeply I didn't really feel like *I* was involved. It was the most strange feeling. And yeah, it was very innocent and playful as we connected on that retreat. So we did go skinny dipping under the full moon and I gave him a massage, but it all it just felt very innocently intimate.

D: Then as the week progressed it was well, just as you say it was magical it was, well, I didn't feel I was really projecting anything at all. I felt a bit *[pause]* I felt very scared actually. About how I was feeling and I'd never experienced sensations like that before. It was like the feeling I got in my spiritual practice but just ten times stronger and all in my heart. And I felt concerned, not because I was projecting romance onto it, but because I know how far we lived apart and I knew it was going to come to an end and feeling so connected; I didn't know how I was going to feel when we went home.

C: And yeah, kind of gut wrenching when I knew we were going home. And so I gave him a locket with a heart that glowed in the dark inside it. I just popped it in his bag to find when he got home. Again, it really didn't have that much intention behind it. I knew he didn't have relationships. It was just wanting to keep the connection. And *[looks at D]* also feeling really scared about it as well.

D: So when, when we, by the time we got home, I felt equal parts um *[pause]* Wanting to push her away and equal parts desperate see her, and I wasn't quite sure how that was going to go. I mean I had no reference point. I didn't know what you were thinking. I didn't particularly think you'd ever been interested me in that way because I knew you did have relationships. So I presumed you weren't interested in a special friendship with me. Because you've never expressed that or …

C: Because it just felt so strong. But anyway, we when we got back, we, I, was still in London doing another bodywork training. And we exchanged texts and emails that was trying to express our feelings. We did meet up, I went to his house for the evening and I was really scared and excited on the way there.

A: *[Interrupting enthusiastically]* It was a much quicker coming together for us.

B: Yes, we have been told that we are 'twin flames' although I don't buy into all that new age bollocks.

A: There was an instant recognition though, outside of the usual attraction dynamic. You could say 'soul mates'.

B: Yes soul mates … two souls instantly recognizing each other. Just wow. She was so familiar to me, I just *knew* her.

A: Our souls knew each other intimately.

B: The rest just took a while to catch up! *[laughs loudly]*

A: *[Chuckles gently]* Hm … yes … you weren't really my type. I used to go for younger men, more effeminate, yet bearded and emotional. Here was this muscular, very masculine man, with a strong physique, clean shaven and really short hair, and yet there was a pull …

B: Not that strong! You avoided me in that hugging session at the end of the workshop.

A: Haha, yes! I hate those, I was just picking all the shy gentle types that I resonated with and hugging them. I think you walked towards me about three times and I managed to side step you.

B: I decided to take the more direct approach.

A: Yes, I remember you came up to me just as I was putting my shoes on and said, "What about that hug?"

B: No escape!

A: Yes, exactly! I quite clearly remember thinking 'who does he think he is?' and 'he can't just let it go'. But at the same time not really wanting you to let it go … I gave him the worst hug ever …

B: But it didn't put me off! I knew already she was the one. I could sense you were rather shut down, but I wasn't going to give up.

A: Yes, I think you being so sure and me being emotionally erratic at the time made it all move very quickly. But I'm sorry, we interrupted you …

B: Wow, we totally did. How did you get together? *[A looks at him and rolls her eyes]* **I mean, sorry you were together, but I mean how did you get together, you know *properly* …**

A: *[Quickly interjects]* I think he means how did you transition into the relationship you have now from the one you started with? …

C: Yeah, we did spend quite a lot of time intensely talking, talking about our friendship, our pasts, relationships or *[looks at D and smiles warily]* lack of. We did movement and breathing exercises together. I guess I was very *very* aware of the fact that D hadn't had a relationship for many years, for all the years that I'd known him and you're discussing that a little. Well we're not really discussing that. I guess just confirming that and talking a little about me, I guess my relationship history and more about how we felt.

B: I'm with you. All that talking is very frustrating at first. It's like, 'can we shut up and get some action?' [laughs bombastically]

C: Hmmm, I would say it wasn't really aiming towards anything but there's this really strong feeling we'd had on the retreat. Being graysexual, my sexual feelings kinda got switched on or off depending on the person. I mean, I could be aesthetically attracted to someone and feel no desire, or intense desire, there's not really an in-between and it doesn't usually change. I was feeling very attracted to D in a 'longing to connect' way, like I had sparkly glasses on, and a heart on fire, but no sexual desire.

A: Yes, yes, that's what I am wondering! How did it happen, I mean how did you come to be together sexually without desire?

C: Well, we had one of our usual evenings. D had cooked me a gourmet meal and then we had the intimate equivalent of a gourmet meal … deep listening and sharing, partner yoga, sitting back-to-back and feeling our breath and energy in sync and I think at that point we turned around… *[looks at D]*

D: Yes, that was when I reached for the chocolate, so we could practice full sensory awareness …

B: What do you mean 'full sensory awareness'?

D: It is where you focus on each sense individually, and intensely – smell, taste, sight, touch, hearing. You can do it as a meditation or in relation to something else – like the chocolate or each other and the chocolate! It focuses and intensifies the experience.

C: Yeah we just naturally started our eye gazing practice, just sat gazing into each other's eyes. And a little bit into it, we did end up, we had some chocolate, and somehow we ended up kissing whilst eating chocolate which was quite an amazing sensation. It was like my sexuality was suddenly on, from not being on, and it was different, just like the sensation of kissing and the chocolate taking over my whole body and mind.

D: Yes, the chocolate moment was quite, um … intense.

C: And after that, he said should we go to bed and it was really, really late and I had my training the next day so that did make sense. And he offered to sleep in the other room and I thought oh how ridiculous ... Obviously, we're gonna have sex.

D: I really did mean I was going to go and sleep in the other room. I wasn't saying it to be polite. That was just what I thought that happened. And again, I still wasn't even projecting anything into the future...

C: It was just the norm, the normal sort of course of action within that situation for me, and I think also part of me thought well, if we don't do it now he probably won't do it because he's a bit relationship adverse, so it's kinda like sealing the deal.

D: But equally, I was just happy to go along with whatever you wanted.

C: Anyway, we went up to his bedroom and we were kissing in the bed and everything but he was he wasn't very responsive so I was more active and yeah, I guess I was, I don't think I'd ever been that much in the lead before. And knowing what I know about consent[138] now I probably would have been a bit slower and spoken a little more but yeah, I mean, he was aroused. *[Speech quickens and cheeks flush]* And I know now that that's not actual consent ... But yeah, so, so I was on top and he was quite passive. And when I woke up in the morning *[voice slows and descends rapidly in volume]* I was kind of worried I basically raped him ... I mean, it wasn't like that, he'd, he kissed me ...

D: *[Emphatically]* No *way* did you rape me! ... And ... I do, I know ... now we've learned about the wheel of consent[139] ... it wasn't ideal circumstances, either of us, and it probably would have been better

---

[138] C is referring to the work on consent by Betty Martin (2021). The 'Wheel of Consent' and the exercise 'The Three Minute Game', which are often utilized in consent workshops at intimacy festivals.

[139] Betty Martin (2021).

to talk about it and set it up in a more equal or understood way. But um, it did feel a bit surreal. I did feel a bit disembodied *[looks up at C]* But nonetheless, I felt connected to you and I wanted to be there with you. And then it did feel lovely and intimate cuddling and kissing in the morning. And by that point, I knew that I wanted, I um realized I wanted to, relationship and I wanted to see you as much as possible and …

C: Yeah, he was kissing me in the morning, and it was all very cuddly and everything else but it was just, *that* feeling, it just felt really wrong.

[All pause, C looks down at hands, D looks at C tenderly. A and B look at each other and B nods gently.]

C: And, yeah, anyway, we obviously, we did end up in a relationship. *[Looks up]* And it was, it is a very intense, beautiful relationship.

D: Coming into it fresh it was, was, it was a lot, um. It was a lot. I mean she had done a lot of sacred sexuality and relationship work and emotional processing. I hadn't done and it felt grueling at times to have to go through all the discussions but the sense of connection and vulnerability, openness … After sharing in a deep way was phenomenal and worth, worth the effort. And I think that, for me it almost became the foreplay. I mean, that was the way that I felt so connected to you. I just felt comfortable becoming one with you physically too, because I felt so one with you emotionally.

C: Yes it …

D: Just felt like the next step.

C: We ended up teaching together so our relationship and our teaching were very much intertwined. It meant we started teaching Yoga for Intimacy and things like that to help other couples. Yeah, what our relationship really consisted of.

D: And then I, once we started to have more sex, I felt that I could direct my energy to that area to make it more pleasurable, whereas maybe before my energy had been more in my solar plexus for getting things done. *[Looks at A and B]* You know?

[A shakes her head, B looks blank.]

C: It was strange because, he had had many years of doing practices that channeled his energy, and then suddenly he realized that he could channel this energy so it became sexual energy in his base and his genitals. So I guess he had been doing something naturally, through his practice, that many yogis take years of practice to perfect.

D: I think, my work ethic, a strong work ethic, so that that was where most of my energy went. So it was it was quite strange for me having to consciously direct my energy sexually.

C: Yeah, and due to my interest in Tantra, that was really interesting, to me, to see that process, and yeah, our relationships are similar. I mean, we valued practice as much as our sexual relationship. So a lot of our time that we spent together was, was spent practicing partner yoga and meditation, breathing exercises. Some neo-tantra exercises like non-sexual conscious touch and conscious communication and yeah, the, the, the sex between us was, was, it was very different. It was …

D: … we came into the middle somehow … and I think the fact that we, we did come from different ends of the scale or different polarity, I guess you would say, which meant that we, I think we found something special.

C: It's very, for me it was very, it was very loving for a start, and we'd always have to process our emotions before because we were coming into such deep connection, that there was no room for any, anything hanging between us that hadn't been said. So it was very intense.

D: Like you say, sex was a spiritual practice, just like our all of our spiritual practices that we shared together and I feel are sharing those practices together. The breathing and the eye gazing and the movement strengthen those practices, and energy exercises particularly, and conscious touch as well. I mean, it will always be strengthened by us, by the strength of our relationship and our staying together. And so equally, yes, sex became one of those practices and because we set it up so much like that.

A: It was soooo different for us. We didn't have those conscious relating and intimacy skills in our tool kit. It was messy, we had to learn as we went along and I came in with a lot of emotional baggage. And B's strength was a positive and a negative really …

B: That's why she had always gone for the effeminate, willowy beardy types!

A: Yes, not just a physical thing, they didn't challenge me for being emotionally erratic and they weren't sexually forceful …

B: That's the thing with soul mates, they are designed to trigger each other, bring up into the light whatever needs to be seen and worked with.

A: I was used to just running with my emotions, I had been going to women's circles where being able to experience depth of emotion and express it was seen as a strength. But I may have misinterpreted this and I used it as an excuse to be emotionally erratic …

B: And I think it triggered you even more that I was able to stay centered and calm and not react to that because of my facilitating skills …

A: Yes, but we are getting ahead of ourselves. All of that was after …

B: Wow indeed, after … I sometimes wonder if we would have stayed together, I'm glad we did but I do wonder …

A: I am demi-sexual, it's all about love for me and sex is only about expressing that love through my body, our bodies …

B: At the time, sex was a very physical thing for me, an urge to be satisfied and I had a wandering eye for the pretty, hippy workshop girls.

A: I wouldn't usually kiss someone so quickly. I think because there was that heart and soul knowing and even though I didn't find him physically attractive, there was this knowing that there was something there, something he was going to help me move through … progress on my path …

B: We kissed soon after that first hug …

A: And it was bad!

B: Not that bad, because we ended up making love …

A: But yes darling, that was the problem wasn't it? It wasn't making love, my heart already knew I loved you on some spiritual level, but that wasn't love making that we did.

B: *[Looks down and shakes his head and speaks more quietly]* I know that now.

A: It made me realize why I wasn't attracted to men like B … I had wounds around the masculine. It wasn't his fault … I … I … I just sort of let go of everything I wanted in the face of his strength and sense of purpose and I knew that about myself, so I didn't go there before.

B: I wish I could change it now, but it is what it is.

A: We can't really say that anyway, it was our path and it's led to where we are now, you didn't hurt me physically, I hurt my own heart by not listening to it and asking to wait or do things differently.

B: We didn't make … have sex again after that first time.

A: We kept seeing each other because we were in a community situation and there was a lot of emotional tension. I appreciate now how you held space for me, but at the time, that also infuriated me, you always being the strong, clear one.

B: I was taking the brunt for a lot of stuff you were carrying before we met.

A: Yes, and we understand that now, how your past conditioning comes up in relationships. I had a lot of resentment and rage towards masculine men from when I was growing up. I threw it all at him and he didn't run way or tell me I was flawed in any way.

B: I triggered you enormously because I reminded you of your dad, but most of the time I could hold space for you and not get too affected by your emotional attacks. There were the times when it went too far and I would crack and snap back at you.

A: Then we got help from others in the community to process what was going on …

B: Just as well we didn't give up …

A: Yes, because I soon discovered I was pregnant!

B: I remember thinking. Wow we really are stuck together now!

A: We did fast track through a lot of relationship work, we used that book, what was it called?

B: *Partnering*[140]. It was powerful work, and just as well because we soon realized that babies don't actually unify you as a couple, like the rosy TV ads or movies, they actually just bring up more of your stuff!

A: With recovering physically for nearly a year after the birth and not feeling fully emotionally unified, I still didn't want to make love, so we were basically celibate for the first two years of our relationship, which I think made it more challenging but also much richer …

B: I can't say it was easy for me, all the touching without sex, I remember one day, I even did a headstand, literally to direct the blood flow and the energy away from my genitals…

D: *[Interrupts eagerly]* I could teach you some great techniques for channeling energy…

B: *[Continuing without acknowledging D at all]* What was funny was that with all of the emotional relationship work we were doing and how deeply I was coming to love A, I was desperate to make love with her, but I had to hold back, I finally understood what it meant to want to physically express love. My roving eye was only

---

140 Stone, H. and Stone S. L. (2000) Partnering: A New Kind of Relationship: Creating Magic and Excitement in Your Relationship, Nataraj: New World Library.

pointing in one direction and it wasn't with lust, it was with devotion…

A: Soooo … this beautiful level of intimacy came in … I think the work we were doing, but also being parents … the type of intimacy you share with a child, together, a different type of physical intimacy, we started to show that to each other.

B: I would get her undressed when she was tired. Run her baths and brush her hair.

A: We would give each other massages … I had never experienced that type of physical, non-sexual attention. It was for me like the ultimate romantic film, where the action stops at a gentle kiss, and as a child I could imagine that was where it stopped, that you wouldn't have to have sex to show that you loved someone, so that you would stay together.

B: At first it was very clear what was pure intimacy and what was sexuality because we were only intimate and not sexual …

A: But then it eventually became more fluid, combined and was exactly what making love *should* be.

B: I admit, I hadn't understood what making love was before … a profound level of connection that is pleasurable, but pleasure is not the aim, and that somehow just makes the pleasure even greater, but on a different level.

C: I totally get that, the level of connection was something that I'd never experienced before and the fact that it was about the connection, and less about the pleasure but somehow that almost heightened the pleasure, really, but it wasn't like seeking pleasure. It wasn't like the end goal. Sometimes we would stop having sex because we felt fulfilled just by laying together with him sort of soft inside me. So there wasn't that seeking urgency so much. And that was something different.

D: It just felt right to me and I don't think it is, well I never, I didn't, you know, I never had a sexual relationship before. I had one sexual experience but not a sexual relationship and it just wasn't really something I was interested in. So I think this is probably the only way I would be interested in it because it fits more with my spiritual focus. How it goes with my work ethic because we're translating what we're doing in our relationship into our teaching. So the relationship becomes like part of my work ... And that was where most of my energy was directed before.

C: Yeah, exactly ... And so gradually, our sex life became more like another spiritual practice in a way because obviously we were having to process our emotions we were reading about and trying different techniques and practices, energy, movement, conscious touch, massage all these things ... eye gazing, constant eye contact whilst making love. And, yes, it was it was kind of almost like sex became a spiritual practice. That's the only way I can describe it. And obviously, that's what Tantra is all about, with neo-tantra anyway. So it was almost like an integration of understanding the Tantra in practice. And yeah, so that was, that was *really* interesting ...

D: Yes, for me, things are sex but don't necessarily come under the usual remit of sexuality, like you said about laying just laying together without moving and me being soft inside you. I mean, it's not the usual idea of sex but it is the ultimate in intimacy and being close to each other. Just breathing whilst your bodies are connected ...

C: ... And it really varying, and for me, it meant that I didn't necessarily, I guess *need* sex the same way. If we weren't having sex, we were doing so many other intimate things... Just holding each other, entwined, pressing my ear into his chest to listen to his heartbeat, allowing my breath to unify with his, our bodily rhythms to synch into one, that sort of unity became more important than simultaneous orgasms. And the quality of our connection in so many other ways was so much more that it became more that we had to set a date to have sex.

D: … I mean, do you define that soft penetration as sexual? I mean, it's not. The goal isn't orgasm, yes there is connection of the sex organs. So that is not necessarily what most people consider sexual. So I think we are creating a different way of being intimate that fits with both of our natural makeups and … and is accelerating our spiritual growth and growth as a couple.

B: **Soft penetration! What on earth?! You're kidding me right?** *[Nudges D's shoulder]*

D: *[Jumps slightly]* No really *[chuckling timidly]* it is actually possible. It allows you to just 'plug in' physically with each other … so you feel joined physically without feeling a need to do anything. A bit like cuddling but totally connected. You lay there and the energy just moves between you, it's delightful! We learned this from a book …

C: *Tantric Orgasm for Women*[141]. It's a must have! So many beautiful intimacy practices that expand the boundaries of physical intimacy and pleasure. We used that one and *The Art of Sexual Ecstasy*[142] *[A screws up her face skeptically]* yeah, although it sounds like a sex guide, it is so much about energy, and we were doing those energy practices together. Which was quite a revelation to me and although I, although I've been practicing moving energy, I

---

[141] Richardson, D. (2004) *Tantric Orgasm for Women,* Rochester, VT: Destiny Books.

[142] Anand, M (1991) The Art of Sexual Ecstasy: The Path of Sacred Sexuality for Western Lovers, New York: Tarcher Perigee. It is interesting to note that the author republished another version of this book in 2013 entitled The Art of Everyday Ecstasy: The Seven Tantric Keys for Bringing Passion, Spirit and Joy into Every Part of Your Life. The description for this book explains, 'Most people think of ecstasy in terms of sexual ecstasy, which Tantric sex expert Margot Anand wrote about in her bestselling The Art of Sexual Ecstasy. Now, in The Art of Everyday Ecstasy, Anand expands our definition of ecstasy and shows how we can harness its energy to help us live, work, and love more passionately, joyfully, and with true spiritual focus'. The co-creator who referenced the first text offered the caveat that 'it isn't really a sex guide'. It is possible that the author had the same realization and that this led to the creation of the second version of this guide.

don't know if I really believed it. I didn't really believe that you transcended sex through practicing tantric sex, that you could really transmute sexual energy... but I wouldn't say we've totally transcended it. I don't know.

D: The movement of energy, I think … I think because it was something I'd been doing in my practice for a long time. I think I brought it naturally into the sexual arena. And it made our practice of tantric sexuality and leading the energy up into the higher energy centers natural …. It is natural, I think …

C: It's just … Yeah, it's not. It's no longer the most important thing but the quality of it when it happens is so astounding. And kind of, I guess, cosmic, you might say, divine maybe, a sense of connection to the universe and a mind-blowing sense of love.

D: … well, we've come across it with our students that 'that'[143] becomes difficult for them because they end up trying to go towards the pleasure at the base, and ending in genital orgasm …

C: That isn't even needed as often either. I guess it's probably like, when you have a fine meal, you don't really do all the time. It's a special occasion.

D: That for me too, all of my spiritual practice has been about moving my energy upwards and the spiritual realization, because I didn't feel sexually driven. That was what was happening in the sexual scenario too. And I think that made it easier for us to experience that as a couple which was beyond anything I'd experienced in my … my individual practice.

C: So yeah, I guess we both sort of changed each other because he became sexual when he hadn't been sexual for many, many, many years or, I mean never really had a proper sexual relationship, was asexual, and, and I've become less sexual. And sex means

---

[143] He is referring to his practice (and the practices he guides students to perform) to move the life force energy or libido to the higher centers, 'transmuting sexual energy', to experience what he describes as 'divine love' and 'universal consciousness'.

something totally different to me now. It's ... it's not, yes, not something I would ever take lightly again. Having that connection with somebody and ...

B: *Totally*. I guess I would now say that I'm emotional-sexual too. Even if we came to the end of our journey together, I don't see myself going back to that ... predatory mode. It would seem pointless, empty.

A: That's what I love, what I love most about us, we are both coming from that demi-sexual place now, but I can feel it, he's not like loads of these new age guys who use emotional literacy as a way to get laid.

B: Relationships are about so much more. Our deep friendship is the glue that holds us and our family together, no matter what is going on. When you are using your partner as a recreation activity or for some kind of emotional hit or physical high that just isn't there.

A: Yes, that true intimacy is worth soooo much, it's not romantic, it's messy and it is hard work. But you know that you are there for each other, because you work through all the shit that comes up so you get this feeling that nothing can tear you down ... You just see it as a challenge to get through together, side by side, even if that challenge is something inside of you, something you would rather hide.

B: I do envy that spark you two have though. How do you do it? I mean, you seem to have that genuine intimacy, I mean that hard work intimacy, but there's an energy between you ... like, I dunno, like a couple that have just met and have the hots for each other, and let's face it – he didn't even used to like sex!!

A: *[Eyes widen, inhales sharply]* B!!!

B: Sorry babe, I'm just interested ... How does this 'tantra sex' thing work?

C: It's not, it's not just a way to have pleasure, it is a way to share your energy with each other, to make it grow, expand throughout the whole of you, so it is very energizing and connecting. It's so much about the connection; setting up the space with candles, flowers, beautiful throws or silk sheets, starting with sharing vulnerably, eye gazing, massage ... I know, you know this ... I guess - looking at the fine dining thing again... you, when you when you go for an amazing meal, it's ... it's, it's about, more about, the connection with the person that you're with. If you ... if you had a bad connection with them, then you're not going to enjoy the evening and the meal won't be pleasurable. And the way that the restaurant looks is really important. I guess the way your date looks as well. But yeah, the way the restaurant looks is important. And the quality and the tableware and the way that the meal is served. Putting in your mouth and tasting it is just the final piece. Yeah. And also you know that it's an experience. It's an intense setup experience that you're not expecting to have every night of the week ... where you are taking time to create beautiful space and have all the trimmings ... and if you did have it every night of the week, it wouldn't be as special so I get I guess that's what it's like with tantric sex. It's like a fine meal you have occasionally and you set a date to, to do.

D: You're always thinking about your stomach!

[All laugh]

C: Very funny. I just thought ... there's so many more dimensions to our relationship. And I don't know that if that's because we came from different angles in the first place. So we've, we've bought the best of both together and made it really into something unique and special, or I don't really know ...

D: I guess if I was going to look at it in that way ... the different angles ... I would also say that my sexuality is more feminine and yours is more masculine. And maybe we've just both come more into the middle now with that as well. I don't really feel that distinction so much anymore but to begin with it, it did really feel like I felt like you were taking the dominant role. I was passive and I think you were probably more penetrating in a way … I know that's really strange but you … it's almost like you took over my penis and I didn't know who it belonged to anymore. And it almost felt like I was being penetrated and you're always more, more … not forceful, but no, dominant…

C: Fat and aggressive, thanks babe!

[A and B laugh, D grins wryly]

D: Not aggressive! Yes, I think I was always more sensual, into the movement side, of the feeling of our bodies touching and the more sensual aspects of oils and yes, so I think maybe that's unusual. I don't know.

C: Yes, I loved that about you, so unusual in a man.

D: I think you take the lead in other ways with the emotional processing and things as well. And I guess that's probably more of a feminine thing, the emotions, but it did mean that you were doing more of the holding in that way. And I think what I brought to the table is the softer intimacy and energy …

C: And with the intimacy things, they're the most important things … to sit together, to come into stillness, to gaze into each other's eyes to touch each other's hearts with a warm palm, to welcome whatever the other one is with and receive it and reflect and hold each other. And then to breathe together.

A: *[Appreciatively]* Mmmmm.

C: To sit back-to-back feeling, yeah, this body moving in time with yours as you breathe. So connecting and so gentle. And sometimes, that's all that's needed. Connection in nature is amazing as well … so playful and some, something else comes through, without talking and sharing, and yeah, kind of magic. I guess it's almost like we become childlike when we share time together … Playing in Autumn leaves and yeah …

D: Yes, that magic, that spark, that isn't anything to do with sex but is full of sparkling lifeforce … it comes through in everything… And what I think is important in our relationship too is that because its not to do just with sex, we can share that love, that sparkle with everyone, and there is no jealousy between us, whether she is sharing her sparkle with another man or a woman, I just love to see her being loving, sharing her magic…

[The dinner bell rings cutting off the conversation. They all get up to join the queue, and the conversation moves to more trivial matters.]

6.3 A journey of many steps

Many of the co-creators had previously found a beautiful, healing, sacred sexual relationship, and yet either decided to move on or their relationship naturally ended, and they wanted to explore being on their own. I also made the decision to be on my own, due to my relationship addiction, I felt the need to go 'cold turkey'. Even 'mindful relationship' felt to me like it was still taking too much of my attention and focus. I wanted to expand the feeling I had within exploring the **nonsexual** polyamory that my 'open' relationship had opened the door to. I wanted to share love indiscriminately, to offer care where it was needed in the moment and to use my creative energy and love to benefit both my family and my community. I felt the shift of energy almost immediately. It was easy to be present and to meet the moment. I had abundant vitality. I shared the following on my Life Coaching Facebook page a few months after making this decision:

> *Facebook post – 18 January 2017*
>
> I am so grateful for feeling radically Alive and connected to Life and all it has to offer ~ these are a few of the questions I ask myself regularly to stay living in this beautiful, open, connected space ~
>
> "What would love do now?"
>
> "How can I maximize the pleasure available to me in this activity or situation?"
>
> "Am I still serving myself whilst being in full service to the other/this situation?"
>
> "Does this situation or opportunity fit with my vision and values?" and if not, but it is necessary "What is needed, what changes can I make or ask for to shift this to fitting more with my vision of life?"

*　　*　　*

Nine of the co-creators in this research had been sexual and became asexual or started to locate themselves on the asexual spectrum. One, like me, through celibacy as a spiritual practice, although he did this purely as a spiritual exercise (he was a tantrika who wished to experience the fullness of tantric practice and did not agree with the Western way of making it all about sacred sexuality). His journey did not include addiction or trauma, and therefore these were not factors in his decision to become celibate in the way that they were for me. He reported in a similar way to me, that the practice simply became a way of being and he was experiencing full body orgasmic states during his somatic awareness and movement practice and deep bliss in meditation. He no longer had any sexual attraction or desire for sex. The other four co-creators that were not in relationships and had 'become' asexual did not practice celibacy. They simply found that they no longer felt compelled to seek sexual relationships due to their spiritual focus and practices (all practiced some type of meditation and somatic awareness/ movement) coupled with an increasing amount of joy and connection in all other areas of their lives. This was a natural process where their last relationship ended, and they simply did not seek another one.

There was a particular moment that I can now identify as when I became 'solidified' in my aromantic asexuality (at the time I had not even heard of asexuality). It was a moment of ecstatic desubjectification, which led to me feeling that the 'hole' I had within had finally been filled, an experience that I shared within the Facebook group:

ONLY YOU CAN FILL THIS EMPTY SPACE

Last year, I fell in love. Deeply. I fell in love with a very special, spiritual being, who touched my heart and soul in a way that no other ever has.

It wasn't supposed to be in this lifetime. The configuration just couldn't work.

During our last, painful, tear-soaked meeting he gently said, 'I invite you to come back to your center, because that's what the world needs right now, Sovereign beings.'

Oh Yes! I thought. And didn't I make a vow to myself last July, I suddenly recalled, a vow of inner union and celibacy!? So why am I giving so much of my attention to you? Our relationship may have been platonic but it sure was taking up a lot of time and headspace!

For the next 7 days I went into total silence, just me, two cats and my recordings of a master somatic awareness training. No internet, no phone, no messaging, no distractions. I filled my heart with love aided by song, harp and harmonium.

I brought myself back to center ~ using those strong and beautiful practices that I love. I won't say it was easy. And what did I find in the center? Grounding ~ yes, stability ~ yes, love ~ yes, an abundant flow of vital energy ~ YES! And … Emptiness. Yes, I found a strange sense of emptiness despite all of that.

There was a hole now that, in human form, only he could fill. He's very special you see.

It was an emptiness I had only experienced before I started along my path and had all these practices to support me. And back then I was numb, and I had toxic habits, so I guess I didn't even feel the empty space.

I sensed that this emptiness must be a gift and decided to meet it, full on. I did not try to fill it with food, alcohol (or any other delicious beverages), Netflix, YouTube or Facebook. I did not even try to fill it by seeing or video chatting with good friends. In fact, in order to meet it fully, I lessened contact with others.

At times it has felt overwhelming. I met the empty space with heartful singing, with mindful movement and breathing, with constant whispers of love. I danced with the empty space with erotic abandon.

And yesterday, the emptiness overwhelmed me and, of course, the world met me with situations to test me in that emptiness.

As I arrived at my caravan the emptiness had turned into exhaustion. I lit the fire, had some tea, said a silent prayer for help and then surrendered totally. I drifted into sleep and when I awoke, I felt fuller and more joyous than I have ever felt.

God, Spirit, all-pervading Love had, during my total surrender, filled the empty space.

Now my inner union has a third party. Oh, and what a party! To feel so full, so complete. I got in the car and put on the radio and the lyrics *'Only you can fill this empty space … space … space, this empty space'* blared out.

I sung, I sung my heart out, but not to my lost love, to God … yes … only You can fill this empty space.

7. Ars Erotica

This chapter includes many poems written in collaboration with co-creators in response to their experiences of non-sexual pleasure. These poems aim to offer an experiential reading of asexual erotic embodiment. They are offered in place of a traditional conclusion. Inspired by Kay Inckle's book (2007), this chapter offers an alternative to a traditional conclusion, by utilizing poems to articulate the experience of erotically embodied asexuality, which is the key theme of this research, and to 'leave open the possibilities of meaning, interpretation and transformation' (Inckle 2006: 14-15).

A shorter version of a traditional conclusion, offering an analysis of the contribution to knowledge, reflections and future research recommendations is offered as a 'Summary' following this chapter.

These poems point towards the redefining of human pleasure, they add a cacophony of voices to the voice that Lorde began articulating in her essay *Uses of the Erotic* (1978). They challenge the discourse that sexuality equals fulfilment, and that asexuality is a lack. They illustrate how the redirection of the life force, also known as libido, leads to a vitalizing and sensitization of the whole bodymind and an increased capacity to experience nonsexual pleasure and, in some cases, spiritual ecstasy. Many are written as a composite of shared experience.

The language used may seem 'sexual' in nature. I have deliberately used the erotic language that (as discussed previously) was originally utilized by mystics to describe their ecstatic experiences. Language that was subsequently purloined and imprisoned by 'sexuality' and its hegemony over the erotic. It is my hope that by reclaiming this language to articulate nonsexual erotic experiences, that I may contribute to the liberation of the erotic and erotic language from its sexual prison.

There has been much theoretical discussion and analysis in the previous chapters to 'frame' these illustrations of experience, and these poems are therefore offered without a theoretical 'frame' or analysis.

This space is a gallery for embodied experiences to speak for themselves. An exhibition of poetic canvases stroked with brushes of experience and hues of meaning.

* * *

Whet dream

She is dreaming of sunflowers
Walking through summer meadows
The sun permeating through clothing
The breeze caressing her skin

Joy floods through her
From feet to brain
Her body shuddering with pleasure

She awakes eyes wide
'Was that sexual?' She thinks
Confused by sexusociety's lies

*   *   *

I'd rather dance[144]

She gently drops inside
Away from busy mind
Her inner eye appreciating
Body's curves
Living spinal liquid
Rippling into bones
Feet like roots
She pushes down
Feeling sap rising
Flowing music pours over skin
As she rivers through the crowd

Beat pulses
Pushing her into meeting edges
Touching boundaries of self
Reaching the stuck places
Excavating mud from the pit
Poking cracks for fresh air
Mining for a lost lode
Jerking rhythms thrust her
Within an urgent liberation of
Discharging bodies

---

[144] This poem is articulating the experience of a 5-Rhythms class. It goes through each of the 'rhythms' in turn. 5-Rhythms is a conscious movement practice, described as 'ecstatic dance', developed by Gabrielle Roth. All the co-creators within this research had experienced the practice of 5-Rhythms.

Tempestuous tempo rises
The atmosphere shifts
She is engulfed in electrification
Smell of sweat and anticipation
Impulsive, frenzied movements
Carrying intensity of feeling
Tremoring over swerving limbs
Undulating her molten spine
Swirling heat in belly
Roaring the intensity
Echoed from around the room
First one, then three
Until they are all united in one tribal
Roar of release

The little death gives way
To lyrical harmony
Sweet swing of lilting cadence
Swaying her body deliciously
No effort necessary, or possible
The body moves freely
Playfully, celebratory
Each greeting the other
With lover's gaze
Seeing the Beloved everywhere
Bodies moving in, and out
Connection without attachment
Suddenly everyone is Beautiful

Music slows

Lilting piano drifts through the air

Touching chords in hearts

Movement slows

Bodies gravitate to closeness

Softly stroking limbs

A group structure of stillness

Breath unifies

Sighs of satisfaction

Bodies spent

Lightly tingling

*   *   *

Sweet solitude

Oh! Sweet solitude

That allows me to notice

Tiny wild strawberries

Trilling flutter of Robin

Gurgling splash of distant brook

Oh! Sweet solitude

That allows me to appreciate

Roses' airborne essence

A blackberry's bittersweet burst

Dewdrops shining rainbows

Oh! Sweet solitude

That allows me to feel

The pulse of my blood

Silk skin on soft cotton

A caress in gentlest breeze

Oh! Sweet solitude

That holds me in Presence

The stillness behind the hum

Ordinary contentment

That overcomes me

* * *

Ars Erotica

She sits naked
Vulnerably present
As he penetrates
Deeply
With his eyes
Through flesh
To soul
Capturing her
Essence

He sees her
Landscape
Curves, crevasses, scars
Arousing
His creativity
Energy pulsing
From hand
To brush
Creating
Beauty

A relationship
Beyond words
Or touch
To see
Beyond seeing
Silently
Surrendering
Boundaries
Dissolving

* * *

The kiss (part 1)

They are kissing
Very gently
Only just Friends
Delicately connecting

It is gentle
Yet opening
Heart warming
Rush inducing

Ankle he touches
Stoking to knee
She inhales
Shuddering deliciously

"What was That?!"
He asks
Full of hope
Of getting more

"An energy orgasm
Full body", she says
As she walks
Out the door

*   *   *

The Kiss (part 2 – The Rose)

Silky, soft sensual
I lean into the Fragrance
Of You

You welcome me In
Right to the Centre
My lips exploring
Your Beauty
My nostrils tingle
Joy runs though me

Your pink petals
Mirroring
The Blossoming
Of my Heart

*   *   *

Heart~gasm

The pastel softness
Encompasses her heart
Warming and glowing
As she smudges chalky pink
Giving an aura of Feeling
To the Fairy of Love

The zestful green
Of Apple Blossom leaves
Bloom from the pencil
Vividly etching
Traces of Joy
River over her hands

She leans back
With happy gaze
Heart expanding
Flourishing vibrating
Tingling Vital
Waves of joy
Encompassing radiating

*   *   *

Orchestral orgasm

Violins thrum in union
Air tingling with sound
Cellos join the play
Sound swells
Engulfing her

She gazes on Harmony
Bodies creating as One
Surrendering to
The moment
Melodiously merging

Vibrancy grows
Tickling toes
Waving upwards
Rousing heart chords into
A Symphony of Sensation

*　*　*

Sacred Union (part 1)

Gazing into your eyes
Transparent awareness
Gazing into
Transparent awareness
Notions of 'you' and 'I'
Merge in shared interiority

Touching your skin
Somatic awareness
Touching
Somatic awareness
Exquisite connection
Melting into sublime pleasure

Moving closer
Magnetic north
Connecting into
Magnetic south
The longing to merge
Drawing bodies together

Energy pulsating
Across poles
Into spine
Spontaneously ascending
The transcending impulse
Drawing energy upwards

Hearts merging
One heart
Melting
Into the other
The fire of Love
Forging Union   *CC*

*   *   *

Sacred Union (Part 2)

I sit
Meditating
Coccyx warm
Gently pulsating
Open to Earth

I breathe
Evenly
Heart soft
Ribs tenderly cradle
Open to Love

I empty
Mindfully
Forehead penetrated
With sparkling spaciousness
Open to Infinity

CC

*   *   *

Sacred Union (Part 3 - The Fire of Love)

Fire of love emerging
Flaring in my belly
Rising upwards
Fanned by the breath of my Heart

Fire burning my thoughts
Consuming the notion of "I"
Clearing the path to Awareness
Of the slightest shiver of a thought

Fire illuminating my Heart
Radiating throughout my being
How can I describe this Bliss
When You have burned away all words?

CC

*   *   *

Stripping

When you strip away everything
You are left with nothing

No thing
     yet
       Every
    Thing

A space
     yet
      not
    Emptiness

A s p a c e
  Filled
With pulsation
  Vibration
Quantum particles Dancing
To The Song that is not sung

Timeless Tremor of Joy
    Reverberating

An Energy

    Love

*   *   *

Summary

The overarching aim of this book was to add to the limited area of asexuality studies that focuses on asexual erotics (Smith 2017, Przyblo 2019) by offering a modern day, erotic, mystic, embodied and experiential narrative of asexuality. I asked the question 'what is the experience of asexuality?' as opposed to it being defined on a lack of experience. I also articulated that it would try to the address the troubling question of 'how can we define and describe an erotically embodied asexuality without utilizing terminology that refers to the sexual?'.

I have also articulated throughout the book, my aim to paint a canvas of stories accentuated with hues of experience, where the brushstrokes of creative methods convey ineffable experience, creating a cubist portrait, that can be interpreted differently depending on the angle from which it is being observed. I aimed to weave a tapestry, not from the threads of meticulous explanations, but in the rich, vibrant threads of erotically charged voices, creating an embroidery of stories that entwine cords of shared experience. I hoped to offer an embodied experiential reading experience that did not offer closed explanations but would be open to the reader's interpretation and temporal understanding.

Through the collaboratively produced creative outputs, this research has told a story of 'platonically erotic' relationships, relationships not only to other humans, but with nature and the divine. It has described asexuality as a 'becoming' an orientation that is formed through the interactions within these relationships. It has described the experience of erotically embodied asexuality. It has shown how asexuality can be a choice, a practice that becomes a way of being. It has illustrated how the lack of asexual representation can lead to asexual individuals trying to 'fix themselves' until they discover that there are other options than sexuality and romance as authenticated ways of being. It has offered examples of non-sexual pleasure and intimacy that, within limited Western discourse, would be conflated with the sexual. It has also illustrated how the pleasure of desubjectification, described in a sexual and 'Godless' way by Foucault (1963) can be a nonsexual and spiritual experience, one which was at the heart of some of the co-creators' narratives.

This research makes an important contribution to challenging cultural assumptions regarding sexuality, relationships, the erotic, and the libido It utilizes vulnerability in order to destabilize compulsory sexuality and highlight the damaging effect of emotional and sexual commodification. It offers a highly personal, engaging account that reaches out to those who have similar experiences. It enables them to feel validated and able to articulate their experience. It offers weight to the expositions of Marcuse, Lorde, hooks, Griffin, Soelle, Gafini and Kincaid, McDaniel and Smith, who all articulate that the sexual is only one small part of the fullness of the erotic; by offering the sensory accounts of erotic experience within individuals who are asexual.

It makes a contribution to existing research on asexual erotics (Smith 2017, Przybylo 2019), compulsory sexuality and couples' culture (Carrigan 2011, 2012, Gupta 2013, 2015, Przybylo 2013) and the commodification of emotion, romance, relationships and sexuality (Illouz 1997, 2007, 2017, 2021, 2022). This work furthers the efforts of these a/sexuality scholars to displace sexuality from its central role in modern Western performances of identity.

This research also furthers the aim of Smith (2017) to describe asexuality as something other than a lack and to describe the orientation without mentioning the word 'sexual', as it is not a *sexual* orientation (this problem with definition is one that he termed the 'asexual paradox'). The co-creators and I offer the possible orientation 'platonically erotic'.

This research offers some insight into Scott and Dawson's (2015) question of how asexual individuals negotiate intimate relationships (especially with sexual people). It also challenges sexual discourse, and furthers the work done to disrupt the notion of universal compulsory sexuality and the resistance of sexual norms, that has been achieved by Przybylo (2013, 2019), Gupta (2013, 2015) and Carrigan (2011, 2012).

The narrative within this book offers a new way of imagining asexuality, via the displacement of sexuality from its current position at center stage in Western society's modern-day performances of identity.

Whilst acknowledging the work of AVEN in validating asexuality, it challenges their notion that asexuality is an innate orientation. It postulates that asexuality can be a 'becoming' (Deleuze and Guattari 1980); the destination of celibate practice, an expression of spiritual devotion and a valid choice for the traumatized who do not wish to 'fix themselves' to fit within 'sexusociety' (Przybylo 2011). 'Erotically embodied asexuality' introduces a new category within the asexual spectrum.

I hope that this research will encourage all asexuals to try to define themselves in terms of asexual flourishing, what they are rather than what they are not, to articulate how they experience their life energy (e.g. through intellectual pursuits, physical prowess, creativity and no doubt many other ways). And to also articulate how they experience pleasure, rather than having the symbol of 'cake'[145] as proposed by the AVEN community, which could produce the idea that the only way asexuals experience pleasure is by eating unhealthy foods.

Smith shared the following in his doctoral thesis conclusion 'we need to consider the possibility that one day, perhaps, people will no longer quite understand all this fuss about sexuality. We need to ponder the chance that eventually people will no longer know why sexuality constituted such a tremendous part of our subjectivity and experience' (2017: 202). I hope that this research contributes to the reformulating of constructs and beliefs that may lead to a new discourse, and that it helps to facilitate Smith's vision being realized.

The analysis of Marcuse's theories regarding capitalism and the suppression of eros, especially when viewed through the lens of asexuality and the experiences shared within this book, point towards how we are manipulated by discourse and media; that promotes a focus on the genitals and sexual instincts. It seems we are living in a society that is obsessed with transforming the human being into a sexual organ, rather than a body that can experience pleasure in every pore.

This research aims to offer an alternative to this obsession with the sexual. An obsession that leads to the problem of people uttering the words 'asexual lump' on terrestrial television, and it not being questioned[146]. Asexual people are often seen as lifeless, as the 'ultimate kink' because they are seen as having no life force in a

---

[145] A slice of cake, colored with the bands from the asexual flag, is the emoji used in the AVEN online community to encapsulate the shared statement 'I'd rather have cake'. This inspired the poem 'I'd rather dance', shared in the Chapter 7. The co-creators and I would use the dancer emoji in a purple, gray, white and black dress, combined with the sparkles emoji, as a symbol of erotically embodied asexuality.

[146] See Chapter 3, section 3.3.

society that has conflated this beautiful energy with the impulse to rub genital organs together.

This research has tried to illustrate that by taking the focus from the genitals the whole body can come alive; energies that once swelled the genital organs can be redirected towards love in action. When the everyday such as 'painting the back garden fence' becomes pleasurable we are no longer prey for consumerist culture. It brings the message that this erotic embodiment is not something gained through attending commercialized spiritual workshops but is something that is free to everyone[147]. It is not something that can be 'bought off a shelf' or read about, and therefore is not attractive to those brainwashed by the lie that more success, more consuming of romantic products, packaged spirituality, or anything that you can buy and instantly consume, is going to liberate you.

This research was limited in its scope by the small community of co-creators selected and the fact that we are largely white and middle class. This means that we have the financial resources which give us the privilege of being able to decide to lessen our participation in capitalist culture through self-employment and part-time working, often in creative, therapeutic, or caring endeavors; lessening the time in which we are a 'unit of production'. This has offered us the time and space for spiritual practice and self-reflection, and work that is inherently erotic; we not have to undertake 'alienating labor' which further suppresses eros, according to Marcuse (1955, 1974). However, the fact that this is the story of a possibility of a way of being, rather than offering a generalization or a 'truth', with the aim of offering hope and recognition and disrupting current discourse, has been articulated throughout the book.

---

[147] As illustrated by the co-creators' experiences, it can be achieved with the freely available disciplined practice of present moment awareness, body awareness, emotional awareness and authenticity in relationship to others and self.

This research offers a resource of embodied asexual narratives and is an important contribution to knowledge for scholars who wish to research the sociology of desire, the sociology of the libido and the sociology of love. It also contributes to the growth of reflexive and creative methodologies such as autoethnography, sensory autoethnography, embodied inquiry, auto/biography, sociological fiction, poetry as method and narrative performative approaches. This book is a fusion of creativity and academic scholarship that challenges academic and doctoral conventions. It can act as a beacon to those who are struggling to fit their work into traditional structures and those who wish to format their work in a layered style, interweaving theoretical and empirical analysis, poetic prose and creative outputs.

There were two themes that I identified following the analysis of my narrative, that did not fit within the main focus of the research as stated at the end of literature review. These were 'the 'motivations for asexuals participating in sex and the consequences of consensual unwanted sex' and 'acknowledgement of the potential link between sexual trauma and asexuality'. These themes have only been explored lightly. It would be useful for more extensive research to be undertaken into these themes. To understand the importance of consent and how this can work in practice[148] and how asexuals experience consensual unwanted sex and the mental health implications. Work that looks at asexuality as a valid choice for traumatized individuals, and how that could work in practice, would also be helpful.

As identified in section 4.6, the training needs of qualitative researchers is an area which perhaps needs to be addressed with research into the experiences of qualitative researchers and

---

[148] Rather than in facilitated workshops or 'conscious relationships', with idealized models such as that articulated by Betty Martin (2021), which were helpful and beneficial to the co-creators, but which are challenging to apply in a natural context.

participants, to see the effects of this 'blurring of boundaries' between qualitative research and therapy.

Research into the point at which the spiritual ascetic practice of celibacy turns into a way of being and becomes asexuality would be interesting, and would add to the discussions and experiences shared within this research. I am also interested in the statement from C S Lewis which refers to the theology about the fall of man (the 'Garden of Eden' story), and that some ancient scriptures say that if man had not fallen our pleasure would be much greater than the sexual pleasure we now experience. This could be an interesting area of study within theology. Perhaps, by returning to erotic simplicity, we can regain this capacity for pleasure and not be such easy fodder for manipulation.

This research has been equally rewarding and challenging. Staying true to my heart whilst meeting academic requirements has made me feel I am riding an 'emotional rollercoaster'. This rollercoaster has had lows of not feeling 'heard' or even 'squashed', with alternating 'highs' when I have managed to use my rational capacities to translate the voice of my heart into academic language.

The collaborative creation of the creative outputs was an expression of the erotic in action. It was thrilling to me to come to shared meanings and interpretations and to find these echoed in the theoretical material. It was also, at times, difficult, when I thought the creative pieces were finalized and a co-creator would come back to me some time later with something that they did not feel comfortable with, after some reflection.

I have found this research personally rewarding, I have found great insight into myself, both who I am and who I want to be. I have connected with like-minded or perhaps like-souled people who have shared experiences and ways of being.

I hope that by revealing these experiences of other ways of being, that new possibilities will be opened for non-sexual individuals to emerge and flourish in unique ways.

Epilogue

*We shall not cease from exploration, and the end of
all our exploring will be to arrive where we started
and know the place for the first time.*
T.S. Eliot

Towards the end of this extensive research, I encountered the rich spiritual traditions of Eastern Orthodoxy. The Orthodox Church, with its profound sense of mystery, the engagement of all the senses within worship, devotion, hesychasm and an emphasis on Theosis (deification), offered me the spiritual depth and discipline I have long sought. The treasures of the Orthodox tradition, particularly the Philokalia, encapsulate the essence of what I had been seeking: a path of circular-attention, deep, heart-centered contemplative prayer, and a way to experience the divine presence in daily life. This collection of texts by Eastern Orthodox Fathers resonates deeply with my quest for a spirituality that embraces the mind, the heart and the body.

My disenchantment began in childhood, mirroring the societal disenchantment Max Weber postulated as the result of rationalization and secularization. This early disenchantment severed my once vibrant connection with Jesus, leaving a void that persisted into adulthood. Weber's theory provided a framework that helped me understand this personal loss as part of a broader cultural phenomenon, allowing me to grieve this spiritual disconnection more fully.

In my academic and spiritual explorations, I found that true spiritual knowledge comes through the heart, not just the intellect, a concept found both in the Philokalia and the direct teachings of Jesus quoted within the bible. These teachings deeply resonated for me with my journey from disenchantment to re-enchantment through embodied experience.

To my delight I also found that my research on the spiritual erotic found profound reflections within Orthodox thought. Two works in particular, *The Eros of Repentance* by George Kapsanis and *Christianity and Eros* by Philip Sherrard, provided invaluable perspectives on nonsexual eros that aligned with the themes of my thesis. These texts explore how repentance and divine love can be experienced as a form of eros—a passionate, all-encompassing love that transcends the purely physical. Kapsanis discusses how repentance itself is an act of returning to one's true self in God, while Sherrard delves into the transformative power of divine love that integrates body and soul.

These books explore the concept of eros as a transformative force that transcends mere physical desire and encompasses a broader, more profound spiritual yearning. Kapsanis discusses how repentance can be a form of spiritual eros, an act of turning towards God with passionate love and desire for union. Sherrard's exploration of Christian eros delves into the mystical dimensions of love, portraying it as a divine gift that can elevate the soul. He also discusses the concept of 'sexual' energy and redefines this as an erotic energy that can lead one to a profound union with a partner and with God. He explains that the union between a couple is sacred when they see God in the other and honor each other as sacred vessels. He explains that as a relationship matures the couple come to experience this eros flowing between them without the need for sexuality.

There is a vast richness to be found within the Orthodox faith and tradition, an exploration I am excited to begin.

Bibliography

Acierno R, Brady K, Gray M, Kilpatrick D G, Resnick H, and Best C L (2002) 'Psychopathology following interpersonal violence: A comparison of risk factors in older and younger adults', *Journal of Clinical Psychology, 8*(1): 13-23.

Ainsley, H. (2020) *Cardi B and Megan Thee Stallion's WAP makes it three weeks at UK Number 1*. Online: The Official UK Charts Company.

Åkerström, M. (2013). Curiosity and Serendipity in Qualitative Research. *Qualitative Sociology Review, 9* (2): 10–18.

Allett, N ,Keightley, E and Pickering, M (2011) Toolkit 16: Using Self Interviewing *University of Manchester*.

Antonsen, A N, Zdaniuk, B, Yule, M & Brotto, L A (2020) 'Ace and Aro: Understanding Differences in Romantic Attractions Among Persons Identifying as Asexual' *Archives of Sexual Behavior 49,* no. 6 (July): 1615-1630.

Arvay, M J (2003) 'Doing reflexivity: a collaborative narrative approach' in R*eflexivity: A Practical Guide for Researchers in Health and Social Sciences*, eds. Finlay, L & Gough, B. New Jersey: John Wiley & Sons.

Asexuality Visibility and Education Network (AVEN) (2022), Overview page, AVEN, viewed 22 February 2022.

Asexuality Visibility and Education Network (AVEN) (2022), Welcome/home page, AVEN, viewed 22 February 2022.

Athanasius, St. (c.338[2017]) *On the Incarnation: De Incarnatione Verbi Dei.* London: CreateSpace Independent Publishing.

Atkinson, P. (1997). Narrative turn or blind alley? *Qualitative Health Research, 7*: 325-344.

Balzer Carr, B, Ben Hagai, E, & Zurbriggen, E L (2017) Queering Bem: Theoretical intersections between Sandra Bem's scholarship and queer theory. *Sex Roles 76*: 655–668.

Barnes, J.W. (2015) *Stories, Senses and the Charismatic Relation': A Reflexive Exploration of Christian Experience*. Doctoral Thesis. Brighton: University of Sussex.

Barounis, C (2014) 'Compulsory Sexuality and Asexual/Crip Resistance in John Cameron Mitchell's Shortbus.' In *Asexualities: Feminist and Queer Perspectives*, edited by Cerankowski, K J and Milks, M: 174–96. New York: Routledge.

Bendelow, G. and Williams S. (1998) 'The 'libidinal' body: psychoanalysis, critical theory and the 'problem' of human desire' in Williams & Bendelow, *The Lived Body: sociological themes, embodied issues.* London: Routledge.

Berger, P. L. (1963) *Invitation to Sociology: A Humanistic Perspective*. NJ: Anchor Books.

Berger, P. L. (1965). TOWARDS A SOCIOLOGICAL UNDERSTANDING OF PSYCHOANALYSIS. *Social Research, 32*(1), 26–41.

Berger, P.L. (1967) *Sacred Canopy: Elements of a Sociological Theory of Religion*. New York: Anchor Books.

Bishop, S (2019) *Touch in Contemporary Tantra: Transgression, Healing, and Ecstasy in Women's Constructions of Selfhood*. Doctoral Thesis. Edinburgh: University of Edinburgh.

Bob-Waksberg R (2020) *BoJack Horseman*. Netflix. Viewed 1 April 2022.

Bogaert, A F (2004) Asexuality: Prevalence and associated factors in a national probability sample. *Journal of Sex Research, 41*(3): 279–287.

Bogaert, A F (2012) *Understanding Asexuality*. Maryland: Rowman & Littlefield Publishers.

Bogaert, A F (2015) 'Asexuality: What it is and why it matters'. *Journal of Sex Research, 52*(4): 362-379.

Bourdieu, P (1994) *Practical Reason*. Palo Alto, CA: Stanford University Press.

Bourdieu, P (1997) 'The forms of capital'. In *Halsey, A H, Lauder, H, Brown, P and Wells, A S (Eds.), Education: Culture, Economy and Society*. Oxford: Oxford University Press.

Breslow A.S., Sandil R., Brewster M.E., Parent M.C., Chan A., Yucel A., Bensmiller N., Glaeser E. (2020) Adonis on the apps: Online objectification, self-esteem, and sexual minority men. *Psychol. Men Masc (21):* 25–35.

Brewer, J (2005) 'The public and the private in C. Wright Mill's life and work', *Sociology (39):* 661-677.

Brintnall, K.L. (2012) *Ecce Homo: The Male-Body-in-Pain as Redemptive Figure*. Chicago: University of Chicago Press.

Brotto, L A, and Yule, M (2017) Asexuality: Sexual orientation, paraphilia, sexual dysfunction, or none of the above? *Archives of Sexual Behavior, 46*(3): 619–627.

Brotto, L A, Knudson, G, Inskip, J, Rhodes, K, and Erskine, Y (2010) 'Asexuality: A Mixed-Methods Approach', *Archives of Sexual Behavior* (39): 599-618.

Brown, N (2019) 'Emerging Researcher Perspectives: Finding Your People: My Challenge of Developing a Creative Research Methods Network', *International Journal of Qualitative Methods:* January 2019.

Brown, P G (2016) *College Students, Social Media, Digital Identities, and the Digitized Self*. Doctoral Thesis. Boston: Lynch School of Education, Boston College.

Browning, J R, Kessler D, Hatfield E and Choo P (1999) 'Power, Gender, and Sexual Behavior'. *The Journal of Sex Research, 36(4):* 342-347.

Budgeon, S (2008) Couple Culture and the Production of Singleness. *Sexualities, 11*(3): 301–325.

Burnam, M A, Stein J A, Golding J M, Siegel J M, Sorenson S B, Forsythe A B, and Telles C A (1988) 'Sexual assault and mental disorders in a community population' *Journal of consulting and clinical psychology, 56*(6): 843.

Burns, E (2010) Developing Email Interview Practices in Qualitative Research, *Sociological Research Online, 15*(4): 24–35.

Burton, N (2012 [2020]) *The Origins of Love*. Online: Psychology Today. Accessed 15/11/2022.

Bury, M (1982) 'Chronic illness as biographical disruption'. *Sociology of Health and Illness, 4(2)*: 167-182.

Bury, M (1991) 'The sociology of chronic illness: A review of research and prospects'. *Sociology of Health and Illness, 13(4)*: 451-468.

Butler, J (1990/2007) *Gender trouble: feminism and the subversion of identity*. New York: Routledge.

Butler, J (1993) *Bodies that matter: on the discursive limits of 'sex'*. New York: Routledge.

Butler, J (2004) *Undoing gender*. New York: Routledge.

Canda E. R., Furman L. D. (2010) *Spiritual Diversity in Social Work Practice: The Heart of Helping*. 2nd edn. New York: Oxford University Press.

Canda, E. and Furman, L.D., (2009) *Spiritual Diversity in Social Work Practice: The Heart of Helping*. US: Open University Press.

Carless, D. and Douglas, K. (2022) 'Collaborative Autoethnography: From Rhythm and Harmony to Shared Stories and Truths'. In *Handbook of Autoethnography: Second Edition*. 2022: 155-165 Eds Adams, T. E., Holman Jones, S. and Ellis, C. New York: Routledge.

Carrigan, M (2011) 'There's more to life than sex? Difference and commonality within the asexual community'. *Sexualities*, *14*(4): 462–478.

Carrigan M (2012) 'How do you know you don't like it if you haven't tried it?' Asexual agency and the sexual assumption. In: Morrison TG, Morrison M A, Carrigan M A and McDermott D T (eds) *Sexual Minority Research in the New Millennium*: 3-20. New York: Nova Science.

Castro Á., Barrada J.R. (2020) Dating Apps and Their Sociodemographic and Psychosocial Correlates: A Systematic Review. *Int J Environ Res Public Health, (18)*: 6500.

Catania, J A, Binson, D, Canchola, J, Pollack, L M, Hauck, W and Coates, T J (1996) Effects of interviewer gender, interviewer choice, and item wording on responses to questions concerning sexual behavior. *Public Opinion Quarterly 60(3)*: 345–375.

Cerankowski, K J and Milks M, eds. (2014) *Asexualities: Feminist and Queer Perspectives*. New York: Routledge.

Chan, L. S. (2017) The role of gay identity confusion and outness in sex-seeking on mobile dating apps among men who have sex with men: A conditional process analysis. *J. Homosex. (64):* 622–637.

Chang, H. (2022) 'Individual and Collaborative Autoethnography for Social Science Research'. In *Handbook of Autoethnography: Second Edition.* 2022: 53-65. Eds Adams, T. E., Holman Jones, S. and Ellis, C. New York: Routledge.

Chasin, C D (2011) 'Theoretical Issues in the Study of Asexuality', *Archives of Sexual Behavior* 40(4): 713–723.

Chasin, C (2013) 'Reconsidering Asexuality and Its Radical Potential', *Feminist Studies, 39*(2): 405-426.

Chasin, C J (2015) 'Making Sense in and of the Asexual Community: Navigating Relationships and Identities in a Context of Resistance'. *Journal of Community & Applied Social Psychology* (25)2, (March/April): 177–80.

Chasin, C J (2019) 'Asexuality and the Re/construction of Sexual Orientation', In *Expanding the Rainbow: Exploring the Relationships of Bi+, Polyamorous, Kinky, Ace, Intersex, and Trans People*: 209–19, eds. Simula, B L , Sumerau, J E and Miller, A. Boston: Brill Sense.

Chen, A (2020) *Ace: What Asexuality Reveals About Desire, Society, and the Meaning of Sex*. Boston: Beacon Press.

Chenail, R. (2018) 'A Guide for Autoethnography Appreciation', Abstracts, Oral, and Symposia Presentation for Qualitative Methods Conference, 2018. (2018). *International Journal of Qualitative Methods, 17*(1).

Chenoweth, E., Stephan, M. (2012) *Why Civil Resistance Works: The Strategic Logic of Nonviolent Conflict (Columbia Studies in Terrorism and Irregular Warfare)*. Columbia University Press.

Chenoweth, E. (2013). *The success of nonviolent civil resistance*. Boulder: TEDx Talks. Published online, 2013: YouTube. Accessed: 20/09/2023.

Chevigny, K and Davenport, B (2012) *(A)Sexual*. FilmBuff. Amazon. Viewed 12 November 2021.

Chia, M. (2009) *Alchemy of Sexual Energy: Connecting to the Universe from Within*. Vermont: Destiny Books.

Chia, M., Winn, M. (1984) *Taoist Secrets of Love: Cultivating Male Sexual Energy*. Kindle Edition: Aurora Press.

Choi E.P.H., Wong J.Y.H., Fong D.Y.T. (2016) An emerging risk factor of sexual abuse: The use of smartphone dating applications. *Sex. Abuse J. Res. Treat:* 107906321667216.

Choi E.P.H., Wong J.Y.H., Lo H.H.M., Wong W., Chio J.H.M., Fong D.Y.T. (2017) Association between using smartphone dating applications and alcohol and recreational drug use in conjunction with sexual activities in college students. *Subst. Use Misuse (52):* 422–428.

Chuck L and Brady, B (2018) *Big Bang Theory*. Online video series, Netflix. Viewed 29 January 2019.

Coduto K.D., Lee-Won R.J., Baek Y.M. (2020) Swiping for trouble: Problematic dating application use among psychosocially distraught individuals and the paths to negative outcomes. *J. Soc. Pers. Relatsh, (37):* 212–232.

Copeland, A. (2022) *Would I lie to you, Series 15, Episode 8,* BBC: Zeppotron. First aired 25 Feb 2022. Rerun: 13 Oct 2023.

Cuesta, M (2006) *Dexter*, CBS Studios International. Amazon. Viewed 22 March 2022.

Cuthbert, K (2019) '"When we talk about gender we talk about sex": (a)sexuality and (a)gendered subjectivities'. *Gender and Society*, 33(6): 841-864.

Davis, E.H. (2021). Ars Romantica. *American Book Review 42*(3): 27.

Dawn, C. (2018) *Reclaiming Eros: A Heroine's Journey.* US: CreateSpace Independent Publishing.

Dawson, M, Scott, S, and McDonnell, L (2018) '"Asexual" Isn't Who I Am": The Politics of Asexuality', *Sociological Research Online*, 23(2): 374–391.

De Ropp, R (1969), *Sex Energy*, Delta, New York.

Decker, J S (2015) *The Invisible Orientation: An Introduction to Asexuality*. New York: Carrel Books.

Deleuze, G. and Guattari, F. (1972) *Anti-Oedipus: Capitalism and Schizophrenia.* Reprint 1983. Minnesota: University of Minnesota Press.

Deleuze, G. and Guattari, F. (1980) *A Thousand Plateaus: Capitalism and Schizophrenia*. Reprint 1987. Minnesota: University of Minnesota Press.

Dempster D, Rogers S, Pope A L, Snow M, and Stoltz K B (2015) Insecure Parental Attachment and Permissiveness Risk Factors for Unwanted Sex Among Emerging Adults, *The Family Journal, 23(4),* 358-367.

Denzin, N K (2001) Interpretive Interactionism. In *Applied social research methods, 2nd ed.* CA: Sage Publications, Inc.

Denzin, N K (2003) *Performance Ethnography Critical pedagogy and the Cultural Politics of Culture.* Thousand Oaks, CA: Sage.

Denzin, N. K. (2022). 'Challenges and Futures of Autoethnography'. In *Handbook of Autoethnography: Second Edition.* 2022: 291-29, Eds. Adams, T. E., Holman Jones, S. and Ellis, C. New York: Routledge.

Dillman, D A, Smyth, J D and Christian, L M (2009) *Internet, mail, and mixed-mode surveys: The tailored design method.* Hoboken: John Wiley & Sons, Inc.

Downing, L. (2013). "Afterword: On 'Compulsory Sexuality,' Sexualization, and History." In *The Routledge History of Sex and the Body : 1500 to the Present,* Toulalan, S., and Fisher, K. eds., Taylor & Francis Group, 2013. *ProQuest Ebook Central*.

Elden, S. (2018). Histoire de la sexualité 4: Les aveux de la chair, Michel Foucault. *Theory, Culture & Society, 35(7-8)*: 293-311.

Elgie, E (2020) *Being and Doing: Interrogating Dominant Narratives of Asexual Kinship in an Amatonormative Culture.* Master's Thesis. University of British Columbia.

Ellis, C. (1999). Heartful Autoethnography. *Qualitative Health Research, 9*(5): 669-683.

Ellis, C and Bochner, A P (2000) 'Autoethnography, Personal Narrative, Reflexivity', in Denzin, N K & Lincoln, Y S (eds.) *Handbook of Qualitative Research.* London: Sage Publications.

Ellis, C. (2000). Creating criteria: An ethnographic short story. *Qualitative Inquiry, 6*(2): 273-277.

Ellis, C and Berger, L (2002) 'Their Story/My Story/Our Story: Including the Researcher's Experience in Interview Research', in Gubrium, J F & Holstein, J A (eds.) *Handbook of Interview Research.* London: Sage.

Ellis, C. (2022). 'Autoethnography in the time of uncertainty: Finding hope and purpose'. In *Handbook of Autoethnography: Second Edition.* 2022: xxi-xxiv. Eds Adams, T. E., Holman Jones, S. and Ellis, C. New York: Routledge.

Ellis-Petersen, H. (2018*) Under Swami's spell': 14 tourists claim sexual assault by guru at Thai yoga retreat.* Online: The Guardian.

Emens E F (2013) 'Compulsory Sexuality', *Stanford Law Review*, 66: 303-386, Columbia Public Law Research Paper No.13-331.

Ewen, S. (2001) *Captains of Consciousness Advertising and The Social Roots of The Consumer Culture*. New York: Basic Books

Ewen, S., Ewen, E. (1992) *Channels of Desire: Mass Images and the Shaping of American Consciousness*. Minnesota: University of Minnesota Press.

Fahs, B (2010) 'Radical Refusals: On the Anarchist Politics of Women Choosing Asexuality', *Sexualities*, 13(4) (August): 445–61.

Fairholm, I & Lench, A (2014) 'Looking back: Freud, the libido and oxytocin', *The Psychologist*, (27)8: 628-631.

Faulkner, S.L. (2009). *Poetry as Method: Reporting Research Through Verse*. Routledge.

Felner, M (1985) *Apostles of Silence: The Modern French Mimes*. Cranberry and London: Associated University Presses.

Ferrer, J (2008) 'What Does it Mean to Live a Fully Embodied Spiritual Life?', *International Journal of Transpersonal Studies*, 27: 1-11.

Filice E., Raffoul A., Meyer S.B., Neiterman E. (2019) The influence of Grindr, a geosocial networking application, on body image in gay, bisexual and other men who have sex with men: An exploratory study. *Body Image, (31):* 59–70.

Fine, M (1994) Dis-tance and other stances: Negotiations of power inside feminist research *(cited in Letherby 2002, p3.7).*

Fosl, P S (2016) 'The many voices of interdisciplinarity', *Cogent Arts & Humanities, 3* (1164949): 1-9.

Foster, S M (2011) *Consensual unwanted sex: Motivations and reservations.* Doctoral Thesis. Greensboro.: The University of North Carolina.

Foucault, M. ([1963] 1977) 'A Preface to Transgression'. *In Religion and Culture: Michel Foucault. Jeremy R. Carrette, ed.*: 57-71. New York: Routledge.

Foucault, M (1978) *The history of sexuality* (1st American ed). New York: Pantheon Books.

Foucault, M. (1983). *Aesthetics, Method, and Epistemology: Essential Works of Foucault 1954-1984.* J. D. Faubion, ed. Reprint, London: Penguin Classics, 2020.

Foucault, M. (1996) 'An Ethics of Pleasure', in *Foucault Live: Collected Interviews, 1961–1984*, ed. Sylvere Lotringer, trans. Lysa Hochroth and John Johnson. New York: Semiotext.

Foucault, M.. 1999 [1980]. 'On the Government of the Living.' In *Religion and Culture: Michel Foucault.* Jeremy R. Carrette, ed: 154-157. New York: Routledge.

Foucault, M. Translated by: Morar, N., & Smith, D. W. (2011 [1978]). The Gay Science. *Critical Inquiry, 37*(3): 385–403.

Frank, A W (2010) *Letting Stories Breathe*. Chicago: University of Chicago Press.

Freud, S (1905) 'Three Essays on the Theory of Sexuality, In Strachy, J & Freud, A (eds.), *The Standard Edition of the Complete Psychological Works of Sigmund Freud, Volume VII (1901-1905): A Case of Hysteria, Three Essays on Sexuality and Other Works*: 123-246, Hogarth Press, London.

Freud, S. (1920 [1955]) Beyond The Pleasure Principle. *The International Psycho-Analytical Library No. 4.* Ed, Jones, E.

Froemming, M W, (2020) *The Relation of Unwanted Consensual Sex to Mental Health and Relationship Variables: The Role of Motivations.* Doctoral Thesis. Ohio: Bowling Green State University.

Fromm, E. (1956) *The Art of Loving*. New York: Harper & Row.

Gafini, M and Kincaid, K (2017) *A Return to Eros: The Radical Experience of Being Fully Alive*. Dallas: BenBella Books.

Gale, K. (2018) *Madness As Methodology : Bringing Concepts to Life in Contemporary Theorising and Inquiry*. ProQuest Ebook Central:Taylor & Francis Group:

Gallop, J. (1984). Beyond the Jouissance Principle. *Representations, 7*: 110–115.

Gautam, S. K. (2016). 'Foucault and the Notion of *Ars Erotica*: Pleasure as Desubjectivation.' In *Foucault and the Kamasutra: The Courtesan, the Dandy, and the Birth of Ars Erotica as Theater in India*. Online ed: Chicago Scholarship Online: University of Chicago Press.

Gibson, L (2010), Toolkit 09: Using email interviews. *University of Manchester.* Online: Accessed 10/10/20.

Giddens, A (1984) *The Constitution of Society: Outline of the Theory of Structuration.* Cambridge: Polity.

Giddens, A (1991) *Modernity and Self-Identity*. Cambridge: Polity.

Gilbert, E (2007) *Eat Pray Love: One Woman's Search for Everything.* London: Bloomsbury Paperbacks.

Gilbert, J. and Pearson, E. (1999) *Discographies: Dance, Music, Culture and the Politics of Sound.* New York: Routledge.

Gleig, A. (2010). Psychospiritual. In Leeming, D. A. (Ed.) *Encyclopedia of psychology and religion:* 738–739. New York: Springer.

Godden, R (1989) *A House with Four Rooms*. London: Corgi Books.

Goffman, Erving (1959) *The Presentation of Self in Everyday Life*. New York: Anchor Books: A Division of Random House, Inc.

Graham, R (2011) 'The health of lesbian, gay, bisexual, and transgender people : building a foundation for better understanding / Committee on Lesbian, Gay, Bisexual, and Transgender Health Issues and Research Gaps and Opportunities'. *Board on the Health of Select Populations, Institute of Medicine of the National Academies*. Washington: National Academies Press.

Green, B. (2016) 'I Always Remember That Moment': Peak Music Experiences as Epiphanies'. *Sociology, 50*(2): 333–348.

Gressgard, R (2013) 'Asexuality: from pathology to identity and beyond'. *Psychology & Sexuality, 4*(2): 179-192.

Griffin, S. (1996) *The Eros of Everyday Life: Essays on Ecology, Gender and Society*. Kindle Edition, 2015: Open Road Media.

Gupta, K (2013) 'Picturing Space for Lesbian Nonsexualities: Rethinking Sex-Normative Commitments through The Kids Are All Right (2010)', *Journal of Lesbian Studies 17*(1): 103–118.

Gupta, K (2015) 'Compulsory Sexuality: Evaluating an Emerging Concept', *Signs 41*(1): 131–154.

Gupta, K (2017) '"And now I'm just different, but there's nothing actually wrong with me": Asexual marginalization and resistance', *Journal of Homosexuality, 64*(8): 991–1013.

Hakim, C (2010) 'Erotic Capital', *European Sociological Review, 26*(5): 499-518.

Halberstam, J. (1998) *Female Masculinity*. ProQuest Ebook Central: Duke University Press.

Hall, S (1997) *Representation: Cultural Representations and Signifying Practices*. London: SAGE Publications.

Hanson, E H (2014) 'Toward an Asexual Narrative Structure'. In *Asexualities: Feminist and Queer Perspectives:* 344–74, Cerankowski, K J and Milks, M (eds.). New York: Routledge.

Hart M.M., Zdravkov J., Plaha K., Cooper F., Allen K., Fuller L., Jones R., Day S. (2016) Digital sex and the city: Prevalent use of dating apps amongst heterosexual attendees of genito-urinary medicine (GUM) clinics. *Sex. Transm. Infect, (92):* A1.

Harvey, A. (2000) *The Way of Passion.* New York: Jeremy P Tarcher.

Heald, J, Hurwitz, J and Schlossberg, H (2021) *Cobra Kai.* Netflix. Viewed 29 December 2022.

Heelas, P. and Woodhead, L. (2005) *The Spiritual Revolution: Why Religion Is Giving Way to Spirituality.* Malden: Blackwell.

Heldman, C., Wade, L. Hook-Up Culture: Setting a New Research Agenda. *Sex Res Soc Policy* **7**, 323–333 (2010).

Herrmann, A. F. (2022) 'Autoethnography as Acts of Love'. In *Handbook of Autoethnography: Second Edition.* 2022: 78. Eds Adams, T. E., Holman Jones, S. and Ellis, C. New York: Routledge.

Hills, R (2012) *Life Without Sex: The Third Phase of the Asexuality Movement.* Online: The Atlantic. Accessed 12/12/21.

Hochschild, A (1979), 'Emotion work, feeling rules, and social structure', *American Journal of Sociology, 85*: 551-575.

Hochschild, A (1983), *The managed heart: Commercialization of human feeling.* Berkeley: University of California Press.

Hodge, D.R., Baughman, L. M., Cummings, J.A. (2006) Moving Toward Spiritual Competency. *Journal of Social Service Research, 32*:4: 211-231.

hooks, b. (1992) 'Eating the other: Desire and resistance', in *Black Looks: Race and Representation*: 21–39. Boston: South End Press.

hooks, b. (2001) *All About Love.* New York: Harper Perennial.

hooks, b. (2010) 'Touch'. In *Teaching Critical Thinking Practical Wisdom*: 153-157. Oxford: Routledge.

Hopkinson, E (2019) *Asexual Fairy Tales.* Bristol: Silverwood Books.

Howell, R (2013) 'I'm not the man I was: Reflections on becoming a widower', *Illness, Crisis and Loss, 21*: 3–13 Routledge, London *(cited in Letherby (2015).*

Illouz, E, (1997) *Consuming the Romantic Utopia: Love and the Cultural Contradictions of Capitalism*, University of California Press, Berkley, CA.

Illouz, E. (2007) *Cold Intimacies: The Making of Emotional Capitalism*. New York: Polity Press.

Illouz, E. (2008) *Saving the Modern Soul: Therapy, Emotions and the Culture of Self-Help.* Berkley, CA: University of California Press.

Illouz, E. (2017) *Emotions as Commodities: Capitalism, Consumption and Authenticity.* London: Routledge.

Illouz, E. (2021) *The End of Love: A Sociology of Negative Relations.* Cambridge: Polity Press.

Inckle, K (2007) *Writing on the Body: Thinking Through Gendered Embodiment and Marked Flesh.* Cambridge: Cambridge Scholars.

Inckle, K (2010) 'Telling tales? Using ethnographic fictions to speak embodied 'truth'', *Qualitative Research, 10*(1): 27–47.

Ingold, T (2000) *The Perception of the Environment.* London: Routledge.

Ingram, N. and Abrahams, J. (2016) Stepping outside oneself: how a cleft habitus can lead to greater reflexivity through occupying the 'third space'. In Thatcher, J., Ingram, N., Burke, C., and Abrahams, J. (Eds) *Bourdieu: The next generation. The development of Bourdieu's intellectual heritage in contemporary UK sociology:* 140-156. London: Routledge.

Jackson, S. (2007) 'The sexual self in late modernity'. In M. Kimmel (Ed.) *The Sexual Self: The Construction of Sexual Scripts*: 3-15. Nashville, TN: Vanderbilt University Press.

James, W (1890)[2021] *The Principles of Psychology: Volumes 1 and 2. Complete works.* Independently Published.

Jiotsa B, Naccache B, Duval M, Rocher B, Grall-Bronnec M. (2021) Social Media Use and Body Image Disorders: Association between Frequency of Comparing One's Own Physical Appearance to That of People Being Followed on Social Media and Body Dissatisfaction and Drive for Thinness. *Int J Environ Res Public Health, 18*(6): 2880.

Johnson, R.A. (1985) *We: Understanding the Psychology of Romantic Love.* San Francisco, CA: Harper & Row.

Jordan, M. D. (2007). 'Religion Trouble'. *GLQ 13(4):* 563-575.

Jordan, M. D. (2015). *Convulsing Bodies: Religion and Resistance in Foucault.* CA: Stanford University Press.

Kann, C (2019) *Let's Talk About Love.* New York: Square Fish.

Kaplan, D. and Illouz, E. (2022) *What Is Sexual Capital?* Cambridge: Polity Press.

Kapsanis, G. (2016 [2000]) *The Eros of Repentance: Four Homilies on Athonite Monasticism.* MA: Pleroma Publishing.

Kim, E (2014) 'Asexualities and Disabilities in Constructing Sexual Normalcy', In *Asexualities: Feminist and Queer Perspectives:* 249–82, Cerankowski K J and Milks, M. New York: Routledge.

Kinsey, A C, Pomeroy, W B, and Martin, C E (1948) *Sexual behavior in the human male.* Philadelphia: Saunders.

Klein, N. (1999) *No Logo : Taking Aim at the Brand Bullies.* Canada: Knopf.

Kripal, J. J. (2007). 'Sexuality and the Erotic', in *The Oxford Handbook of Religion and Emotion* John Corrigan (ed.). Online ed: Oxford Academic, 2009.

Kubo, T and Yuyama, A (Translators) (2007) *The Lotus Sutra (Bdk English Tripitaka).* Honolulu: University of Hawaii Press.

Kurowicka, A (2021) 'Asexuality', in Dodd, S. (ed), *The Routledge International Handbook of Social Work and Sexualities.* London: Routledge.

Lacan, J. ([1959] 2007) *The Ethics of Psychoanalysis: The Seminar of Jacques Lacan: Book VII: 7* Abingdon: Routledge.

Lacan, J. (1966) *Écrits – The First Complete Edition in English.* Reprint 2007. New York: W. W. Norton & Company.

Laing, R D (1990) *The Divided Self.* London: Penguin.

Lang, C (2018) *Intimacy and Desire Through the Lens of an Aro-Ace Woman of Color.* Honors Thesis. Bates College.

Laslett, B.(1999) Personal Narratives as Sociology. *Contemporary Sociology, 28*(4): 391–401.

Leavy, P (2020) *Method Meets Art, Third Edition: Arts-Based Research Practice,* New York: Guilford.

Leigh, J and Brown, N (2021) *Embodied Inquiry.* London: Bloomsbury Academic.

Leigh, J. S. (2023) *Borders of Qualitative Research: Navigating the Spaces where Therapy, Education, Art and Science Connect.* Currently in press (2023). Bristol: Bristol University Press.

Leigh, Jennifer S (2018) Where are the boundaries around research? *International Journal of Qualitative Methods. International Journal of Qualitative Methods. 17* (1).

Letherby, G (2002) 'Claims and disclaimers: Knowledge, reflexivity and representation in feminist research', *Sociological Research Online*, 6(4).

Letherby, G (2015) 'Bathwater, babies and other losses: a personal and academic story', *Mortality, 20*(2): 128-144.

Letherby, G, Scott, J and Williams, M (2013) *Objectivity and Subjectivity in Social Research.* London: Sage and Reid-Boyd.

Lewis, C S (1952) *Mere Christianity.* Glasgow: William Collins Sons & Co.

Lorde, A (1978) 2007, 'Uses of the Erotic: The Erotic as Power.' In *Sexualities and Communication in Everyday Life: A Reader:* 87-91, Lovaas and Mercille (eds.). Berkeley, CA: Sage Publications.

Lorde, A. (2017) *The Master's Tools Will Never Dismantle the Master's House.* UK: Penguin Random House.

Love, L. (2022) *Asexual epiphanies – Rewriting the past and crafting the future from the omnipresent vantage point of realisation.* Conference Abstract. British Sociological Society, Autobiographical Summer Conference 2022.

MacCartney T, (2007) *Finding Earth, Finding Soul: The Invisible Path to Authentic Leadership.* Cambridge: Green Books.

MacInnis, C C. and Hodson, G (2012) 'Intergroup Bias Toward 'Group X': Evidence of Prejudice, Dehumanization, Avoidance, and Discrimination Against Asexuals'. *Group Processes and Intergroup Relations 15*(6) (November): 725-43.

Marcuse, H. (1955) *Eros and Civilization: A Philosophical Inquiry into Freud* (2nd ed.). Reprint: Routledge, 1987.

Marcuse, H. (1974). 'Marxism and Feminism'. *Women's Studies, Vol. 2:* 279-288.

Martin, B. and Dalzen, B. (2021) *The Art of Receiving and Giving: The Wheel of Consent.* Oregon: Luminare Press.

Marx, K. (1843) A Contribution to the Critique of Hegel's Philosophy of Right: Introduction. Written: December 1843-January 1844; First published: in Deutsch-Französische Jahrbücher, 7 & 10 February 1844 in Paris; Transcription: the source and date of transcription is unknown. It was proofed and corrected by Andy Blunden, February 2005, and corrected by Matthew Carmody in 2009. (Accessed 7/7/23).

Maslow, A.H. (1943) 'A theory of human motivation'. *Psychological review*, Vol. 50(4): 370.

Masters, R.A. (2010) *Spiritual Bypassing: When Spirituality Disconnects Us from What Really Matters*. US: North Atlantic Books.

Masters, W. and Johnson, V. (1970) *The Pleasure Bond.* Reprint 1976. New York: Bantam.

McCutchen, J (2015) *Conscious Writing: Discover Your True Voice Through Mindfulness and More.* London: Hay House.

McDaniel, J. (2018) *Lost Ecstasy: Its Decline and Transformation in Religion*. Online: Palgrave Macmillan.

McDougall, G. (2021) *Madness to Memoir: The Creative Cure. Critical Studies*. Doctoral Thesis. University of Glasgow.

McIlveen, P (2008) Autoethnography as a Method for Reflexive Research and Practice in Vocational Psychology. *Australian Journal of Career Development*, *17*(2): 13–20.

McWhorter, L. (1999) *Bodies and Pleasures: Foucault and the Politics of Sexual Normalization.* Bloomington: Indiana University Press.

Mead, G (1934 [2015]) *Mind, Self, and Society*. Chicago, USA: The University of Chicago Press.

Merton, T. (1979) *Love and Living*. Kindle Edition: Farrar, Straus and Giroux.

Mills, C W (1959/1999), *The Sociological Imagination* (Fortieth Anniversary Edition). New York: Oxford University Press.

Mitchell, H, and Hunnicutt, G (2018) 'Challenging accepted scripts of sexual "normality": Asexual narratives of non-normative identity and experience', *Sexuality and Culture*, *23*(2): 507–524.

Moors A C, Gesselman A N and Garcia J R (2021) 'Desire, Familiarity, and Engagement in Polyamory: Results From a National Sample of Single Adults in the United State'. *Frontiers in Psychology. 12*:619640.

Morano, M. (2020) *Like Love*. Ohio: Mad Creek Books.

Mostafa, V. (2015). *Rumi and Shams' silent rebellion: Parallels with Vedanta, Buddhism, and Shaivism.* New York: Palgrave Macmillan.

Nowen, H.J.M., (1986) *Reaching Out: The Three Movements of the Spiritual Life.* New York: Bantam Doubleday Dell.

Odier, D. (1999) *Desire: The Tantric Path to Awakening.* Vermont: Inner Traditions.

Olund, E. (2015) 'Afterword: When Has Sexuality Ever Been About Sex? A Review of Historical Geographies of Sexualities. *Historical Geography, Volume 43*:15: 106-121.

Oseman, A (2020) *Loveless.* London: HarperCollins Children's Books.

Pargament, K. I. (1997). *The Psychology of Religion and Coping.* New York: Guilford Press.

Pargament, K.I., Koenig, H.G. and Perez, L.M. (2000), The many methods of religious coping: Development and initial validation of the RCOPE. *Journal of Clinical Psychology., 56*: 519-543.

Parsons, J (2018) 'Narrative re-scripting: Reconciling past and present lives'. *Auto/Biography Review,* 2018.

Parsons, J. (2014) 'Ourfoodstories@e-mail.com', an Auto/Biographical Study of Relationships with Food', *04 University of Plymouth Research Thesis.*

Parsons, J M, and Chappell, A (2020) Chapter 1: 'A Case for Auto/Biography'. In Parsons, J and Chappell, A (eds.), *The Palgrave Handbook of Auto/Biography.* London: Palgrave McMillan.

Peck, M. S. (1978) *The Road Less Traveled: A New Psychology of Love, Traditional Values and Spiritual Growth.* London: Arrow.

Pedalino F, Camerini AL. (2022) Instagram Use and Body Dissatisfaction: The Mediating Role of Upward Social Comparison with Peers and Influencers among Young Females. *Int J Environ Res Public Health, 19*(3): 1543.

Peele, S., with Brodsky, A. (1975), *Love and Addiction.* New York: Taplinger.

Pelias, R. J. (2004). *A Methodology of the Heart: Evoking Academic and Daily Life.* Lanham, MD: AltaMira Press.

Pelias, R. J. (2022) 'Writing Autoethnography: The Personal, Poetic, and Performative as Compositional Strategies'. *Handbook of Autoethnography: Second Edition.* 2022: 121-132. Eds Adams, T. E., Holman Jones, S. and Ellis, C. New York: Routledge.

Pfaus, J.G., Tsarski, K. (2022) A Case of Female Orgasm Without Genital Stimulation. *Sexual Medicine, (10)*2: 100496.

Pink, S (2015) *Doing sensory ethnography* (Second ed.). London: SAGE Publications.

Plieger, T., Groote, O., Hensky, R., Hurtenbach, L., Sahler, S.,Thönes, L., and Reuter, M. (2021) The Association Between Sexism, Self-Sexualization, and the Evaluation of Sexy Photos on Instagram. *Front. Psychol Sec. Personality and Social Psychology Volume 12.*

Plummer, K (2001) *Documents of Life 2: An Invitation to a Critical Humanism.* London: Sage.

Plummer, K (2013) A Manifesto for Social Stories in Stanley, L (ed.) *Documents of Life Revisited : Narrative and Biographical Methodology for a 21st Century Critical Humanism*, (pp. 209 – 2019). Farnham: Taylor & Francis Group.

Prabhavananda, S. (1963) *The Sermon on the Mount According to Vedanta.* US: Vedanta Press.

Pratt, S F (2017) 'A Relational View of Ontological Security in International Relations'. *International Studies Quarterly, 61*: 78-85.

Przybylo, E (2011) 'Crisis and safety: The asexual in sexusociety', *Sexualities, 14*(4): 444–461.

Przybylo, E. (2013). Producing facts: Empirical asexuality and the scientific study of sex. *Feminism & Psychology, 23*(2): 224–242.

Przybylo, E (2019) *Asexual Erotics: Intimate Readings of Compulsory Sexuality.* Columbus: The Ohio State University Press.

Przybylo, E. (2020) *An Erotic Toolkit: Asexual and Aromantic Critiques of Heteronormativity.* Online: American Studies Colloquium Series. Accessed May 28, 2020.

Quinn, J (2011) *Learning Communities and Imagined Social Capital: Learning to Belong*, Bloomsbury Publishing Plc, ProQuest Ebook Central.

Hall, D and Estrada, C L (directors) (2021) *Raya and the Last Dragon.* [Film]. California: Walt Disney Animation Studios.

Reay, D. (2004) 'Gendering Bourdieu's notions of capitals? Emotional capital, women and social class'. *Sociological review, Vol. 52 (2)*: 57-74.

Renninger, B J (2015) '"Where I Can Be Myself . . . Where I Can Speak My Mind": Networked Counterpublics in a Polymedia Environment', *New Media and Society 17*(9) (October): 1513–29.

Renzetti C M and Lee, R M (1993) *Researching Sensitive Topics.* London: Sage Publications.

Rich, A. (1981) *Compulsory Heterosexuality and Lesbian Existence.* London: Onlywomen Press.

Rifkin, M (2012) *The Erotics of Sovereignty: Queer Native Writing in the Era of Self Determination.* Minneapolis: University of Minnesota Press.

Robbins, N K, Low, K G, and Query, A N (2016) 'A qualitative exploration of the "coming out process" for asexual individuals'. *Archives of Sexual Behavior, 45*: 751–760.

Ronai, C R (1995) 'Multiple reflections of child sex abuse: An argument for a layered account', *Journal of Contemporary Ethnography (23)*: 395-426.

Rubin, G (1984) 'Thinking Sex', In Vance, C., *Pleasure and danger: Exploring female sexuality*: 143-178. Boston: Routledge, Boston.

Sadlier, A C (2017) *Women Dancing on the Edge of Time: Reframing female (a)sexualities through Zorbitality.* Doctoral Thesis. London: King's College.

Satchwell, C., Larkins, C., Davidge, G., & Carter, B. (2020). Stories as findings in collaborative research: making meaning through fictional writing with disadvantaged young people. *Qualitative Research, 20*(6): 874-891.

Sauthoff, P J P (2019) *Protective Rites in the Netra Tantra*. Doctoral Thesis. London: SOAS, University of London.

Scheff, T (2015) Toward integration: Disciplines, specialties and journals. *The American Sociologist, 46*(1): 116-121.

Scherrer, K (2008) 'Coming to an Asexual Identity: Negotiating Identity, Negotiating Desire' *Sexualities 11*(5) (October): 621–41.

Schrader, E. (2020) *The problem with normalizing TikTok – opinion.* Jerusalem Post: online edition. Accessed 01/10/2023.

Scott, S and Dawson, M (2015) 'Rethinking asexuality: A Symbolic Interactionist account'. *Sexualities, 18*(1–2): 3-19.

Scott, S., McDonnell, L. and Dawson, M. (2016), Stories of Non-Becoming: Non-Issues, Non-Events and Non-Identities in Asexual Lives. *Symbolic Interaction, 39*: 268 - 286.

Dawson, M., Scott, S., & McDonnell, L. (2018). '"Asexual" Isn't Who I Am': The Politics of Asexuality. *Sociological Research Online, 23*(2), 374-391.

Scully, P. (2010). Peripheral Visions: Heterography and Writing the Transnational Life of Sara Baartman. In: *Transnational Lives*. Deacon, D., Russell, P., Woollacott, A. eds. The Palgrave Macmillan Transnational History Series. London: Palgrave Macmillan.

Seidler, V. (1994) *Unreasonable Men: Masculinity and Social Theory,* London: Routledge.

Seidman, S (2014) *The Social Construction of Sexuality*. New York: W.W. Norton & Company.

Seidman, S. (1989) 'Constructing sex as a domain of pleasure and self expression: sexual ideology in the sixties'. *Theory, Culture and Society 6*: 293–315.

Shandas, V, and Brown, S E (2016). An empirical assessment of interdisciplinarity: Perspectives from graduate students and program administrators. *Innovative Higher Education, 41*(5): 411-423.

Sherrard, P. (1976) *Christianity and Eros*. London: SPCK.

Shri Shashikumar S (2003) *The Philosophy of Tantra with Special Reference to Osho: A Study*. Doctoral Thesis. Dharwad: Karnatak University.

Shteynberg, G, Hirsh, J B, Garthoff, J, and Bentley, R A (2022), 'Agency and Identity in the Collective Self', *Personality and Social Psychology Review, 26(1)*: 35–56.

Sinwell, S (2014) 'Aliens and asexuality: Media representation, queerness, and asexual visibility', in Cerankowski, K J and Milks, M (eds.), *Asexualities: Feminist and queer perspectives:* 162–173. London: Routledge.

Sire, J W (2004) *Naming the Elephant: Worldview as a Concept.* USA: IVP

Smith, G W H (2006) *Erving Goffman*. Abingdon: Routledge.

Smith, M A (2017). *Bypassing the Asexual Paradox: A Strategic Retelling of the History of Asexuality*. Doctoral Thesis. Georgia: Emory University.

Smith, S B (2018) *The distinctive relationship between sexual ecstasy and spiritual ecstasy for heterosexual, lesbian, gay, bisexual and transgendered clergy of the Church of England: Integrating Transpersonal Awareness with an Interpretative Phenomenological Analysis*. Doctoral Thesis. Liverpoool: John Moores University.

Soelle, D. (2001) *The Silent Cry: Mysticism and Resistance.* Kindle Edition: Augsburg Fortress Publishers.

Sovatsky, S J (2009) 'Complete maturation of the ensouled body', *The Journal of Transpersonal Psychology, Vol. 41*(1): 1-21.

Sovatsky, S J (2018) 'The Grand Unfolding Yogaverse', *Journal of Conscious Evolution 11*(11), Article 4.

Sovatsky, S. (2000) *Passions of Innocence: Tantric Celibacy and the Mysteries of Eros.* Vermont: Inner Traditions Bear and Company.

Sparkes, A C (2002) 'Autoethnography: Self-Indulgence or Something More?' in Bochner, A P and Ellis, C (eds.) *Ethnographically Speaking: Autoethnography, Literature & Aesthetics*. Walnut Creek: Altimira Press.

Sparkes, A. C. (2000). Autoethnography and narratives of self: Reflections on criteria in action. *Sociology of Sport Journal (17):* 21-43.

Sparkes, A. C. (2022) 'When Judgement Calls: Making Sense of Criteria for Evaluating Different Forms of Autoethnography'. In *Handbook of Autoethnography: Second Edition.* 2022: 263-276. Eds Adams, T. E., Holman Jones, S. and Ellis, C. New York: Routledge.

Sprinkle, A, Stephens, B, Klein J, Chaudhuri, U, Preciado, P B, and Montano, L (2021), *Assuming the Ecosexual Position: The Earth as Lover*. London: University Of Minnesota Press.

Stanley, L (ed.) (2013) *Documents of Life Revisited : Narrative and Biographical Methodology for a 21st Century Critical Humanism*. Farnham: Taylor & Francis Group.

Stanley, L. (1993). On Auto/Biography in Sociology. *Sociology, 27*(1): 41–52.

Stone, H. and Stone S. L. (2000) *Partnering: A New Kind of Relationship: Creating Magic and Excitement in Your Relationship*. Nataraj: New World Library.

Stone, P. (2018) *Confronting Myself: An Auto/Biographical Exploration of The Impact of Class and Education on the Formation of Self and Identity*. Doctoral Thesis. Canterbury Christ Church University.

Strauss, A., & Corbin, J. (1994). Grounded Theory Methodology: An Overview. In N. Denzin & Y. Lincoln *Handbook of Qualitative Research:* 273–284. New York: Sage Publications.

Stryker, R. (2011) *The Four Desires*. UK: Hay House.

Swash, R (2012) 'Among the Asexuals' *The Observer*. Online: Accessed 12/12/21.

Tagirov, Philip. (2018) Sexuality, Love and Eroticism: Methodology of Distinguishing. *Conference: Proceedings of the International Conference on Contemporary Education, Social Sciences and Ecological Studies (CESSES 2018).* Atlantis Press.

Thoreau, H.D. ([1854] 2016) *Walden*. Macmillan Collector's Library.

Turban, J. (2018) *We need to talk about how Grindr is affecting gay men's mental health.* Online: Vox Media. Accessed 22/09/23

Urban, H. (2000) 'The Cult of Ecstasy: Tantrism, the New Age, and the Spiritual Logic of Late Capitalism'. *History of Religions 39* (3): 268-304.

Urban, H. (2003) *Tantra: Sex, Secrecy, Politics and Power in the Study of Religion.* California: University of California Press

Urban, H. (2022) 'Modernity and Neo-Tantra'. In *The Oxford Handbook of Tantric Studies*, eds. Hayes, G. and Payne, R. Oxford: Oxford University Press.

Vance, C. (2018). 'Towards a Historical Materialist Concept of Asexuality and Compulsory Sexuality'. *Studies in Social Justice, Volume 12*(1): 133-151.

Vares, T (2018) '"My [Asexuality] Is Playing Hell with My Dating Life": Romantic Identified Asexuals Negotiate the Dating Game', *Sexualities, 21*(4) (June): 520-36.

Venkatesh, P (2010) *Art of Natya and the Science of Tantra: A Correlative Study.* Doctoral Thesis. Manasagangotri, Mysore: University of Mysore.

Vera, H. (2016). Rebuilding a Classic: The Social Construction of Reality at 50. *Cultural Sociology, 10*(1): 3–20.

Villarroel, M A *et al* (2006) 'Same-gender sex in the United States: Impact of T-ACASI on prevalence estimates', *Public Opinion Quarterly 70*(2): 166-196.

Villegas, D (2018) 'From the self to the screen: a journey guide for auto-netnography in online communities', *Journal of Marketing Management* 34 (3-4): 243-262.

von Franz, M L (1964) 'The Process of Individuation', *in Jung, C G, Hendeson, J L, Jaffe, A and Jacobi, J, (1964 [1997], Man and His Symbols*. New Jersey: Laurel Press.

Walker, S J (1997) 'When "no" becomes "yes": Why girls and women consent to unwanted sex', *Applied & Preventive Psychology, 6*, 157-166.

Wall, S. (2008) 'Easier Said than Done: Writing an Autoethnography', *International Journal of Qualitative Methods, 7(1):* 38-52.

Wardley, L J, and Bélanger, C H (2015) 'Interdisciplinarity: Suffering from a lack of effective marketing?' *International Journal of Higher Education, 4*(4): 45-52.

Watson, A (2021) 'Writing sociological fiction', *Qualitative Research, 22*(3): 337-352.

Weatherall, R. (2019). Writing the doctoral thesis differently. *Management Learning, 50*(1): 100-113.

Weber, M. (1905 [2014]) *The Protestant Ethic and the Spirit of Capitalism*. New York: Angelico Press.

Weber, M. (1920 [1993]). *The Sociology of Religion*. Boston, MA: Beacon Press.

Wegner, P.E., (1999) *Consuming the Romantic Utopia: Love and the Cultural Contradictions of Capitalism* Eva Illouz. *Utopian Studies (10)*2: 264-268.

Weis, R *et al* (2020) *2017 and 2018 Asexual Community Survey Summary Report,* Ace Community Survey. Accessed 14/02/22.

Wexler, P. (2013) *Mystical Sociology: Toward Cosmic Social Theory.* New York: Peter Lang.

White, D G (2000) *Tantra In Practice: Princeton Readings in Religions*. Oxford: Princeton.

Wilkinson, E (2012) 'The Romantic Imaginary: Compulsory Coupledom and Single Existence', in *Sexualities: Past Reflections, Future Directions:* 130–45, Hines, S and Taylor, Y (eds.). London: Palgrave Macmillan.

Williams S. and Bendelow, G. (1998) *The Lived Body: sociological themes, embodied issues.* London: Routledge.

Winfield I, George L K, Swartz M, and Blazer D G (1990) 'Sexual assault and psychiatric disorders among a community sample of women'. *American Journal of Psychiatry, 147(3)*: 335-341.

Winnicott, D W (1960). 'Ego distortion in terms of true and false self', in *The Maturational Processes and the Facilitating Environment 1965*: 140–152. New York: International Universities Press.

Women's Health (2016) Here's what actually happens at 'cuddle parties'. New York Post. Online: Accessed 14/5/23.

Wong, D, and Guo, X (2020) 'Constructions of asexual identity in China: Intersections of class, gender, region of residence, and asexuality' *Feminist Formations, 32*(3): 75-99.

Index

accessible academics